# THE CAPTIVE PRESS
## in the Third Reich

# THE
# CAPTIVE PRESS
# in the Third Reich

## BY ORON J. HALE

PRINCETON UNIVERSITY PRESS
PRINCETON, NEW JERSEY
1964

PN
5214
R7013064    O9
H3

Copyright © 1964 by Princeton University Press
All Rights Reserved
L.C. Card No. 64-12182

Printed in the United States of America
by The Colonial Press Inc., Clinton, Mass.

2699

TO STUDENTS PAST AND PRESENT
IN MY *HISTORY 144*

# Preface

While detained at Nürnberg, in September 1947, Max Amann was given a copy of Fritz Schmidt's *Presse in Fesseln* (The Press in Chains), a sensational exposure of Amann's role in the Nazi party conquest of the German press, and was requested to comment on the author's charges and allegations. In a twenty-five page memorandum Amann attacked Schmidt furiously as a turn-coat employee whose object was to curry favor with the occupation authorities and build a defense for his impending denazification trial. It was easy for Amann to point out numerous errors of fact where his personal history and actions were involved, but he made a lame defense of Nazi press policy and the operations of the Eher Verlag. In his concluding remarks, Amann referred to "an American general" who had interrogated him at the Seckenheim detention center near Heidelberg in August 1945, with a view to writing a book on the German press during the National Socialist period. "The book by the general should be shortly published and will doubtless be an objective and scientifically valuable treatment in contrast to the political smear-book *Presse in Fesseln*." While two grades below a general officer in 1945, I confess to being the interrogator referred to by Amann. The book has been considerably delayed and both Schmidt and Amann are deceased, but I doubt that there is much in what I have written that will serve to rehabilitate either of the principals in the controversy of 1947. I have endeavored to be "objective and scientific" in my approach, which, owing to the evidence presented, excludes any possibility of rehabilitating Max Amann and his associates in the Nazi rape of the German press.

To professional colleagues I have jestingly described this work as "my second doctoral dissertation," although my acquaintance with many of the persons involved gives it the character of both memoir and monograph. My interest in the newspaper press and the publishing trade began with research for my doctoral dissertation and was extended in the preparation of a larger work published in 1940 (*Publicity and Diplomacy; with Special Reference to England and Germany, 1890-1914*). As chief of the Foreign Press Section, War Department General Staff, during World War II, my knowledge of the European press was further deepened and broadened. On special assignment in Germany in the summer and autumn of 1945, I used the opportunity to interview Nazi party officials concerned with the publication and direction of the German press during World War II. Using ordinary prudence I have drawn on the records of these conversations while always giving priority to available contemporary documents and publications. A two-year tour of duty, in 1950-1952, with the High Commission for Germany brought me into close contact with many of the editors and publishers of the new German press, which exemplifies, with some inevitable exceptions, the highest values and standards of pre-Nazi journalism.

Dr. Joseph Goebbels is not prominently presented in this study. This does not result from willful neglect on the part of the author, but rather from the established fact that he played a minor role in building the Nazi party's monopoly of the newspaper press. If this were a study of publicity and propaganda that emanated from the publishing mechanism, Goebbels would occupy a central position, although even in this respect his flair for self-advertising has given him stature and notoriety out of proportion to his actual achievements and importance. The men who erected the giant party monopoly in the newspaper publishing industry are admittedly less interesting but scarcely less important. Their work was performed in board rooms, lawyers' offices, and management suites, and hence out of the public eye. Owing to the destruction of records it has not been possible to illuminate every aspect of the Nazi party's publishing operations. But the main features, I trust, have been made clear. And if a major conclusion needs to be drawn it is that any degree of socialization or nationalization of the press, either democratic or authoritarian, is incompatible with true freedom of the press.

I have incurred substantial obligations to a number of persons and institutions in the preparation of this work, and for their assistance I wish to make generous and grateful acknowledgement. These include in Germany, Dr. Walther Jänecke, dean of German publishers; Heinrich Walter, historian of the German Newspaper Publishers' Association; Oberregierungsrat Wallner of the Bavarian Restitution Office; Dr. Karl Schwend and Philip von Brand, of the Bavarian State Chancellery; Dr. Martin Löffler of Stuttgart; Prof. Hanns Braun and Dr. Heinz Starkulla, of the Institute of Journalism, University of Munich; Mr. Ernst Langendorf, Radio Free Europe, Munich; Prof. Paul Klucke, and Drs. Helmut Krausnick, Thilo Vogelsang, and Sonja Noller, of the Institut für Zeitgeschichte, Munich; Dr. Isaac Stone, former chief of the Berlin Document Center, and his obliging staff; Herr Emil Goldshagg, of the *Süddeutsche Zeitung,* Munich; and Rechtsanwalt Rolf Rienhardt, and Herr Willy Imhoff, who were impressively frank in responding to many probing questions. I should acknowledge also the hospitality and assistance of the directors and staffs of the Manuscripts Division of the Library of Congress; the National Archives; the World War II Records Center, Alexandria, Virginia; and the Alderman Library, University of Virginia.

A study of this kind is not completed without substantial material aid. I wish to acknowledge such support from the Virginia University Center, Richmond, Virginia; the Institute for Research in the Social Sciences, of the University of Virginia, and the University Research Committee. Mr. David Harrop of the Princeton University Press has given expert assistance in matters editorial and typographical; and my wife has done what only wives dare do—criticize a husband's prose and carry the argument to the point where improvement results. And only a wife can sustain the last act —the making of an index.

*Charlottesville*                                    ORON J. HALE
*Virginia*

# Contents

# THE CAPTIVE PRESS
## in the Third Reich

# GLOSSARY OF TERMS AND ABBREVIATIONS

| | |
|---|---|
| AG | Aktiengesellschaft (Joint stock company whose shares are publicly offered and traded) |
| BDC | Berlin Document Center, U. S. Mission Berlin |
| BWB | Bayerische Wiedergutmachungs Behörde (Bavarian Restitution Office) |
| Fachverband | Trade or occupational association |
| Generalanzeiger | Non-partisan popular newspaper |
| Gleichschaltung | Coordination |
| GmbH | Gesellschaft mit beschränkter Haftung (Private joint stock company with limited liability) |
| Heimatpresse | Local or home-town press |
| Kampfzeit | Combat years of the N-S party before 1933 |
| Kopfblatt | Local edition of a newspaper under separate title |
| KPD | Kommunistische Partei Deutschland (German Communist Party) |
| LV | Landesverband (Provincial association) |
| NA | National Archives, Washington, D. C. |
| NSDAP | Nationalsozialistische Deutsche Arbeiter Partei (National Socialist German Workers' Party) |
| N-S | National Socialist |
| OKW | Oberkommando der Wehrmacht (Armed Forces High Command) |
| RKK | Reichskulturkammer (Reich Chamber of Culture) |
| RPK | Reichspressekammer (Reich Press Chamber) |
| Reichsleitung | Reich Directorate of the National Socialist Party |
| RVDP | Reichsverband der Deutschen Presse (Reich Association of the German Press) |
| Rundschreiben | Circular report or directive |
| RVDZV | Reichsverband der Deutschen Zeitungsverleger (Reich Association of German Newspaper Publishers) |
| Schriftleitergesetz | Editor's Law |
| SPD | Sozialdemokratische Partei Deutschland (German Social Democratic Party) |
| Spruchkammer | Denazification court |
| Verlag | Publishing house |
| Verwaltungsamt | Administrative Office of the Reich Leader for the Press |
| V-B | *Völkischer Beobachter* |
| VDZV | Verein Deutscher Zeitungsverleger (Society of German Newspaper Publishers) |

# INTRODUCTION. Structure and Problems of the German Press

Since the invention of printing with movable type by Gutenberg and the development of the mechanical power press by Friedrich König, Germany appropriately has been the world's leading producer and consumer of the printed word. Books, newspapers, illustrated weeklies, scientific journals, trade and commercial publications, and magazines for sports, fashions, entertainment, and family life—all became highly developed, numerous, and widely distributed. During the 1920's 7,000 periodicals in all fields of interest and knowledge, approximately 4,000 daily and weekly newspapers, and 30,000 books annually were published in Germany. Sparing of paper for wrapping and other purposes, the Germans squandered it in printing. The number and variety of popular publications offered the traveling public by the railway newsstand as an antidote to boredom was ever a matter of astonishment to the foreign visitor.

Of the types of printed materials produced, the newspaper is most expressive of the cultural, political, and economic life of the nation. A translated book may find a wide audience in another country; a translated newspaper would have little popular appeal. For example, a standard German newspaper established in London and published in English would require continuous subsidization. A London newspaper published in Germany and endowed with a half million subscribers would, nevertheless, go under in a short time. The newspaper is like the national diet—a person of another culture must acquire the taste in order to appreciate it. No institution in the modern world expresses and represents more positively the differences between national cultures than the newspaper press.

A prominent feature of the German press in the 1920's

was its decentralization. Nothing comparable to London's domination of British journalism existed in Germany. Berlin, to be sure, was a political news center and every important paper in the Reich maintained a bureau in the capital, but of the six or seven German papers with European reputations, only three were published in Berlin. The *Frankfurter Zeitung, Hamburger Fremdenblatt,* and *Münchner Neueste Nachrichten* were quite as likely to be quoted abroad as the Berlin papers.

In the amount of printed material offered to subscribers, the German journals outdid all others. Besides general news and reports, the German newspapers published quantities of material on literature, art, music, and the theater, sports, business, religion, science and fashion, entertainment sections for women, and a large amount of advertising. These features were usually published in special supplements to the first or main news section and they represented one of the more praiseworthy qualities of German journalism. Weak on objective news coverage, as compared to Anglo-American journalism, the German press surpassed that of any other country as an educational and cultural medium. The German press was, above all others, a "serious press."

To appreciate fully the impact of the National Socialist revolution on the publishing industry requires a brief description of the structural features of the German press, its political divisions, its leadership, and its internal problems. The ease with which the Nazis effected the coordination and subjection of the press can be explained in part by the lack of unity among the segments of the publishing industry, and by the historic discord between the editors' and publishers' associations. Other factors that contributed to the weakening of the press as an institution in Weimar Germany were the undeniable overcrowding of the field, the undermining effects of the depression, and the policy of the government toward the daily press.

One topic should be disposed of at the outset. From

Nazi propaganda assertions is derived the impression of a large Jewish-owned press in Germany. This is quite erroneous. The Ullstein publishing house in Berlin was one of the largest producers of newspapers, periodicals, and books; the Mosse firm operated the largest advertising agency and published the liberal *Berliner Tageblatt,* a journal of national and international distinction; and the Sonneman-Simon family published the *Frankfurter Zeitung,* a leading liberal-democratic daily. These enterprises were no larger or more potent than the Hugenberg concern or the newspaper chains operated by the Huck and Girardet families. Excluding the Ullstein, Mosse, and Sonneman-Simon companies there was little Jewish capital invested in the newspaper trade. Also, in contrast to England and the United States, there were few large combinations or newspaper chains. Consolidation, trustification, and the liquidation of the small-town press had made but slight inroads in the field prior to 1933.

Germany published more newspapers than any other industrially advanced country. Particularism, confessional differences, and the multiple party system in the political life of the country contributed to the maintenance of a large number of papers with modest circulations. In 1932, there were 4,703 daily and weekly newspapers, including local editions of parent papers (Kopfblätter). Each metropolitan center had several dailies: Hamburg 10, Cologne 8, Stuttgart 8, Leipzig 5, Frankfurt 6, and Berlin 20, including suburban journals. Provincial centers generally supported two or three dailies, while there was scarcely a town that lacked a locally owned paper. The small-town press, designated as "Heimatpresse" in German journalism, was a distinctive feature of the publishing scene. Newspaper ownership was usually local and therefore widely dispersed. Eighty-one per cent of the newspapers in 1928 were family-owned undertakings.

A feature of German journalism that contributed to the

multiplication of papers was the well-developed press of the political parties. In this group the Social Democratic and Catholic Center papers were the oldest, followed by the Communist publications, and lastly the press developed by the NSDAP. These papers were party-owned or in the hands of prominent party members; they were political instruments rather than purveyors of news. Speeches of party leaders, political announcements, news of party activity, and polemical attacks upon opposing groups made up the bulk of the material offered to readers who were mainly faithful party members. For other news most of them were content to reproduce the colorless news agency reports and what they could reasonably take from the larger journals. True, not all party papers were so narrow and unimportant. The *Kölnische Volkszeitung*, a leading Catholic organ, had a creditable news service, was ably edited, and had a large general circulation; but for one such party paper there were ten that merited the appellation Käseblatt—that is, useful mainly for wrapping cheese. Although these papers could not wholly disregard the economics of publishing, their goals and functions were political, social, or confessional rather than journalistic and commercial.

An important section of the German press was composed of papers that described themselves as non-party, neutral, or independent. Some indicated a general political orientation such as liberal, national, democratic, or simply "middle class." In 1932, of the 4,703 newspapers, 52 per cent were classified as independent or non-partisan. In other words, for these papers publishing was essentially a business. None better exemplified this orientation than the Generalanzeiger press, urban mass circulation papers, which developed in Germany at the end of the nineteenth century in response to a wide demand among the literate masses for news, entertainment, and popular reading material. Politically colorless, these papers sought to please everyone and offend no one. Crime, catastrophe, divorce, and human interest stories, together with special features, such as household and kitchen columns, legal advice, and the serialized novel, constituted the staple fare offered to this new reading public. By 1932 the cultural level of these papers had been substantially raised and they gave more prominence to political affairs, but in general they remained basically business enterprises, striving to reach the widest public, selling advertising, and enjoying the largest circulations in the metropolitan centers and their suburbs. The publishers of the mass circulation press were in business, their undertakings had survived war, revolution, and inflation and since they had maintained their basically non-partisan standing during 1932—Germany's year of decision—they confidently expected to continue on the old lines under the new regime.[1]

A distinctive weakness of the German press manifested itself in the period after the first World War, when banks, industrial firms, and other economic interests began to participate in the ownership of newspapers. The history of this "special interest press" (Interessentenpresse) extends back to the 1870's, but penetration into the field by non-publishing interests was greatly advanced by war and inflation, and made easy by adoption of the corporate form of organization by publishing firms. Shares were sold, traded, and acquired, and properties transferred without the true ownership being revealed. In these instances the shares would appear as vested stock in the hands of a legal trustee or bank representing an unknown, but not always unsuspected, owner. Critics of the press and champions of the public interest roundly condemned this "campaign by industry to conquer public opinion" as subversive of the inde-

[1] The statistics are from E. Dovifat, *Zeitungslehre*, II, 33 ff.; *Jahrbuch der Tagespresse* (1928); on the mass circulation press, Otto Groth, *Die Zeitung*, I, 223-38; and on the party press, Groth, II, 370-541; also Walter Kaupert, *Die deutsche Tagespresse als Politicum*, Chap. III, "Die politischen Parteien und die Presse."

pendence of the press and a nullification of its public responsibilities. Hugo Stinnes's newspaper acquisitions during the inflation period and the development of the giant Hugenberg concern, representing Ruhr industry, were examples frequently cited by critics and reformers. This condition presented a visible target of criticism for respected journalists, spokesmen for the public interest, and the left-wing political parties. Inevitably critical voices were raised and demands made that this unhealthy condition be remedied by a law to protect the independence of the press and the professional journalists in the discharge of their public trust. The Nazis too had taken up the issue and made it a part of their party program and propaganda.[2]

Sternly opposed on principle to state intervention in this area were the publishers of the most substantial and responsible newspapers. Often described as "the political press," their papers were not bound to any party. Devoting much space to politics, they sought to inform and influence the public in foreign and domestic affairs. In their ranks were to be found Germany's best known journals—the *Vossische Zeitung, Berliner Tageblatt, Kölnische Zeitung, Frankfurter Zeitung, Münchner Neueste Nachrichten, Stuttgarter Neues Tagblatt, Bremer Nachrichten, Hamburger Fremdenblatt,* and *Hannoverscher Kurier.* Politically they ranged from democratic to national conservative, but all were distinguished for their sense of responsibility, their efforts to influence and guide political opinion, and their registered disapproval of demagoguery and adventure in the political life of the nation. With varying degrees of firmness and intensity, and sometimes at considerable cost in circulation

[2] The history and literature of this issue are reviewed in detail in Groth, ii, 566-620. It might be noted that in the United States a newspaper to benefit from second class mailing privileges must file annually with the Postmaster General an attested statement giving the names of the publisher, the responsible editor and owner, and, if a corporate enterprise, the actual holders of the shares.

and income, these papers had endeavored to stem the Nazi tide that engulfed Germany in 1932. When Hitler came to power the proprietors of these journals were keenly aware that they faced an uncertain future in the publishing world.

Germany also had its publishing elite. In this group were the owners of above-mentioned papers, and they provided leadership in the Association of German Newspaper Publishers (Verein Deutscher Zeitungsverleger) and its subordinate provincial associations. Chairman and co-chairmen were Heinrich Krumbhaar (Liegnitz), Julius Wolff (Dresden), and A. Neven DuMont (Cologne), while the board membership included such leading figures as Walther Jänecke (Hanover), Carl Esser (Stuttgart), Martin Carbe (Berlin), Kurt Simon (Frankfurt), A. Knittel (Karlsruhe), and Franz Ullstein (Berlin). A. von Boetticher was director of the VDZV with headquarters in the association's stately Press House in Berlin. In its twenty provincial associations were enrolled approximately 2,600 newspapers and their publishers. Broadly based, the VDZV included in its membership the entire range of the daily press, without regard to political affiliation, confessional orientation, or ideological tendency. The SPD publishers were well represented in the membership and on the board; only the Communist and Nazi publishers lived in self-imposed isolation. For flagrant infractions of the publishers' code the VDZV had several suits pending against Nazi publications in 1932. Like any industry or trade association, the VDZV was concerned with the business and technical aspects of publishing, with the relation of the press to the state, with the maintenance of standards of conduct and ethics in newspaper publishing, and in the general social and economic welfare of the industry. To a greater extent than was customary with trade organizations it was inspired by a sense of high past achievement, of service and obligation to the public and the nation, and of standards that transcended the business balance sheet and the profit and loss statement.[3]

Not so firmly rooted and enjoying less prestige and potency was the professional organization of German editors and journalists. Founded in 1910, the Reich Association of the German Press (Reichsverband der deutschen Presse) had approximately 3,600 members grouped in nineteen provincial associations. The board of directors included Georg Bernhard, a leading journalist and editor of the *Vossische Zeitung*, Emil Dovifat, director of the Institute of Journalism of the University of Berlin, Paul Baecker, Curt Mossner, and M. A. Tönjes. The executive secretary and director was Gustav Richter. Although the scope of its interest and activities was broad, the association concerned itself especially with the problems of contractual relations between editors and publishers, and the arbitration of disputes arising out of these relationships. The association also maintained a job register, promoted professional training objectives, provided legal advice and protection to its members, and administered a variety of social welfare programs.[4]

In the 1920's these two associations were the protagonists in a furious dispute over the respective rights and responsibilities of editor and publisher in determining the form, content, and policies of the newspapers which they jointly produced. The independence of the editor, the rights of the publisher—this was an old battlefield in the history of German journalism and one to which each generation of newspaper people returned. The problem is encountered in the early nineteenth century and it was a subject of hot debate in the 1850's. The basic Reich law on the press, of May 7, 1874, made the editor legally responsible for the textual content of the paper and chargeable under the law for

[3] *Jahrbuch der Tagespresse*, pp. vi-x; and H. Walter, *Zeitung als Aufgabe—60 Jahre Verein Deutscher Zeitungsverleger, 1894-1954*; Groth, IV, 46-51. A more critical view of the publishers' association is presented in E. Dovifat, *Die Zeitungen*, pp. 104 ff.

[4] *Jahrbuch der Tagespresse*, pp. x-xv; Groth, IV, 300-306.

offenses of a public or private nature. The law did not, however, define the relationship between editor and publisher or protect the professional rights and independence of the editor vis-à-vis the employer. Basically the dispute arose from the dual nature of the newspaper as a private economic enterprise which also serves a public function. Traditionally, as the canons of the journalistic profession developed, the editor and his functions represented a public trust, while the publisher, who provided the mechanism, was concerned with the newspaper as an economic undertaking. This proved oftentimes an unhappy marriage.

As the press became an economic power, with emphasis upon news collection and dissemination, advertising, and circulation, the functions and importance of the publisher overshadowed those of the editor. The trend was distinctly toward the subordination of editor to publisher, the latter becoming in the embittered description of some publicists, the "work-giver and bread master" (Arbeitgeber und Brotherr). Does the editor take his orders from the publisher? Does the publisher determine in detail the textual content of his paper? Does he lay down minutely the policy line to be followed and perhaps pitch the editor into a serious conflict of conscience? And who represents and interprets the public interest, the editor or publisher? The dispute has many ramifications as the extensive literature on the subject reveals. It suffices to note that as newspaper publishing became "big business" in Germany, the publisher moved into a position of overriding authority. This found expression in the individual employment contracts of editors and in the practice that developed in the majority of newspapers. In the "business press"—papers of the Generalanzeiger type—the editor's function was reduced almost to that of a technician, since the paper was concerned exclusively with news, entertainment, and advertising. The public interest was scarcely discernible in these publications.

Through the Reich Association of the Press, editors and professional journalists sought the protection of the state. They demanded legal definition of the editor-publisher relationship and protection for the journalist in discharging his professional duties. Against such a law, which in their view would impair the right of private contract, the publishers fought tooth and nail. In 1924 the issue developed to the point where a draft law, the "Journalist's Law," was presented by the Reich ministry of the interior for consideration by the trade and professional organizations of the press. The preamble to this proposed law stated: "The editorial part [of a publication] serves the public interest. An editor who misuses his position by mixing private with public interests in order to deceive the public, or in violation of truth seeks at the expense of the public welfare to advance private interests, is betraying his public trust." The measure sought, further, to clarify the rights and obligations of publisher and editor toward one another and toward the public interest. Paragraph 4 specified that: "The general political, economic and cultural tasks, and the orientation of the publication, are determined by the publisher. This determination shall be made prior to the conclusion of the employment contract [with the editor]." This, it should be noted, was scarcely any infringement of the rights and powers asserted by newspaper publishers. Paragraph 5 dealt with the duties and responsibilities of the editor: "Within the limits of the agreement specifying the general political, economic, and cultural orientation of the publication, the shaping and representation of the intellectual content is the responsibility of the editor. . . ."[5] Although the law aimed at a compromise between editor

[5] Text of the draft "Journalistengesetz" in Groth, ɪv, 30-33, 82-83. The issues are presented objectively by Groth, ɪv, 3-46, 74 ff.; the publishers' position is represented by Walter, *Zeitung als Aufgabe*, pp. 100-102; and the legal aspects by Martin Löffler, *Presserecht—Kommentar*, pp. 26-30, 78-80.

and publisher, the VDZV at the annual conference and through its spokesmen flatly rejected any legal definition and clarification. With a turnover in the Reich cabinet (Dr. Hans Luther succeeding Chancellor Wilhelm Marx) the publishers' objections prevailed. The draft of the Journalist's Law was returned to the ministry files, and a truce was concluded between editors and publishers. Some of the journalists' demands were conceded in the model contracts which were then formulated and accepted as standard by the two contending organizations. There the issue rested until 1933 when Goebbels and the jurists in his propaganda ministry resurrected the Journalist's Law and grafted on it Italian Fascist provisions in such manner as to deprive the publisher of all rights in directing his paper, and making of the journalist a "press coolie" in the service of the Nazi state.

Another aspect of the newspaper publishing scene during the Weimar period requires brief mention. In the struggle for the preservation of the Republic the principle of freedom of the press was a major casualty. The law for the defense of the Republic and its implementing ordinances, promulgated in 1922, gave the Weimar government the means of curbing excesses in the press of the revolutionary and anti-state parties. Even sharper and more restrictive were the emergency decrees issued under Article 48 during the severe political and economic crisis of 1931-1932 (Pressenotverordnungen of March 28, July 17, August 10, 1931, and June 14, 1932). In their practical application these measures required police approval for public placards and handbills possessing a political content. Further, newspapers which through their excesses of language threatened public order and security could be suspended for a maximum of eight weeks, and periodicals for six months. These measures were subsequently extended to protect public officials and institutions and symbols of the state from slander and vilification by their political enemies. However, an editor or publisher could appeal a suspension of his journal to a competent court. Whose dogs were whipped under these decrees is shown by a classification of suspensions imposed in Prussia upon the political newspapers in the crisis years. During Brüning's chancellorship, there were 284 newspaper suspensions of which the Nazis incurred 99, the Communists 77, and radical rightist journals 43. Under Von Papen (June 14 to November 17, 1932) there were 95 suspensions of which the Nazis incurred 20, the Communists 39, and the Socialists 10. Significantly there were few suspensions of nationalist papers under the Papen government.[6]

A more serious invasion of the area of freedom of opinion and expression resulted from the ordinance of July 17, 1931. Under this measure the authorities could require a responsible editor or publisher to print in his paper an official pronouncement or corrective explanation in rebuttal to unfounded political charges or misrepresentations. Such official pronouncements had to be published in the first issue following receipt by the editorial office, and a rejoinder could not be printed in the same issue. This extraordinary provision was a product of the political crisis which threatened to extinguish the parliamentary republic. To attack the government and misrepresent its policy pronouncements was an established tactic of the extremist political papers. An official correction or explanation would be passed over in silence by the journal concerned, so that its readers had no opportunity to judge between the original allegations and the explanations of the government. The power of the press is oftentimes "the suppress." This official procedure against abuse of freedom of the press established a dangerous precedent and was sharply criticized by editors and publishers because it forced opposition newspapers to make propaganda for the government. Whether

[6] Kaupert, *Die deutsche Tagespresse als Politicum*, p. 256.

it was ethically and constitutionally justified to enforce in this manner the right of the government to be heard, even against the will of the destructive circles that ringed the tottering state, can be eternally debated. But this kind of "press direction," foreshadowing a state directed press, did not go unnoted by the bright young propagandists in the Nazi party leadership.[7]

Observing the structure and problems of the German press in the crisis years that produced the Third Reich, these critical weaknesses are manifest: economic foundations that were seriously eroded by the depression; penetration of the press by special interest groups, political and economic; a deep rift between journalists' and publishers' associations that prevented cooperation; and a sharp abridgement of freedom of the press through the emergency decrees of the Brüning and Papen governments. The press mirrored the mood and condition of the country—confusion, uncertainty, and fear, and the clash of irreconcilable parties and ideologies.

In the revolutionary period that began with Hitler's appointment as chancellor, the working press—editors and journalists—was one of the first bodies to be "cleansed," coordinated, and subjected to state control. This was accomplished by Dr. Goebbels through his ministry of propaganda. But the publishers of the newspapers, the owners of the rights and titles of the German press, the proud publishing houses representing capital investments running into millions, these were not so easily coordinated with the new regime.

[7] See especially Theodor Lüddecke, *Die Tageszeitung als Mittel der Staatsführung*, pp. 145-53, published in April 1933. An excellent legal study of the press law, emergency decrees, and control measures is the Harvard dissertation by Peter J. Fliess, *The Freedom of the Press under the Law of the German Republic, 1918-1933* (Cambridge, 1951). Kaupert, *Die deutsche Tagespresse*, pp. 184-95, makes a fair and sober examination of the emergency decrees affecting the daily press.

It is axiomatic that a totalitarian system must control the media of mass communication—press, films, radio, and now television. In Soviet Russia the press became an integral part of the administrative apparatus of state and party; in Fascist Italy the journalists were organized in a state-controlled guild subservient to the political regime; in Nazi Germany the newsmen and editors were likewise subjected to stringent control, but going beyond that the regime largely despoiled the publishers of their rights and properties. This was a significant part of the calculated Nazi program to employ the press not only for propaganda but also as an instrument of social control and integration.

How the privately owned press was despoiled and replaced by a giant Nazi publishing monopoly is the theme of this study. In summary, it presents these features: the acquisition by the party of the Eher Verlag and the *Völkischer Beobachter*; the development of the local Nazi press by the Gauleiters; the confiscation of the Socialist and Communist publishing properties; the conversion of the newspaper publishers' association into an instrument of party control and exploitation; the enforcement of special ordinances to effect the transfer of hundreds of privately owned papers to the party publishing combine; and the further acquisition and trustification of newspaper properties under the guise of wartime necessity during World War II. In all these phases policy and guidance came from Adolf Hitler. Max Amann, director of the Party's publishing house, and his staff assistants, worked with a large degree of autonomy, but always along lines and toward goals approved by the Führer.

# I. The *Völkischer Beobachter*—
# Central Organ of the Nazi Party

## The Nazi Party Acquires a Newspaper

Two pleasing bridges over the Isar River and the massive Palace of Justice were Friedrich Thiersch's principal contributions to the public architecture of Munich. In grateful recognition the city government named a street for him. Thierschstrasse begins at the Maximilian II monument ("Max-Zwei Denkmal") and parallels the left bank of the Isar for two hundred yards, leading to St. Luke's Evangelical Church. There it takes a new start at a slight angle, conforming to the direction of the river, and after two blocks terminates as it intersects with Zweibrückenstrasse. This is not a working class district, neither is it a fashionable one. It is plainly middle class, with three and four storied structures giving space to shops and offices on the street level and modest apartments on the floors above. If it were closer to the Bavarian State Library and the University, it would doubtless be a favored student quarter. Thierschstrasse is important in this book only because the Eher Verlag, the Nazi party publishing company, had its offices at No. 11 and Hitler lived in rented rooms at No. 41, until he moved in 1929 to Prinzregentenplatz in the more fashionable district of Bogenhausen. Ten years after the Nazis came to power, a visitor to No. 11 Thierschstrasse would not have imagined that these modest quarters housed one of Germany's largest business enterprises. With a half dozen subsidiary corporations controlling 150 publishing companies, employing an estimated thirty-five thousand persons, with net profits of over a hundred million marks in its best year, the annual volume of business transacted by the Eher Verlag probably exceeded that of the I. G.

Farben concern. It published books, periodicals, illustrated magazines, and over twenty million newspapers daily in Germany and throughout Europe. With only slight exaggeration it has been described as the world's largest "poison gas factory."

There was no printing plant in the headquarters building of the Eher Verlag in the Thierschstrasse. At some twenty minutes' distance, occupying the corner of Schelling and Barerstrasse, near the Alte Pinakothek, was the establishment of M. Müller and Son, printer of the Nazi party's *Völkischer Beobachter*, Hitler's *Mein Kampf*, and all officially sponsored books, serials, and pamphlets of the Nazi movement. Near the Müller plant on Schellingstrasse was located the editorial offices of the *Völkischer Beobachter* and, in the early days of the party, the Eher Verlag, before it moved to larger quarters in the Thierschstrasse. The relations between Adolf Müller and Hitler's party had so developed by 1933 that M. Müller and Son was in fact the printing and production apparatus of the Eher Verlag. The dominant figure in the Nazi party's publishing enterprises was Max Amann, director of the Eher Verlag and Reich Leader for the Press. Hitler held him in highest regard, according him unstinted praise for his development of the V-B and the party's giant newspaper trust. "As regards Amann," Hitler said in 1942, "I can say positively that he's a genius. He is the greatest newspaper proprietor in the world. . . . Today the *Zentral Verlag* owns from 70 to 80 per cent of the German press. Amann achieved all that without the slightest ostentation." [1]

Like the party itself, this great publishing power had rather shabby and insignificant beginnings. The *Völkischer Beobachter*, Reich organ of the N-S party, was the first German newspaper to achieve a million circulation in all editions. This was in no way due to its excellence as a

[1] *Hitler's Secret Conversations*, pp. 268-69.

publication but rather to its position as the official organ of the party. The early history of this newspaper, principal property of the Eher Verlag, has been ably narrated by Dr. Sonja Noller.[2] Only the most significant facts should be presented here.

The predecessor of the V-B, the *Münchner Beobachter*, began publication on January 2, 1887, as a four-page suburban weekly in small format. Both the ownership and the title changed several times before the paper was acquired by the publisher Franz Eher in 1900. Shortly after Eher's death in 1918, the edition circulating outside Munich was retitled *Völkischer Beobachter*, which became the title of the main edition a year later. Meanwhile the Eher heirs had sold the V-B and the Verlag to Rudolf Freiherr von Sebottendorff, a central figure in the Munich Thule Society and other counterrevolutionary and rightist organizations which flourished in the turbulent winter of 1918-1919. Incorporated by the new owners, the principal stockholder was Fräulein Käthe Bierbaumer, reputedly Sebottendorff's mistress as well as his financial backer. Frau Dora Kunze, Sebottendorff's sister, was a minority stockholder. Rightist and strongly racial in its direction, the paper served during this period as a general organ of the *völkisch* movement in South Germany and in the Austrian and Sudetenland areas. It also accumulated debts and required new infusions of capital. Some of this came from members of the Nazi party and its sympathizers and supporters. A list of the stockholders, entered in the Munich corporation court register on March 20, 1920, shows the amounts of their capital participation:

[2] *Die Geschichte des "Völkischen Beobachters" von 1920-1923* (Diss., Munich, 1956). Georg Franz-Willing, whose study of the early history of the Nazi party has recently appeared, adds significant details on the acquisition and the financial expedients resorted to in supporting the paper. *Die Hitler Bewegung: Der Ursprung, 1919-1922*, pp. 180-85.

Käthe Bierbaumer (Freiburg/Breisgau)     46,500 RM
Dora Kunze (Lauban)                      10,000 RM
Gottfried Feder (Munich/Murnau)          10,000 RM
Franz Xaver Eder (Munich)                10,000 RM
Franz Freiherr von Feilitzsch (Munich)   20,000 RM
Dr. Wilhelm Gutberlet (Munich)           10,000 RM
Theodor Heuss (Munich)                   10,000 RM
Karl Alfred Braun                         3,500 RM

Of the listed stockholders, Feder was active in the Nazi party leadership, Gutberlet was a financial supporter, Eder was business manager of the Verlag, and the others were assuredly sympathizers if not active party members.

With dwindling income and mounting debts, the Verlag was on the brink of bankruptcy by December 1920, when a controlling interest was acquired by the National Socialist party. The purchase price was 120,000 RM and assumption of debts amounting to 250,000 RM. On December 18, 1920, it was announced in the V-B that the paper had been purchased by the NSDAP. Although Anton Drexler was still party chairman, Hitler was the driving force behind the venturesome move. Dietrich Eckart, Hitler's friend and sponsor in the party, played the decisive role in that he found the money to make the down payments on the majority shares. Eckart got the cash—60,000 RM—from Reichswehr General Ritter von Epp, acknowledging receipt and pledging repayment in a personal note dated December 17, 1920.[3] Hitler, who was convinced

[3] It is generally assumed that Von Epp used special Reichswehr funds. In 1923, when the matter was exposed in the Social Democratic press—Von Epp called it a "stink bomb"—he claimed that this was a personal loan which had been repaid, a statement of doubtful validity. The relevant documents are in the Von Epp papers, National Archives, Micro-copy T-84, R-24, fr. 9692, and R-25, frs. 9695 ff. See also Franz-Willing, *Die Hitler Bewegung,* pp. 180-81; Freiherr von Sebottendorff, *Bevor Hitler kam,* pp. 192-95; Konrad Heiden, *Geschichte des Nationalsozialismus,* p. 43; and Noller, pp. 235-43.

that acquisition of a party paper was essential to advancement of the movement, was immeasurably happy and Eckart received from him a note of ecstatic thanks for his decisive help.[4] While the loan from Epp was decisive, others also contributed. Dr. Gottfried Grandel, an early financial supporter of the party, and Simon Eckart, an official of the Hansa Bank, advanced part of the purchase money or pledged their credit to consummate the deal. Grandel, as late as 1940, sued the Eher Verlag to recover the warranty money which he had put up in 1921. In a party devoted to the "breaking of interest slavery," financial loans were commonly regarded and treated as gifts!

An entry in the corporation court register (December 17, 1920) reflected the change in ownership. Listed as the principal stockholders were Bierbaumer, Kunze, and Anton Drexler, chairman of the incorporated National Socialist German Workers Society (Nationalsozialistische Deutsche Arbeiterverein, e. V.), the organization which actually held the shares as trustee for the unincorporated NSDAP.[5] Within the year the shares held by the former owners, Bierbaumer and Kunze, passed to the N-S Workers Society and an entry in the corporation register (November 16, 1921) listed Adolf Hitler as chairman of the board, who "declares that he possesses all the shares of the Eher company." The corporation registers subsequent to 1921, which might have thrown additional light on the problem of

[4] Reproduced in Franz-Willing, *Die Hitler Bewegung*, p. 181.

[5] The N-S Arbeiterverein e. V., was registered and its constitution filed with the Amtsgericht München on October 10, 1920. As a corporate body it could hold and administer property, safeguard party funds, and enter into contracts. Membership in the NSDAP carried membership in the N-S Arbeiterverein. The statutes of the Verein were altered in July 1921, when Hitler gained control of the party, ousted Drexler from the chairmanship, and made himself independent of the decisions of the executive committee. Franz-Willing, *Die Hitler Bewegung*, pp. 99-102, reproduces and analyzes the constitution and by-laws of the incorporated Verein.

transfer and ownership, were destroyed during the war.[6] How and when the minority stockholders—Feder, Gutberlet, Braun, Heuss, Eder, and Feilitzsch—were bought out cannot be exactly determined. There are indications that sometimes shares were pledged as dubious security for emergency loans. Reminiscing years later about the daring acquisition of the V-B, Hitler said that Dr. Gutberlet had made him a present of shares valued at 5,000 RM, and he had bought other shares.[7] Amann, whose memory was not infallible, stated in 1951 that when he became director of the Verlag the stock was held by Gottfried Feder, Freiherr von Reitzenstein of Garmisch, and the N-S Workers Society.[8] In 1929, Amann was made a party to a suit against the Eher Verlag, and on this occasion Hitler published a statement on the ownership of the V-B and the publishing company. Amann, he declared, was not a private stockholder in the enterprise. "The firm of Eher is an incorporated company whose total shares are held by the National Socialist Workers Society, a registered society in Munich. There are no private stockholders in the firm." [9]

In the absence of complete corporate records, it is reasonable to conclude that by 1923, or 1926 at the latest, all the capital stock of the Eher company was in the possession of the N-S Workers Society, the trustee organization of the Nazi party. This legal and property relationship was maintained until December 1933, when the "Law for the Safeguarding of the Unity of Party and State" was promulgated. Paragraph I of this Reich statute declared the NSDAP a legally incorporated body whose constitution was

[6] Noller, pp. 232-36; and a study made by Dr. Wilhelm R. Beyer for the Bavarian Restitution Office: "Die Gesellschaftsrechtliche Geschichte des Eher-Verlages," March 1, 1949, pp. 1-3; File 3820-b, BWB.

[7] *Hitler's Secret Conversations*, p. 282.

[8] In an appeal from his sentence by the Munich denazification court, filed Nov. 2, 1951; Amann Spruchkammer file.

[9] *Völkischer Beobachter*, April 11, 1929.

determined by the Führer. A subsequent ordinance implementing this law was issued on March 20, 1935. It declared the N-S Workers Society dissolved and its assets transferred without liquidation to the newly incorporated NSDAP. The constitution and by-laws of the predecessor organization remained in force, however, until a new constitution was published on April 29, 1935. This instrument made no change in the status of the Eher Verlag and the V-B, which remained outside the property and financial control of the party treasurer. Like other property, the stock of the Eher Verlag was legally held by the N-S Workers Society and later by the incorporated NSDAP.[10] As chairman of the board of the Eher Verlag, Hitler exercised sole authority, which he later delegated to Amann. His name appeared as publisher on the masthead of the V-B from 1925 to 1933. But contrary to the common assumption Hitler did not personally own or hold shares in the Eher Verlag.

## Max Amann—Hitler's Business Dwarf

From the time of its acquisition, Hitler personally interested himself in the direction and management of the *Völkischer Beobachter*. Because of his addiction to drugs and alcohol, Dietrich Eckart, who took charge of the party's paper in 1921, was an unreliable editor. Gradually he was shunted aside and Alfred Rosenberg, his principal assistant, became editor-in-chief when he acquired German citizenship in 1923.[11] Hitler has described the financial

[10] Text of the statute, the implementing ordinance, and the new constitution are printed in the *Organisationsbuch der NSDAP*, (7th edn. 1943), pp. 489-91, 492-97. On the title page of official party publications, the inscription "Zentralverlag der NSDAP, Franz Eher Nachfolger," was commonly used. The Zentralverlag, however, was a party agency; in the corporation register the title remained "Franz Eher Verlag Nachfolger."

[11] *Memoirs of Alfred Rosenberg*, p. 70; and Heiden, pp. 121-22.

plight of the V-B and the Eher Verlag when they were acquired by the party. "When I took it over the *Völkischer Beobachter* had no more than seven thousand subscribers, not a single advertising contract . . . and not a penny in the till for the purchase of the paper it was printed on." Hitler did not exaggerate the difficulties encountered in the first year of party ownership. The position of business manager changed hands several times until Max Amann, who had been business manager of the party since the previous August, became director also of the Eher Verlag on April 4, 1922.[12]

It was not an easy task that Amann undertook, and his gifts for organization, economy, and calculation were put to a severe test. A person with less energy and determination would have been discouraged. Unfamiliar with publishing problems, he learned the business as he went along, and it must be said he learned it well. He maintained the V-B on a sound financial basis, he founded and developed the book department of the Verlag, and after 1933 he was the driving force, if not the creative brain, of the party's monopoly of newspaper publishing. Hitler never ceased to praise Amann and his astuteness as a publisher and business man.

Born in Munich, November 24, 1891, Amann attended business school and served an office apprenticeship in a Munich law firm. He served five years in the Bavarian army and for a time during World War I he was Hitler's company sergeant. Demobilized in 1919, he married and took employment in a Munich mortgage bank. Regarding his reencounter with Hitler and entry into the Nazi party Amann had two versions—one which he propagated in party circles before 1945, and the other after 1945. In the first version, a chance meeting in the street and an invitation to attend one of Hitler's meetings brought him into

[12] *Hitler's Secret Conversations*, pp. 376-77; Noller, pp. 239-40.

the movement in February 1920. In the summer of 1921, after he had gained control of the party apparatus, Hitler offered Amann the position of business manager. Amann hesitated as he had job commitments and pension prospects. Hitler gave him a two-hour lecture on the dangers of Bolshevism and closed with an impassioned plea to switch jobs. He asked: "What good will your pension rights do you if some day the Bolsheviks string you up to a lamp post?" Amann took three days to think it over, then resigned his secure job and took the position offered by Hitler.[13] After 1945, under interrogation, Amann was less heroic. He posed as a business man and Germany's leading publisher; he was completely disinterested in politics and scorned impractical ideologues; his connections with Hitler, the party, and the movement were strictly business relationships; he understood nothing of politics.[14] The record, however, shows Amann to have been not only an effective business manager and Verlag director, but an active member of the party. His political services fully justified his later appointment as a Reichsleiter and the award of the highest party honors.

The details of his party activity need not detain us. His role in the Beer Hall Putsch was that of a trusted lieutenant. Together with other party activists, Amann was arrested and jailed from November 19 to December 12, 1923, and charged with "aiding and abetting high treason." It

[13] *Max Amann: Ein Leben für Führer und Volk*, pp. 9-10. Also Franz Hartmann, *Die Statistische und Geschichtliche Entwicklung der N-S Presse, 1926-1935*, pp. 209-10, statement supplied by Amann. This work prepared under the direction of Dr. Uetrecht, director of the Hauptarchiv der NSDAP, is a rich mine of information on the early history of the Nazi press. The typescript volume is presently in the Library of Congress, Manuscripts Division, Eher Verlag collection, carton 474. The work is cited hereafter as Hartmann, *N-S Presse*.

[14] Amann, Interview notes, Aug. 23, 1945; and depositions in his denazification records.

appears that at Hitler's orders, on the night of November 8-9, he forcibly seized quarters in the bank building where he was formerly employed with a view to using them as central offices for the new "national government" which had been proclaimed at the Bürgerbräukeller. At his trial on April 15, 1924, Amann threw up a great smoke screen, asserting that he was uninformed in advance by Hitler of the plot and thought that he was carrying out orders of a legal authority. He got off lightly with a fine of 100 gold marks, or ten days' imprisonment, for "illegal assumption of official authority." Amann was interrogated again by the police on June 2, 1924, concerning the source of party funds, particularly as to whether large sums had been given to Hitler just prior to the Putsch. Amann denied this and went on to state that as business manager he handled membership dues and contributions, and transmitted through Julius Schreck to Göring sums for payment of the SA—all on Hitler's orders. He admitted that substantial gifts were made to Hitler by German admirers but he denied that these channeled through his office; they were expended by Hitler personally for "party propaganda" purposes. He refused to give the names of any donors and stated that the party's bank account was with the Hansa Bank.[15]

Although dwarf-like in stature, Amann was the aggressive, rowdy type of Nazi. This was publicly demonstrated by an incident that occurred in the Munich city council, to which he had been elected as a NSDAP candidate. At a council meeting in 1925, Amann attacked the city and state authorities for refusing his request for a pistol permit and loud taunts were exchanged between Nazi members and Social Democrats. One of Amann's party associates

[15] Amann, Spruchkammer file, Handakten; copy of judgment and rationale, May 22, 1924; and sworn statement by Amann made to Polizeidirektion Abt. vi-a, Nov. 19, 1923, describing every move made on the night of Nov. 8-9.

was escorted from the council room by Mayor Scharnagl. Later when Amann denounced city councillor Nussbaum as "Jew Nussbaum and *provocateur*," Thomas Wimmer, who served as mayor of Munich after World War II, seized Amann by the throat and forced him down upon the council table. Wimmer was only restrained from further violence against the Nazi tormentor by the intervention of his colleagues.[16]

Other and even more discreditable instances of Amann's brutality and propensity for brawling were presented in his denazification hearing. While these were not all judicially established, altogether eleven instances, some serious and some trivial, were alleged. They mainly concerned the use of his party position and power to play the bully, oppressor, and persecutor; but one involved denunciation to the Gestapo, one personal assault, and another suspicion of murder. It was brought out in the denazification hearing that Amann had caused a young student, who was friendly with his secretary, to be arrested and then personally gave him a merciless beating. The general prosecutor, in summing up, declared that "in his entire life Amann was never anything more than a brutal sergeant." [17]

Behind a jovial Bavarian exterior, Amann was temperamental, brutal, domineering, and materialistic in his personal and business relationships. Toward his subordinates he was dictatorial and ruthless. Personally greedy, it was shown from tax records during the denazification proceedings that his income increased from 108,000 marks in 1934 to 3,800,000 in 1944. His country house at Tegernsee cost nearly a half million marks. This was one of the principal charges against him—that he had enormously enriched himself through his position in the Nazi party. This charge

[16] *Augsburger Abendzeitung*, Feb. 18, 1925.
[17] *Süddeutsche Zeitung*, Dec. 7, 1948. Amann was pronounced a "major offender," sentenced to ten years' hard labor, confiscation of all but 5,000 marks of his property, and loss of civil rights.

was well founded. After the war it was revealed that
Amann, besides his substantial salary from the Eher Verlag and five per cent of the net profits, also owned a one-
third interest in the Müller and Son printing company, and
that his business assets for tax purposes in 1943 amounted
to over ten million marks. Whether Hitler was aware of
Amann's participation in the Müller company cannot be
determined. When the party press was reorganized in 1933-
1934, an order by Hitler forbade party officials to retain
any financial interest in the party press. Only Hitler could
have made an exception in Amann's favor, for the order
was enforced even against the powerful propaganda minister Goebbels.

Apart from membership in the Munich city council and
attendance at important party meetings and rallies, Amann
was not conspicuous in the political leadership of the party.
Neither was he a regular member of Hitler's personal entourage, and socially they do not seem to have been close.
In the splits and feuds that were chronic in the leadership
after the November 1923 fiasco, Amann remained unshake-
ably loyal to Hitler. Although its business dwindled almost
to extinction and the employees had to be furloughed,
Amann saved the Verlag when the party was banned, and
he was able to resume publication of the V-B when the
prohibition was lifted. With the refounding of the party
in February 1925, Franz Xaver Schwarz became party
treasurer and took over the duties previously performed by
Amann as business manager. When this reorganization
took place, the Eher Verlag was given independent status
at Hitler's insistence and Schwarz was relieved of responsibility for its financial oversight and control. Here Hitler
gave Amann a free hand and he reigned supreme.[18]

After the party came to power, Amann continued to
enjoy Hitler's favor and confidence. He was moved into

[18] Statement by Schwarz, May 15, 1945.

the key position in the national publisher's organization, and his jurisdiction and responsibilities were further extended, in 1934, when the N-S Gau press was reorganized and placed under the control of the Eher Verlag. In 1935, with the introduction of the publishing ordinances, frequently designated "Amann ordinances," the Eher Verlag acquired a hundred or more important publishing properties, placing it in a position of complete dominance in the German publishing scene. Amann defended his empire fiercely and drove off all poachers. In any jurisdictional conflict he could usually count on a favorable decision from Hitler. However, Goebbels and Otto Dietrich, the Reich press chief, were the two with whom Amann stood in closest relationship and with whom friction and rivalry developed. He usually avoided direct collisions with Goebbels, who was his intellectual superior in every respect; in disputes with Dietrich, Amann could usually prevail. And Robert Ley, leader of the labor front, who sought to force all Eher employees into his organization, was easily blocked by Amann. "I never had any of Ley's Labor Front Leaders in my printing plants," he boasted in 1945. "The greater part of my workers never joined the Labor Front." [19]

Amann maintained his office and residence in Munich, going to Berlin only on business trips. When he visited the capital he was always invited to join the Führer's circle at lunch in the chancellery. As director of the Eher Verlag, Amann was immediately responsible to Hitler, and made no periodic reports to the party chancellery or party treasurer. What Amann called "plenipotentiary powers" were given him by Hitler in 1936.[20] Not only was Amann Hitler's business agent in publishing matters, he also served as Hitler's banker. The large income from royalties on *Mein Kampf* remained in the Eher accounts and when Hitler

[19] Amann, Interview notes, Aug. 22, 1945.
[20] Amann, Interview notes, Aug. 22, 1945.

required funds he simply called on Amann. When money was needed for personal or party purposes, Amann could usually produce it.

As a party man and political activist, Amann's talents and interests were severely limited. He was not a speaker or debater, nor could he express himself well in writing. Addresses, articles, official announcements, and important letters were usually prepared by his subordinates. Anything resembling an abstract idea baffled him. He was not wholly insincere when he insisted that politics, programs, ideas, and ideologies did not interest him. He could function effectively as general director of an enterprise where he only had to issue or bawl orders to subordinates. He gained a thorough knowledge of the publishing business and the techniques of corporate finance, but he wisely left important business negotiations requiring finesse to others better qualified than he. A passionate hunter, he spent much time in the fields and forests of Bavaria. In 1931 he suffered the loss of his left arm in a firearms accident while hunting with an old crony, Ritter von Epp.[21]

A perceptive appraisal of Amann in his later years was made by one of the panel judges in a post-war publisher's restitution case in which Amann testified as a witness. The judge noted that "The witness, Max Amann, one of the most prominent National Socialists in the Third Reich, and on reliable testimony of other witnesses one of Hitler's most trusted associates, still gives the impression of a brutal personality with inclinations toward outbursts of anger. His statements are absolutely untrustworthy where they run counter to other principal witnesses or depositions. . . .

[21] Fritz Schmidt in his exposure of Amann and the Nazi party publishing trust was in error when he stated that "He [Amann] did not lose his arm in the first World War but in one of his numerous automobile accidents, which cost the lives of several people." *Presse in Fesseln*, p. 10.

One can imagine how he must have conducted himself at the height of his power. Apart from obvious untruths . . . the witness displayed a certain directness and simplicity, and a view of things that is in marked agreement with views current during the Third Reich." [22] Greedy and eager to amass wealth, Amann gained a large fortune through service to Hitler and the Nazi party. In the end he lost his property, his business holdings, his job and pension rights, and died in extreme poverty.

## Amann and the *Völkischer Beobachter*

Although inexperienced in newspaper publishing Amann brought order into the chaotic affairs of the *Völkischer Beobachter*. Prior to its acquisition by the Nazi party, the paper had publicized the activities of all parties and associations in the German *völkisch* movement. A bi-weekly, it appeared on Wednesday and Saturday and was limited customarily to four or six pages. After the Nazis acquired the paper, it lost its broader representation and became a typical party organ, an exclusive megaphone for the leadership of the NSDAP. Hitler published his first article in the paper on January 1, 1921—"The Völkisch Idea and the Party." After Dietrich Eckart became chief editor, Hitler's personal publicity as party chairman and leader was notably increased. For anti-Semitic excesses the paper incurred a ten-day suspension in 1920 and was suspended again for nearly a month in 1921. On February 8, 1923, the V-B converted to daily publication.

During that turbulent winter, Hitler's notoriety was spreading in Munich and Bavaria, the inflation soared, discontent and confusion spread, and people flocked to the party meetings and enrolled for membership. The move-

[22] Case of Ilse Pielenz vs. Finance Ministry of Baden-Württemberg, Sept. 28, 1953, p. 40.

ment needed a daily journal to spread its views more widely
and effectively. Hitler tapped the resources of some of his
wealthy supporters to finance the conversion. The risk was
taken and the venture succeeded.[23] A further advance was
made in August 1923, when at Hitler's insistence the paper
was changed from the traditional small format to the larger
Berlin size.[24] On the eve of the Beer Hall Putsch the circulation reached thirty thousand daily. The official ban on the
party, after this event, included its principal newspaper.
The Verlag, however, continued in business although its
operations were limited to the small book department
which Amann had added in 1923. In subsequent years this
department was developed cautiously, publishing Nazi
authors, and yielding a considerable profit which supported
the development of the V-B as the national organ of the
Nazi movement.[25]

When the ban on the party was lifted, Amann resumed
publication of the paper, first as a weekly, and a month
later as a daily (March 24, 1925). Its circulation now was
barely 4,000. Henceforth the growth in circulation, like the

[23] According to Rosenberg, the principal benefactor was Frau
Gertrude von Seidlitz, who helped with a gift of shares in a Finnish
paper mill. (*Memoirs of Alfred Rosenberg*, p. 79.) "Putzi" Hanfstaengl also contributed an interest-free loan of one thousand dollars,
a small fortune in inflated marks. (Hanfstaengl, *Unheard Witness*,
pp. 55, 144-45.) On the party's finances and its principal bene-
factors, many of whom were foreigners, see also G. Franz-Willing,
*Die Hitlerbewegung*, pp. 190-98.

[24] Hartmann, *N-S Presse*, pp. 215-16. Hitler regarded the adoption of the large format as a daring and distinctive innovation.
*Hitler's Secret Conversations*, pp. 115-16.

[25] *Max Amann: Ein Leben für Führer und Volk*, pp. 36, 40;
Hartmann, *N-S Presse*, pp. 215-16; and an informative article by
Hermann Esser, "Die Entwicklung unseres Parteiverlages," in the
V-B, Dec. 12, 1928. Hitler credited Amann with saving the Eher
Verlag from enforced liquidation when the party was suppressed.
(*Hitler's Secret Conversations*, pp. 281-82.)

party's membership, was steady but not spectacular, amounting to only 18,400 in 1929. Then came the great depression. The spreading confusion and discontent yielded to the Nazis not only votes but also subscriptions to their leading paper. With the South German and Berlin editions added in 1930, total circulation rose to 39,600. In 1931, circulation in all editions reached 128,800, dropping to 116,200 in 1932.[26] After the Nazi victory in 1933, and the acquired prestige of a government organ, circulation of the V-B forged ahead for two years at a sharp rate and then settled down to steady but substantial annual gains. A North German edition was added in 1933 and a complete editorial and printing establishment was set up in Berlin. In 1938 with the Austrian Anschluss, the Vienna edition made its prompt appearance. In all editions, circulation between 1933 and 1939 gained about 100,000 per year, reaching 741,714 in 1939 and 1,192,542 in 1941.[27]

Circulation in the newspaper publishing business does not necessarily guarantee a paper's financial position. Amann maintained that financial difficulties were considerable for the first two or three years after the refounding of the party, but that the phenomenal sales of *Mein Kampf*, beginning in 1929, relieved the Eher Verlag of all financial troubles. By that time the V-B had cleared its considerable indebtedness and was financially independent. This was an unusual condition for a political party paper and convincing proof of Amann's ability as a manager. In the

[26] The Munich and South German editions lost 23,000 circulation in 1932 while the Berlin edition doubled. In 1933 the Munich edition dropped to 11,645 and then quadrupled its circulation in 1934.

[27] These statistics are taken from the charts in *Max Amann: Ein Leben*, p. 50. They correspond roughly but not exactly to the statistics given in Hartmann's *N-S Presse* for the period 1925 to 1939. Hartmann's figures are slightly higher than those given in the Amann volume.

presidential, Reichstag, and state elections of 1932, the V-B contributed 3,900,000 RM to the party's campaign funds.[28]

Much of the success of the V-B was due to the paper's position as the organ of the party leadership. All party officials were required to subscribe to it, and the ordinary members were under pressure to support the movement by taking its leading paper. In the early years the V-B was simply an instrument of indoctrination and political combat. After 1933, people subscribed because they hoped to learn what their masters were thinking and saying. The quality of the paper was low judged by ordinary standards of journalism. The masthead proclaimed that it was the "Combat Organ of the National Socialist Movement of Germany," and, despite improvements in news service and coverage, such remained its predominant character. When Rosenberg became chief editor in 1923, the V-B had only four editorial staff members, no local representatives, and was dependent for much of its material upon occasional contributors. Hitler complained that under Rosenberg's editorship the paper was dull and lacked popular appeal. Rosenberg, he said, retrospectively, "gave us deeply philosophical treatises written by professors, and mostly on Central Asia and the Far East." He ought to have called the paper "Münchner Beobachter—Baltic edition." [29]

Between Amann as business manager and Rosenberg as editor there was constant friction. The rough Bavarian extrovert loathed the pseudo-intellectual Balt who would sit for hours in a café reading and writing when he should

[28] Hartmann, *N-S Presse*, p. 216; *Max Amann: Ein Leben*, pp. 36, 40, 46-47. On the annual sales of *Mein Kampf* and Hitler's income from this source see, Oron J. Hale, "Adolf Hitler: Taxpayer," *Amer. Hist. Rev.*, July 1955, pp. 836-37. Amann stated in 1945 that *Mein Kampf* had total sales of fifteen million copies in all German editions.

[29] *Hitler's Secret Conversations*, p. 527; *Memoirs of Alfred Rosenberg*, p. 79.

have been producing a good newspaper.[30] Amann, when supported by Hitler, would give Rosenberg instructions on content and makeup and bellow orders over the telephone to his chief editor. In his turn, Rosenberg would write long letters of dignified protest. Both would bombard Hitler with complaints and charges against one another, and Hitler, in the crossfire, would take evasive action. On one occasion, and probably on others as well, Rosenberg offered his resignation because relations between the editorial staff and the Verlag (Amann) had become intolerable.[31] In 1927, much of the daily routine of editing the paper was placed in the hands of Wilhelm Weiss, who was appointed Rosenberg's assistant and supervisor of the editorial staff. An experienced journalist, Weiss was soon promoted to deputy editor, and in 1938 succeeded Rosenberg as editor-in-chief. Weiss, because of his pliant personality, served as an effective buffer between Amann and Rosenberg.

## Wilhelm Weiss—Managing Editor

Wilhelm Weiss, like many of the early Nazi journalists, came from middle class *völkisch* nationalist circles. Born in Stadtsteinach, Bavaria, March 31, 1892, Weiss served in the World War, and reached the grade of captain. He was severely wounded and suffered the amputation of his left leg. He was then posted to the Troop Office of the Bavarian war ministry where he began to write military commentaries for the press department. Later he wrote for several

[30] Albert Krebs, *Tendenzen und Gestalten der NSDAP*, pp. 179-80, quoting Amann's comments on Rosenberg as editor.

[31] Rosenberg to Hitler, Dec. 29, 1926; NA Micro-copy T-81, R-667, frs. 5061-2. This file of Rosenberg's correspondence contains a number of letters recording clashes with Amann. One letter from Amann, Dec. 8, 1925, is a rejection of a Rosenberg book on the grounds that it was too long, too costly to produce, and the party members too poor to buy it.

veteran's papers. His work for the daily press began with contributions to the *Bayerische Staatszeitung*. He was a registered student in the University of Munich from 1918 to 1920 but took no degree. A rabid nationalist, he joined one after another of the quasi-military and veterans' organizations, which flourished in Munich and Bavaria— the Einwohnerwehr, Altreichsflagge, Reichskriegsflagge, Deutsch-völkischen Offizierbund, Freikorps Oberland, and Ernst Röhm's Frontbann, serving in the latter as staff officer for political affairs. In 1922 he edited the *Heimatlandbriefe* in which he denounced "Marxism, Jewry, and political Catholicism." An artificial leg did not prevent him from marching with Hitler from the Bürgerbräukeller to the Feldherrnhalle in 1923. Weiss gradually withdrew himself from the veterans' organizations as they had no effective political leadership, and developed his contacts with the National Socialists. When the V-B was banned after the November Putsch, Weiss published the *Völkischer Kurier* as a substitute. On January 1, 1927, he joined the V-B, becoming deputy editor in 1933 and editor-in-chief in 1938, a position he had filled for some years without the title.

Up to 1933 Weiss had ten convictions for infraction of the press laws, participation in the Beer Hall Putsch, violations of the law for the defense of the Republic, and glorifying the murder of Walther Rathenau. Among various editorial assignments with the Eher Verlag was the editorship of the anti-Semitic periodical, *Brennessel*. Of this publication it can only be said that, compared to Julius Streicher's *Sturmer*, it was satirical rather than sadistic. Weiss was also the organizer and publisher of the Nazi party correspondence service—the N-S Korrespondenz —of which Otto Dietrich later became the editor. Weiss was the possessor of many party honors, including the Golden Party Badge, the Blood Order, the Service Cross,

Reichsleiter Max Amann

DR. MAX WINKLER, Trustee and Business Agent of the Eher Verlag

WILHELM WEISS, Editor-in-Chief of the *Völkischer Beobachter*
and President of the Reich Press Association

and the rank of Obergruppenführer in the SA.[32] Weiss was a good example of how high one could go in the Nazi system with only moderate intelligence, capacities, and drive. Hired, as it were, to labor in the vineyard from the first hour, he received more than the biblical penny for his labors.

As editor of the official party organ, later the largest newspaper in the Reich, Weiss became a leading figure in German journalism. Although the Berlin, Munich, and Vienna editions of the V-B had separate editorial staffs, Weiss in his capacity of managing editor bore general responsibility for personnel and policy, as well as the foreign and domestic news services. In 1934, Goebbels appointed Weiss head of the Reich Association of the German Press, the agency of control and coercion imposed by the Nazis upon the journalistic profession.

In his denazification hearings and in numerous depositions, Weiss criticized the coercive system imposed by the political leadership upon the press. There is supporting evidence of disillusionment and dissatisfaction with the strait jacket which he and other Nazi journalists found themselves compelled to wear. But this aversion was not evident before or immediately after the Nazis came to power. At the annual conference of the journalists' association, in 1934, Weiss made the principal address in which he declared: "The press in the old liberal sense is dead and will never be called to life again. It must remain dead because the spirit of that epoch, which lies behind, is also dead. . . . Journalism today is no longer a middle class business, and those who inwardly remain Philistines will

[32] Weiss, Interview notes, Aug. 31, 1945; Spruchkammer file, including autobiographical depositions, Munich political police record, and Fragebogen; also Hartmann, *N-S Presse*, pp. 213-14; and *Völkischer Beobachter*, Aug. 7, 1931, on the founding of the *N-S Korrespondenz*.

certainly not be encouraged by us to clothe their tender souls in National Socialist garments. We cannot use such persons in the future in the German press, because at the first intellectual or moral testing they would fail utterly. . . . The German press is dead—Long live the German Press!" [33] By 1937 Weiss was considerably disillusioned. That he wanted to resign his position as the leading party editor is probably true, but his commitments and character were such that he never repudiated or distanced himself in any way from the Nazi system.

It was not in Weiss's nature to attempt to play a major role in party affairs. He lacked the aggressive toughness required for the game as played by Hitler's associates. Even in the direction of the affairs of the V-B and the journalists' association, Weiss was the *routinier*, maintained in his position by the forces of contention that emanated from Otto Dietrich, Goebbels, Amann, and the party chancellery. Both Amann and his deputy Rolf Rienhardt put pressure on Weiss to keep him in his position when he wanted to resign. If the key post were vacated, Weiss's successor would undoubtedly have come from Goebbels' ministry, Dietrich's apparatus, or Himmler's circle. His relations with Dietrich, both personal and official, were particularly bad and the press chief tried on several occasions to effect Weiss's removal. This was sufficient reason for Amann and Rienhardt to work for his retention because the rivalry and conflict between Amann and Dietrich was of long standing. On one occasion, Weiss, goaded beyond endurance, effected the dismissal of Helmut Sündermann, Dietrich's deputy and editor of the N-S Correspondence. Dietrich intervened with Hitler. The latter called Amann on the carpet and the dismissal notice was withdrawn.[34]

[33] *Völkischer Beobachter*, April 21, 1934.
[34] Weiss, Spruchkammer file, "Beiakten," deposition by Rolf Rienhardt, Aug. 26, 1948; also Interview notes, Wilhelm Weiss, Aug. 31, 1945.

By nature Weiss was quiet, reserved, and conciliatory. His staff associates were aware that he avoided at all cost collisions and difficulties with the party leaders. Amann could bully him, and his services were cheap. He supported and carried out the Editor's Law, first as president of the Landesverband Berlin, and then as head of the Reich association of journalists. Instances of tolerance in applying the law and maintaining the professional list, even in cases involving Jewish journalists, speak for his humanity. By dilatoriness, or looking the other way, Weiss made it possible for many journalists to remain in the profession and in employment. Under more rigorous enforcement many would have been stricken from the list. A number of non-Nazi journalists testified on his behalf in the denazification hearing. Weiss was not a fanatical, brutal, vindictive type of Nazi, and instances of tolerance and decency in professional relationships are not absent from his record. However, there is no evidence that he ever recognized the truth about National Socialism, or dissociated himself from its ideology and program. The Munich denazification court came to the same conclusion and placed him in the category of "activist." [35]

Until 1933, little effort or money was expended in developing the news and information services of the V-B. Party politics was its *raison d'être* and its meager cultural, economic, and intellectual offerings were designed for the converted and the dedicated. With the party's accession to power, the V-B had fulfilled its original mission as a combat organ and spokesman for the movement. Could it now become a newspaper in the accepted sense? Weiss undertook to convert a weapon of political combat into an informa-

[35] He was sentenced—July 15, 1949—to three years' imprisonment, which he had already served in internment camps, confiscation of thirty per cent of his property, loss of civil rights, and suppression of professional rights for ten years. Weiss died on Feb. 24, 1950, as an appeal was pending. (Weiss, Spruchkammer file, "Verdict and Rationale.")

tional newspaper by broadening its interest and offerings, improving its journalistic personnel, and extending its news service and coverage. It must be admitted that he accomplished much between 1933 and 1939, but the war brought new restrictions and difficulties that made it impossible to publish an interesting and informative newspaper in Nazi Germany.

## II. The Nazi Party Press, 1925-1933

## Reichsleitung and the Party Press

Before 1933, National Socialist press propaganda was decentralized to the Gau and district areas and their official leaders. Financing of the propaganda organs was likewise a local or regional responsibility. The V-B was the official organ of the party directorate; through it was communicated the party line and news of party action. It served also as a combat organ in the arena of national politics. Party officials were obligated to subscribe to the V-B, and its dominant position was jealously guarded by Hitler and Amann, the latter having a particularly sharp eye for potential rivals among the regional party papers. The editorial production of the staff of the V-B was likewise rigorously controlled. The Bavarian political police reported in November 1926 that three staff members had been dismissed because they refused to sign an agreement not to write for other papers, not to use material for private purposes, or to communicate information to other N-S papers. Three of the editors—Buchner, Stolzing-Czerny, and Gengler—had rejected the conditions but Rosenberg had signed. Hitler, it was reported, had approved the action.[1]

The monopoly position and control enforced on behalf of the V-B was likewise demanded for the *Illustrierte Beobachter,* which was launched as a monthly (later weekly) in 1926, on the initiative of Amann and the photographer, Heinrich Hoffmann—the two whom Konrad Heiden dubbed "Hitler's business dwarfs." When the Verlag "Die Flamme" in Bamberg announced that it would publish periodically an illustrated supplement for party

[1] Report of Nov. 3, 1926, Akten des Staats-Ministeriums des Innern (Bayern), File 1768; Hauptarchiv der NSDAP, Berlin Document Center.

members, the publisher Gottfried Feder received a sharp communication from party headquarters in Munich. He was reminded that all publications designed for sale and circulation among the membership required the specific approval of the Reichsleitung. This approval would not be forthcoming for an illustrated periodical, which would compete with the *Illustrierte Beobachter*, established under a mandate from Hitler. "If every private publisher in Germany, even one authorized to publish an official party paper, should seek to imitate or surpass a publication established with great effort by the central party office, then soon we should have a dozen or two illustrated papers, and the *Illustrierte Beobachter*, which was begun in the first place as a support to our central party organ, would go to the wall." [2] It might be noted here that the concept of monopoly was inherent in the Nazi press from its inception.

Officially, until 1933, the control and organization of the party press rested upon resolutions adopted at the 1928 party congress in Weimar. To insure unity of purpose and expression, authority to supervise and control the party organs was vested in the central party directorate. Likewise only the party directorate could designate papers as official and authorize the use of the swastika emblem on the masthead. Withdrawal of this permission canceled the official status of the organ. The central authority also approved new editions of established papers and exercised a right of concurrence in editorial appointments. The Propaganda Section of the Reichsleitung in Munich was charged with responsibility for interpreting and applying these resolutions. [3]

At the end of 1928, three years after refounding of the NSDAP, the Nazi press consisted of two dailies, twenty-

[2] Bouhler to Verlag "Die Flamme," Oct. 16, 1926; Propaganda Abtl., Hauptarchiv der NSDAP, BDC.

[3] The resolutions are reproduced in Otto Groth, *Die Zeitung*, II, 466.

seven weeklies, one monthly, and one fortnightly publication. Seven of the weeklies were published by Gregor and Otto Strasser through their Kampfverlag in Berlin, and circulated in the various districts of North Germany. Three, or four (it is not possible to determine), were published by the Eher Verlag, and the remainder were local private or party undertakings. Nineteen of the thirty-one carried the swastika emblem, which gave them the status of official organs, while the remainder were "officially recognized" by the party. All were subject to the regulations adopted at the party conference in Weimar. From time to time the Reichsleitung would announce that official status had been given to a paper or would circulate a list to all party agencies. Official recognition by the Reichsleitung implied acceptance of certain conditions: First, the editor must observe the party line and the directives issued by the party propaganda office; second, editors and publishers were subject to reprimand and disciplinary action for infractions of regulations or breaches of party discipline; third, the papers must publish free of charge party announcements and notices emanating from the departments of the Reichsleitung; fourth, they could not accept advertising from Jewish firms. The disciplinary sanctions available against both editors and publishers were expulsion from the party, withdrawal of party recognition—the use of the swastika emblem was covered by law—and finally, boycott by the membership. Editors and publishers were obligated to send to the propaganda office a copy of each edition, which was carefully scrutinized, sometimes criticized, and sometimes made the basis of suggestions for notices or articles. The propaganda office also distributed clippings and recommended republication.[4]

[4] This summary of the control and direction of the press is based on the letters, memoranda, and circulars contained in the records of the Propaganda Abteilung der Reichsleitung for the years 1926-1930. For this period Himmler was the section chief with the title

One of the principal activities of party members was the promotion of their literature and publications. Like some religious sects, with their door-to-door canvassing, the Nazis, and particularly the SA, solicited subscriptions for their local and national organs. This activity was promoted by the party directorate to the point where one sometimes has the impression that Hitler was more interested in new subscribers for the V-B than in new party members. Typical is a communication to all "recognized party papers" dated February 1, 1927, requesting reprinting of a special supplement of the V-B in which Hitler announced the launching of a propaganda campaign for new subscribers to the party's central organ. Copies of their reprints were to be returned to the Reichsleitung.[5]

Another concern of the central directorate was the advertising that appeared in the party papers. A letter to Gregor Strasser's Kampfverlag called attention to the unauthorized use of the party emblem by an advertiser who was competing with the party sales outlet in providing SA uniforms, emblems, and insignia. Also advertisements of weapons, particularly of pistols, were not to be carried in official party papers as the possession and carrying of weapons had been repeatedly prohibited![6]

As with all political party journals propagating a distinctive ideology, the suppression of intra-party strife and the maintenance of ideological discipline was a continuing

Deputy Reich Propaganda Leader, and most of the communications are signed or initialed by him. (Himmler was also available for speaking assignments at party meetings and usually asked an honorarium of twenty marks!) Some of the communications are signed by Philip Bouhler in his capacity as Reichsgeschäftsführer der NSDAP. This file is from the party Hauptarchiv now in the Berlin Document Center.

[5] Circular, Feb. 1, and *Völkischer Beobachter*, Jan. 26, 1927; Prop. Abtl., Hauptarchiv, BDC.

[6] May 25, 1927, copy to all recognized party papers; Prop. Abtl., Hauptarchiv, BDC.

problem, requiring repeated admonitions from Hitler and the Reichsleitung. On February 9, 1927, a circular directive to all editors reminded them that on current political questions the position taken by the V-B must be observed as authoritative.[7] An admonition from Hitler, several times repeated, also warned party editors to refrain from conducting intra-party strife in the papers; the N-S press was a weapon to be used against opponents, not against party members. He expressly forbade attacks upon fellow members through the press, either openly or camouflaged as letters to the editor.[8] On another occasion a stiff reprimand was issued to Gauleiter Erich Koch and the *Ostdeutscher Beobachter* for anti-Catholic articles and attacks upon the papacy. In view of "the positive Christian posture of the Party as stated in the Party program," it was highly undesirable to raise religious issues that divided rather than united the membership. Koch was reminded that what might be acceptable in East Prussia could evoke adverse reactions in Catholic Bavaria. The *Ostdeutscher Beobachter* should observe party discipline in this important matter. The reprimand delivered to Koch appears to have resulted from a strong complaint lodged by Gauleiter Grohé with Rudolf Hess, calling attention to the anti-clerical excesses of the *Deutsche Wochenschau*, the *Ostdeutscher Beobachter*, and particularly a recently published article in the latter by Count Reventlow, entitled "The Crusade against Soviet Russia." [9]

Echoes of the Goebbels-Strasser feud in Berlin are also discernible in the records of the propaganda section of the

[7] Bouhler to all N-S papers, Feb. 2, 1927; Prop. Abtl., Hauptarchiv, BDC.

[8] Sept. 17, 1928; Prop. Abtl., Hauptarchiv, BDC.

[9] Grohé to Hess, April 13; Bouhler to Koch, May 8, 1930; Prop. Abtl., Hauptarchiv, BDC. There is a perceptive sketch of Count Reventlow and his position in the Nazi party in Albert Krebs, *Tendenzen und Gestalten*, pp. 220-25.

Reichsleitung. In 1927-1928, next to the Eher Verlag, the Kampfverlag, founded by Gregor and Otto Strasser, was the principal publisher of party papers in North Germany. At the height of the feud between Goebbels and Gregor Strasser, the latter wrote a sharp letter to the Reichsleitung asserting that for three weeks the Berlin Gauleiter had withheld from Strasser's *Berliner Arbeiter-Zeitung* the party calendar of meetings, discussions, and assemblies for Gau Berlin-Brandenburg. He reminded the Reichsleitung that the BAZ was the official paper for Gau Berlin and that party members looked to it for official notices and announcements. Strasser went on to air his suspicion that withholding of official announcements was a trick to force party members to buy or subscribe to Dr. Goebbels' "neutral" Monday paper, *Der Angriff*, where the complete calendar of weekly meetings for the Gau was to be found. He closed by saying that he would appreciate being informed of the action taken by the Reichsleitung.[10]

While not so acute as in Berlin, similar friction and feuds developed elsewhere as Gauleiters and Kreisleiters founded their own publications to compete with older N-S organs. Since subscribers were largely recruited through solicitation by party members, the appearance of a new paper frequently created serious local discord. The central party organs had a preferred position, but miniature subscription wars broke out at the lower levels with the appearance of competing publications. Gottfried Feder, author of the concept of "interest slavery" and the party economist and theoretician before 1933, was active on the publishing scene. In 1929 he was registered as the responsible editor of six

[10] Letter, Oct. 14, 1927. *Der Angriff*, founded by Goebbels in competition with Strasser's paper, was published on Monday, when the regular Berlin newspapers did not appear. Although *Der Angriff* was an "officially recognized" paper, it was not the official Gau organ and did not carry the party emblem. The file in the Hauptarchiv contains no reply to Strasser's communication.

N-S weeklies which appeared in Franconia, the Saar, and the Palatinate. The founding of papers by members of the party was not altogether welcome to the Parteileitung in Munich and the subject was hotly debated at the Nürnberg party congress in 1929. This arose in part from a local squabble between Streicher and Feder over the circulation of their respective publications in Franconia. Streicher partisans had openly sabotaged the sale of Feder's *Die Flamme* in Nürnberg, and in defiance of the Reichsleitung, and without the swastika emblem, Streicher had continued publication of *Der Stürmer* as a private journal.[11]

Continued strife in this sector of party activity finally evoked from Hitler a long clarifying circular stating the Reichsleitung's position on competition among party publications. Directed to all Gau and district offices, and all N-S papers, Hitler began by reiterating the directive of September 17, 1928, prohibiting personal feuding in the party press and threatening expulsion for violators. He then turned to the main subject of the directive:

"With the further expansion of our ideology (Gedankenwelt) and with our increase in membership, the desire and need for new local party papers finds expression. By dealing with daily occurrences such papers deepen our ideology in the local area and bring us new members. It is obvious that through newly established papers, those already appearing in the area will be adversely affected, since part of their readers take the new paper which more nearly satisfies their interests. It is possible that thereby the older paper loses subscribers if it cannot meet the increased demands of this competition. Likewise the new paper will only survive in competition with the older if it satisfies the needs of its circle of readers better than the older one.

"This is a manifestation which every competitive struggle

[11] Reports June 6, 1929, and March 20, 1930, Akten des Staats-Ministerium des Innern (Bayern), File 1768; Hauptarchiv, BDC.

produces in all fields of nature and in all life. The stronger
will prevail. In the free play of forces the weaker always
succumbs and the stronger has the victory. A struggle thus
develops in which both parties must put forth the maximum effort to survive. The performance of both is thus increased. *Und das ist gut so.* This applies also to competition
among newspapers. The free play of forces determines and
reveals which is the stronger. Therefore it is to be unconditionally rejected that any party agency, in promoting a
newspaper, should forbid party members under its jurisdiction to circulate or subscribe to another paper that is published with the knowledge and approval of the Reichsleitung. No party member can be forced to read a certain
paper or constrained not to read another paper. Interference in this direction signifies a limitation upon personal
rights, for which no party agency is empowered. On the
other hand, such a prohibition would be an untenable action against an established paper, which at one time, like
its new competitor, was created with great sacrifice and
which has rendered faithful service to the movement. If the
older paper does not actually meet any longer the demands
of its readers, then the new paper will prevail through its
better performance without any intervention by a party
agency. The Parteileitung therefore prohibits all intervention by party authorities either to promote or impede competition among journals which have been authorized by the
Parteileitung, according to the party resolution of 1927."

There then followed a list of thirty-one officially recognized
publications; nineteen were designated official organs of the
party to be indicated by the use of the swastika emblem,
and twelve were designated "officially recognized" papers.[12]

[12] The following are listed: 1) *Völkischer Beobachter* (daily);
2) *Illustrierte Beobachter*; 3) *Der Nationalsozialist*; 4) *Der Nationalsozialist für Norddeutschland*; 5) *Der N-S für Westdeutsch-
land*; 6) *Der N-S für Mitteldeutschland*; 7) *Der N-S für Rhein
und Ruhr*; 8) *Der N-S für Ostmark*; 9) *Der N-S für Sachsen*;
10) *Berliner Arbeiter-Zeitung*; 11) *Niedersächsischer Beobachter*;

With reference to the situation in Berlin, about which Strasser had protested so strongly, the circular went on to state: "With regard to official pronouncements requiring publication, the party authorities are obligated to make these available *without delay* to the papers in their area bearing the party emblem. It is improper and forbidden to provide these announcements only to publications which do not bear the party emblem, while newspapers with this emblem are passed over. Under no circumstances is it permissible to use membership dues to promote the circulation of newspapers." The circular closed with a "puff" for the central party organs and a reminder that it was the duty of all party offices and party members to promote the distribution of the V-B and the *Illustrierte Beobachter*.[13]

12) *Westdeutscher Beobachter*; 13) *Saardeutsche Volksstimme*; 14) *Volksstimme*; 15) *Der Stürmer*; 16) *Der Streiter*; 17) *Der Führer*; 18) *Die Flamme*; 19) *Hitler Jugend Zeitung* (monthly); 20) *Der Donaubote*; 21) *Der Angriff*; 22) *Hamburger Volksblatt*; 23) *Frankfurter Beobachter*; 24) *Nassauer Beobachter*; 25) *Die Neue Front*; 26) *Der Kampfruf*; 27) *Der Weckruf*; 28) *Niederdeutscher Beobachter*; 29) *Reichswart*; 30) *Weltkampf*; 31) *Nationalsozialistische Briefe* (bi-monthly). Those numbered 1-19 were official party organs, authorized to carry the swastika; the remainder were "officially recognized" organs. Those numbered 4-10 were published by Strasser's Kampfverlag. All were weeklies unless otherwise designated.

[13] Nov. 2, 1928, signed by Hitler, authenticated by Bouhler; Prop. Abtl., Hauptarchiv, BDC. Unauthorized publication of books and pamphlets in the name of the party was also a recurring problem. On Feb. 13, 1930, Hitler published in the V-B the regulations which henceforth were to govern non-serial publications. In summary, these provided that any party member publishing a book, pamphlet, or brochure dealing with basic matters concerning the NSDAP must have prior approval of the Reichsleitung. The approved item must bear the inscription "Published with the approval of the Reichsleitung"; previously published items not bearing this inscription must carry it in new editions; and sale and distribution within the party of unauthorized material was strictly forbidden. All N-S papers were instructed to reprint this announcement in three successive editions.

Despite Hitler's apparent support of Strasser, the Kampf-verlag was effectively undermined by Goebbels in Berlin. In July 1930, when Otto Strasser broke with his brother Gregor and resigned from the Nazi party, Hitler forced the liquidation of the Kampfverlag and the Strasser papers were replaced by publications founded by local Gau leaders. Goebbels had great ambitions to make *Der Angriff* the dominant Nazi daily in North Germany, with the other Gau papers restricted to weekly publication. In this he was thwarted by the "Munich group," which began in 1930 to circulate a Berlin edition of the V-B, as a Nazi morning paper, following this in 1933 with a branch of the Eher Verlag for the production of the Berlin and North German editions. This may explain Goebbels' waspish remarks to Albert Krebs, Gauleiter in Hamburg, about "Sergeant director Amann," and "almost Rosenberg." [14] Goebbels' *Angriff* became the official Gau organ, but as an afternoon journal it never achieved a large circulation. When it got into financial difficulties—corruption was strongly indicated —it was salvaged by Amann and incorporated in the Eher Verlag. Goebbels' reputation as a militant Gauleiter and master propagandist should not be extended to newspaper editing and publishing.

Hitler's experience with Gregor and Otto Strasser, with Feder and Streicher, and other private owners of official papers, together with the complex of problems encountered in developing and controlling the Gau press, gave him the landmarks for the publishing policy which he imposed upon the party after 1933. On more than one occasion Hitler confronted the problem of a dissident or deviationist party leader using, or threatening to use, his personal paper in an intra-party feud, or challenging the policies of the leadership. If he left the party or was ejected, he carried his paper

[14] Krebs, *Tendenzen und Gestalten*, p. 166. On the affairs of the Kampfverlag and its liquidation see Otto Strasser, *Hitler and I*, pp. 94-96, 98-102, 114-20.

with him. The defection of a powerful feudal baron together with his private army is an approximate analogy. This was one of the dangerous rocks around which Hitler had to steer in dealing with Gregor Strasser. Secession from the party could also mean the loss of substantial propaganda weapons, which could be turned against the leadership. Whenever possible, therefore, Hitler required the Gauleiters to acknowledge in a formal statement that the papers they published were the property of the party and that they would make no claims against these papers if they left their positions.[15] When the Gau press was reorganized in 1934, all private participation in party newspapers and publishing houses was banned.

## The Gau Press

Development of its own press by a political party was not a new phenomenon in Germany. Newspapers as adjuncts to political parties had been a feature of public life since the revolution of 1848. The Kulturkampf not only evoked the Center party but the Center press as well. The Social Democrats had a highly developed press for the propagation of their doctrines among the working class. The Communists likewise developed their newspapers as instruments of leadership and propaganda. Establishment of journals by militant political interest groups was a common practice. What was distinctive about the Nazi press was its sudden appearance on the scene, like the party itself, and the rapidity with which it developed between 1928 and 1933. Gau-

[15] Wilhelm Murr, Gau Württemberg, gave the following pledge: "I declare on my word of honor that the paper published by me, the *Nationalsozialistische Zeitung für Württemberg und Hohenzollern*, is solely the property of Gau Württemberg, and therefore the property of the NSDAP and under the control of the Reichsleitung; and in the event of a later separation from the post of Gauleiter I personally will make no claim upon the paper." (Aug. 12, 1930; Hauptarchiv, BDC.)

leiter and Kreisleiter usually took the initiative in founding
party organs at the local level. The capital and credit available were negligible, nor was much needed. In Mannheim,
the *Hakenkreuzbanner* was launched with only 1,300 RM
capital. Sometimes the Gauleiter persuaded the more substantial members to put up a small amount of cash. Other
expedients for fund raising involved selling certificates or
"building bricks" to the local membership.

Franz Hartmann, in his "Statistical and Historical Development of the National Socialist Press," presents for
each Gau sketches of the history of the Nazi papers. There
is striking uniformity. Almost without exception they began
as weeklies between 1925 and 1930; between 1930 and 1933
they converted to daily publication; and they became substantial papers only after the party's accession to power.
Hartmann's sketches of the launching of individual papers
have a monotonous similarity—no capital, no regular subscribers, no advertising; the office established in one or two
rooms with borrowed furniture; a single telephone connection, and a printing contract with any sympathizer who
would extent credit. Primarily propaganda organs, these
papers had no news service, no local correspondents, and
few advertisers. Many had no regular subscribers but only
sent bundles of their papers to the local groups for distribution to the faithful. Editorial and management staffs were
recruited from local members, usually serving on a volun-
teer or part-time basis. Few were trained or experienced in
journalism or publishing, and most were from the ranks of
the fanatics, the salvation seekers, the rootless, and the un-
employed.

Violent in language, as the Brown Shirts were in action,
these early party papers were crude almost beyond belief.
The worst of them scarcely resembled a weekly newspaper
but rather a badly printed brochure of ten to twenty pages
filled with the wildest and meanest diatribes, poisonous, bit-

ter, and in every way repulsive in content and appearance. These early Gau smear sheets could have been the work of juvenile delinquents. It is not surprising that they were frequently suspended by the authorities under the emergency decrees for the preservation of public peace and order. Indeed, Hartmann, in compiling his history of the N-S press, listed the number of suspensions incurred by each journal —the greater the number the greater the kudos. Frequently, however, a ten-day suspension was a relief from the critical financial problems of continued publication. The time thus afforded was used to solicit contributions and to straighten out the paper's affairs with its creditors.[16]

Many local papers sponsored new journals in nearby districts. Such a sub-edition would have an appropriate name, identifying it with the community, and a local editor with one or two pages at his disposal for local developments— the rest of the paper came ready-made. If the venture prospered and the party gained membership, the paper frequently separated from the parent organ and became an independent enterprise with its own local staff. To illustrate how party papers multiplied, we may cite the examples of *Der Alemanne* of Freiburg and the *Bodenseerundschau* of Constance, both of which originated as sub-editions of *Der Führer* in Karlsruhe.[17]

In important centers where the party made little headway, the establishment of a daily paper was effected as a means to overcome local resistance and infiltrate the community. This was sometimes accomplished by the Gauleiter with the support of the Reichsleitung. Frankfurt am Main, solidly liberal and Social Democratic, was a case in point. All previous N-S publications in Frankfurt and Wiesbaden

[16] Hartmann, *N-S Presse*, pp. 281, 288, and *passim*.

[17] Hartmann, *N-S Presse*, pp. 55, 63. Hartmann cites numerous other instances of this amoeba-like reproduction in all parts of Germany.

had failed. In the summer of 1930, shortly before the September elections, Gauleiter Sprenger took the initiative in founding a party-owned Verlag to publish the *Frankfurter Volksblatt*. The Eher Verlag supplied sixty per cent of the capital—12,000 RM—while the Gau administration undertook to raise 8,000 RM. Alfred Gutbrod, who became a prominent figure in Nazi publishing circles, claimed to have raised 3,000 RM among party sympathizers and members, and the remainder from his mother and brother. With this limited capital the paper was launched. As no Frankfurt printer would accept a Nazi contract, the printing was done in Darmstadt. The *Frankfurter Volksblatt* was by no means an immediate success, achieving an average daily circulation of only 8,000 copies in 1931. It distinguished itself by incurring ten suspensions between October 1930 and August 1932. After the Nazis came to power circulation shot up to 70,000. Gutbrod became the paid Verlag director in October 1933, and by January 1936 when he was replaced by Konrad Goebbels, brother of the propaganda minister, circulation had reached 86,000.[18]

By no means all the Gau press projects were as successful as the *Frankfurter Volksblatt*. Robert Ley's failure with the *Nationalblatt* in Coblenz was frequently cited by Hitler as

[18] Hartmann, pp. 133-34, 146-47; also letter from Gutbrod, June 4, 1936, Hauptarchiv, File 1021, BDC. Owing to difficulties with the Gauleiter, Gutbrod was transferred from Frankfurt to the post of director of the Stuttgart *N-S Kurier*. An ambitious, self-advertising fellow, Gutbrod had joined the SS, in which he held the rank of Sturmbannführer. Informed unofficially that he had been promoted in grade, he appeared at the next assembly in the uniform and insigne of the higher rank. Instead of a promotion, however, he was relieved of his SS assignment pending investigation of his past career and affiliations. The investigation revealed that Gutbrod, before becoming a Nazi, had been in and out of a number of questionable organizations, including the Stahlhelm and a Masonic lodge! This appears to have blighted his career in the party and the SS, although he remained an important figure in the Gau publishing field.

an object lesson in party publishing policy[19] The Gau was large and Ley was an optimistic plunger. He put his personal funds and all that he could borrow from friends into a large printing plant complete with linotype machines, rotary presses, and other modern equipment. The first edition of the *Nationalblatt* appeared in Coblenz on June 1, 1930, but the financial management of the enterprise was unrealistic and the paper became bankrupt in the spring of 1931 with heavy losses for all involved. Ley was more successful in the Cologne-Aachen area, where he converted his weekly *Westdeutscher Beobachter* to a daily in September 1930. With numerous local editions, this paper after 1933 became, next to the V-B, the most widely circulated of the Nazi dailies.[20]

One of the most revealing accounts of the early history of a Nazi publishing enterprise is presented in Albert Krebs' memoir of early party days in Hamburg.[21] Krebs was a staff member of the Deutschnationaler Handlungsgehilfenverband, a strong national union of business employees with a membership of 345,000. His indulgent superiors permitted him to devote most of his time to NSDAP affairs in Hamburg. Krebs also functioned as a political link and communications channel between the DHV and the Nazi

[19] Ley's failure according to Hitler was his inability to see that a party printing establishment meant death to a party-owned paper, because all the local groups expected to have their posters and handbills printed on credit. (H. Picker, *Tischgespräche*, p. 279.) What Hitler had learned was not wholly new—that political groups everywhere are notoriously poor credit risks from a printer's standpoint.

[20] Hartmann, *N-S Presse*, pp. 242-43.

[21] Krebs, *Tendenzen und Gestalten*, especially the sections entitled "Die N-S Presse im Hamburg," and "Hauptschriftleiter des Hamburger Tageblatts." A detailed study of the evolution of the Nazi press in Hamburg has been published by Roland V. Layton, "The Early Years of the Nazi Press in Hamburg," University of Virginia, *Essays in History*, Vol. vii (1961-1962), pp. 20-36.

party leaders. With the support of Gregor Strasser he became Nazi Gauleiter in Hamburg in 1926, when the party membership numbered barely six hundred. When he retired from this post in 1928, he gave his attention to party journalism. He began by contributing articles on social policy to the *Hamburger Volksblatt*, a weekly founded and owned by a party member. It purchased most of its material from Strasser's Kampfverlag in Berlin and the local party covered the moderate deficit which the owner-publisher incurred. When the contract with the Kampfverlag was canceled and the paper faced bankruptcy, Krebs and Edgar Brinkmann took over the journal and, as editor and publisher respectively, continued its publication. Sometime later they acquired a rival party weekly, the *Hansische Warte*, and merged the two. In great detail Krebs narrates his experiences as editor—failures and successes, disagreements and difficulties with the Gau organization, and the suspicions aroused in local party ranks by the private ownership and publication of a party paper. In 1930 the subscriptions, sales, and advertising began notably to increase and freed the enterprise from its chronic financial difficulties. It was this flush of success, after the September elections, that led Krebs and Brinkmann to convert their weekly paper to a daily, the *Hamburger Tageblatt*. Optimistically they estimated that the 140,000 Nazi voters in Hamburg would easily support a daily journal. Strong objections were raised by the Gauleitung to an official daily, privately owned and edited. An agreement was finally reached whereby fifty per cent of the profits were to go to the local party, the political wishes and directives of the Gauleiter would be observed in the editorial and news policies, and the paper would publish all official news and announcements. In the event of disputes over fulfillment of the agreement, Gregor Strasser would act as arbitrator.

The critical difficulties—political, technical, and financial —encountered during the first year and a half are richly illustrated in Krebs' account. Two problems were chronic: Strained relations with Gauleiter Kaufmann and his staff, and inadequate financial support. "It happened almost every fortnight, Friday being payday, that a deputation from the printing plant would appear and threaten to quit if they were not paid. Then Brinkmann, to insure the appearance of the paper, would get a taxi and go around and beg the needed 800 or 1,200 marks. Mostly he called on personal acquaintances and party members for this help. Two or three times, through my personal efforts, the DHV, or more exactly the Deutsche Ring, made us a small loan on thirty day terms, never exceeding 3,000 marks. Under such pressure we survived from week to week, from month to month. Conditions became increasingly unfavorable, however, and the race between slowly increasing income and unpostponable fixed payments threatened to go against us." [22]

Finally, in June 1931, the Gauleitung intervened and delivered an ultimatum—either convert the paper to a party-owned organ or face a boycott and the competition of an official Gau paper. Preferring to have their masters in Munich rather than in the Gauleiter's office, Krebs and Brinkmann journeyed to Munich, followed within a few days by Kaufmann and his lieutenants. By agreement reached there with the party leadership the paper and its debts were taken over by Amann and the Eher Verlag, while Krebs and Brinkmann remained as editor and Verlag director. This solution was regarded as an intolerable defeat for the Gauleiter and the relations between Krebs and the Hamburg leadership became acutely strained. Not inclined to echo the *Völkischer Beobachter* and take orders from the Gau propaganda office, Krebs deviated sharply on several occasions from the party line. Marked for the kill, his resignation was forced in May 1932, and after a stormy interview

[22] Krebs, p. 99.

with Hitler in Frankfurt he was thrown out of the party.[23] Brinkmann, who remained as Verlag director, later served as president of the Nazi reorganized newspaper publishers' association.

The founding of the *National-Zeitung* in Essen is another example of an ambitious newspaper enterprise that floundered in financial difficulties. This paper was frequently quoted abroad in the 1930's as the mouthpiece of Hermann Göring, who was a close friend and ally of the founder, Gauleiter Terboven.

Essen was a stronghold of the SPD, KPD, and Center parties. Here the Nazis had only a weekly publication until November 1930 when, encouraged by the September elections, Terboven founded the *National-Zeitung*. Departing from the usual practice, Terboven, with only 20,000 RM capital, purchased and equipped on credit a printing plant costing more than 200,000 RM. The first edition of the paper appeared on December 15, 1930. From the beginning the enterprise encountered stormy financial weather. The company was reorganized in March 1931 and some assistance was given by the Reichsleitung; but the financial position worsened in 1932. The creditors would have foreclosed had they seen a chance of recovering their money. By the end of 1932 the directors of the enterprise saw no way of continuing beyond February 1, 1933. Then occurred the miracle of resurrected political and financial credit. In the words of the local chronicler: "The salvation of our *National-Zeitung* was the appointment of the Führer as Chancellor by Field Marshal Hindenburg. With this one stroke confidence in the economic reliability of the National Socialists was restored. All the creditors who, in order to save something, were prepared to go to extremes, were again quieted, since through the Party's accession to power res-

---

[23] Krebs, pp. 99-105, 114-15, 155-56. Using Munich idiom, Amann commented to Brinkmann: "Er [Hitler] hat ein Sauwut auf den Doktor."

toration of the paper's solvency could be expected, and they again had hopes of getting their money back." This frank historian then tells how the Gauleiter raised 350,000 RM from a "friendly group," which enabled him to satisfy the more pressing debts and keep the paper going. This did not end the financial difficulties. Some of the company shares were in private hands; these were recovered in 1934 so that the enterprise was completely party-owned. The capitalized company was reorganized in October 1933 and again in 1935, but it was not until 1936 that "a certain degree of solvency with regard to obligations was noticeable." [24]

The only Nazi paper in Saxony, in 1930, was Otto Strasser's *Sächsische Beobachter*. When Strasser defected, taking his paper with him, Gauleiter Mutschmann and other local party leaders in Dresden organized a company to publish the *Freiheitskampf*. The contract printer was a Freemason. A year later the company became bankrupt amidst scandal followed by much dust throwing. A new party Verlag for Gau Sachsen was organized and the publication of the *Freiheitskampf* resumed on August 1, 1931. The circulation reached 31,000 the first year, and in 1932 local editions were established for East and West Saxony, Leipzig, and Chemnitz. Total circulation reached 58,000 in January 1933, and more than doubled by December (164,900). In 1936 the average daily circulation in all editions reached 196,370. In June 1933, the contract with their Freemason printer was canceled and the *Freiheitskampf* moved into the printing and publishing house formerly belonging to the Social Democratic *Dresdner Volkszeitung*. In Chemnitz and Zwickau the SPD publishing plants were taken over for the local editions of the *Freiheitskampf*.[25]

[24] Hauptarchiv, File 1066, BDC. Circulation figures reflected the changing political and financial fortunes of the paper: December 1930: 16,000; 1932: 27,800; 1933: 180,000; 1934: 133,000; 1935: 130,000; 1936: 138,000.
[25] Hauptarchiv, File 1013, BDC; "Geschichte der sächsischen N-S Presse von der Gründung 1930 bis Juni 1935."

It would be tedious to recount the early history of each provincial Nazi paper which formed the group of political journals referred to as the "Gau press." The period of greatest expansion began in 1929 when Hitler allied with Hugenberg in the campaign against the Young plan, and thus tapped for the party the rich resources of Hugenberg's industrial and financial backers. While the campaign against the Young plan failed, Hitler and the Nazis benefited substantially from this marriage of convenience with the Nationalists. In 1929 the Nazis made surprising gains in the provincial elections in Thuringia, Saxony, Brunswick, and Baden. The same year marked the beginning of the great economic crisis in Germany and the rise of unemployment. As the depression deepened the Nazi party increased its strength with the voters. Thus encouraged, a campaign of agitation and propaganda was begun which continued without cessation to the fateful Reichstag election of September 1930. The expansion of the Gau press kept pace with the party victories at the polls. In 1928 the Nazis had only two daily papers with a combined circulation of 22,800. Beginning in 1929 there was a sharp surge forward in the conversion of Gau weeklies to dailies and the founding of additional papers. Among the daily journals founded immediately before or shortly after the 1930 elections were the *Westdeutscher Beobachter* (formerly a weekly) in Cologne, the *Freiheitskampf* in Dresden, the *Niederdeutscher Beobachter* in Lübeck, the *Nationalblatt* in Coblenz, the *Schlesische Tageszeitung* in Breslau, the *N-S Kurier* in Stuttgart, and the *Frankfurter Volksblatt*. Seventeen dailies were founded in 1931, among them the *Hamburger Tageblatt*, the *Rote Erde* in Dortmund, the *Niedersächsische Tageszeitung* in Hanover, the *Preussische Zeitung* in Königsberg, the *Nationalsozialist* in Thuringia, the *Coburger National-Zeitung*, and the *Heilbronner Tagblatt*.

Twenty-three additional dailies made their appearance in 1932 and twenty-seven in 1933.[26]

Some significant conclusions can be drawn from the appearance of a new political press in Germany. First is the fact that although the party had fifty-nine daily journals in 1932, their combined circulation was barely three-quarters of a million. The circulation successes of the Nazi press came after and not before the accession to power. A second judgment is that the founding of all these papers in depression-ridden Germany had no economic justification; they owed their existence solely to the political forces which they served. They had only the flimsiest of economic foundations. Five major election campaigns in 1932 made the support of these propaganda organs a nightmare of financial

[26] The following table shows the growth in number and circulation of the "recognized" and "official" party press, based on Hartmann's history of the N-S press and his statistical reports for the period 1926-1939.

| Year | Number of Daily Papers | Daily Circulation |
|---|---|---|
| 1926 | 1 | 10,700 |
| 1927 | 3 | 17,800 |
| 1928 | 4 | 22,812 |
| 1929 | 10 | 72,590 |
| 1930 | 19 | 253,925 |
| 1931 | 36 | 431,444 |
| 1932 | 59 | 782,121 |
| 1933 | 86 | 3,197,964 |
| 1934 | 97 | 3,375,757 |
| 1935 | 100 | 3,900,080 |
| 1936 | 100 | 4,328,140 |
| 1937 | 100 | 4,556,755 |
| 1938 (Incl. Austria) | 127 | 4,726,266 |
| 1939 (Incl. Sudetenland) | 200 | 6,120,057 |

The circulation of the non-party press, of which a substantial portion was controlled by the Eher Verlag, amounted to 10,322,000 at the end of 1938.

expedients. Millions of copies were printed for which there were no subscribers or street sales, but which were distributed simply for purposes of political propaganda.[27] The November 1932 Reichstag election was a severe setback to Hitler and the party. The Nazis lost heavily in popular vote and their Reichstag mandates dropped from 230 to 196. In the sketches of the many papers reproduced by Hartmann, the narrators tell how the creditor's axe hung ominously over their publishing activities. Worst of all, they agree, was the period from November 1932 to March 5, 1933. Despite the three million marks contributed by German industrialists to the "Fund for the March Elections," administered by Hjalmar Schacht, the Gau press had exhausted its last resources of cash and credit.[28] Obviously, if Hitler had not come to power early in 1933, the party press would have withered and disappeared quite as rapidly as it had blossomed.

Only in time of deepest economic depression was it possible to start these papers with such slender resources. Millions of skilled men suffering unemployment would turn to anything in the hope of relieving their condition. This was especially true of young men seeking any kind of work. Printers, too, would take great risk in extending credit in the hope that the enterprise would be successful. How unemployment played a role in the founding of party papers is illustrated by the *Hamburger Tageblatt*. It had an editorial staff of six persons, of whom three were volunteers and three received salaries "not large enough to live on, but not small enough to die on." In the composing and press rooms the workers hardly knew from one payday to the next whether their wages would be forthcoming. Yet the paper survived and became an established journal in the

[27] Typical of what went on at the Kreis level was the example of the *Hessische Volkswacht*, which printed 5,000 copies daily but had only 2,800 subscribers. (Hartmann, *N-S Presse*, p. 164.)

[28] Hjalmar Schacht, *Confessions of an Old Wizard*, pp. 275-76.

Hansa city.[29] Like the phenomenal sales of Hitler's *Mein Kampf*, which began in 1929, the burgeoning of the Nazi press in depression-ridden Germany was a gauge of the political unsettlement and the demand for radical solutions that pervaded the country.

## The Socialist and Communist Press in 1933

Three developments enabled the Gau press to surmount the financial crisis of the winter of 1932-1933 and escape liquidation: First, with Hitler in power, credit at the banks and with contract printers became available again to the Gauleiters. Second, there was an enormous rush by opportunists and 'reinsurers' to subscribe to the Nazi papers and advertise in their columns. Third, and even more important, the Gau press received a great windfall with the confiscation by the state of the extensive publishing enterprises of the Socialist and Communist parties. Most of the confiscated property—land, buildings, machinery, vehicles, and bank accounts—was sold at bargain prices to the Gau press. Soon the Nazi papers were nested into the former premises of the so-called Marxist press and for the first time began to publish their papers from well-equipped printing plants and business offices. Approximately 120 SPD printing plants were confiscated and converted to Nazi party use. The KPD owned or controlled from twelve to fifteen printing plants and publishing houses, and these too were treated as the spoils of victory.

Numerous and formidable tasks confronted the Nazi editors and publishers, and especially the Gauleiters, who bore the major responsibility for the party press in their districts. These papers could not be continued in the old pattern of the "combat organ" because the political battle had been won. It was also inconceivable that the party press apparatus would be dismantled after victory. Either they

[29] Hartmann, p. 126; Krebs, pp. 78-99.

had to turn their propaganda weapons into acceptable newspapers or lose the advantages that came with the Nazi triumph; and they had to establish these papers in a crowded, sharply depressed, and highly competitive economic field. How they would have performed under conditions of fair competition with the established press is a matter of conjecture, but they now had the power and prestige of the national leadership, the Gauleiters, the Kreisleiters, and the SA leaders at their disposal. The party did not hesitate to use this power to take over the lion's share of the newspaper publishing business in Germany.

The Social Democratic press which the Nazis confiscated was not a narrow sectarian political institution. As the Socialists emerged from World War I the strongest party in Germany, great efforts were made to expand, modernize, and broaden the appeal of the labor press. It would not be incorrect to say that a political press became a mass circulation family press, with new features reflecting the total interest of workers—sports, news photos, business section, entertainment, and even women's features. In the party publishing committees the ideological opposition to commercial advertising was rapidly eroded. The greatest period of expansion occurred between 1924 and 1929. In the latter year, the peak of SPD press development, the party published 203 newspapers (including 75 sub-editions) with a total circulation of 1.3 million.[30]

The SPD press was uniquely a creation of the party membership, developing as the party grew in numbers and influence. Excepting the Communist papers, it was the most tightly structured and controlled political press in Germany. Ownership was vested in the party, although the

[30] Kurt Koszyk, *Zwischen Kaiserreich und Diktatur: Die Sozialdemokratische Presse von 1914 bis 1933*, p. 177. This is a commendable scholarly study of the political and publishing history of the SPD press. (Cited hereafter as Koszyk, *Sozialdemokratische Presse.*)

usual corporate or cooperative forms were employed for the individual enterprises. Members of the national and state executive committees usually occupied the board positions. As a capstone to the party press organization, which became more capitalistic in spirit and form, a management and holding company was established in 1925. With the title of Konzentration AG, the majority of the party publishing enterprises were brought under centralized control and direction. An auditing and central purchasing bureau had existed previously as an offshoot of the party central committee. Its functions now passed to the Konzentration AG, which also provided technical and business aid, advice in tax matters, and financial support. This marked a further advance toward centralization and strengthening of the powers of the central committee over the party press.[31] While in spirit they were poles apart, the capital and management structure of the SPD press, in its main features, was not unlike that imposed by Hitler upon the Gau press after 1933.

An exact valuation of the SPD newspapers and printing plants at the time of confiscation is not available. In 1925 the total value of property and assets under control of the Konzentration AG amounted to 36,577,526 RM, which included land, buildings, machinery, book and paper stocks, vehicles, and bank accounts.[32] In 1930 the value of all assets was estimated at approximately 70 million RM book value, or 100 million RM market or actual value. The real value of SPD publishing enterprises in 1933 has been variously estimated at 100 to 120 million marks.[33] By 1933 the market value was certainly considerably less than in 1929.

[31] Otto Groth, *Die Zeitung*, ii, 412 ff.; Koszyk, *Sozialdemokratische Presse*, pp. 170-73.

[32] Groth, ii, 410-11. The machine inventory showed 126 rotary presses, 353 "Schnellpressen," 394 linotype machines. The total persons employed—editorial, business, and technical—was 6,641.

[33] *Zehn Jahre Konzentration*, p. 16. This anniversary brochure of the reorganized Konzentration provides much interesting in-

The economic crisis bore as heavily upon socialist enterprises as upon capitalist concerns. Max Grünbeck, an authority on the economics of publishing, has described the early effects of the depression on circulation and advertising: "The decline in the general economy, which in the course of the year 1929 assumed the character of a crisis, was manifested quickly and sharply in the publishing business. Almost immediately the newspapers in the rural areas, in consequence of the far-reaching recession in agriculture, reflected the impact of the depression. Gradually toward the end of the year the larger newspapers also felt the effects. The decline in advertising became increasingly noticeable and the alarming rise in unemployment brought significant losses in subscriptions." [34] As a workers' press, the Socialist newspapers were especially vulnerable to urban unemployment. In the first three years of the depression they lost one-fourth of their subscribers and the number of newspapers declined from 203 to 135. Twelve SPD publishing plants were closed. Although part of the decline resulted from consolidation and rationalization, the SPD press, like the commercial press, suffered heavy losses in advertising, subscriptions, and contract printing.[35] Never-

---

formation on the history of the pre-1933 organization. More exact statistics on the value of SPD publishing properties confiscated in 1933 are not presently available. Fully one-third were in the East Zone and therefore a total loss; those located in Berlin and West Germany, all heavily damaged and depreciated, are today the subject of restitution and indemnity suits in German courts. As long as litigation continues officials of the Konzentration are reluctant to provide more than general estimates of the 1933 property values.

[34] Max Grünbeck, "Die Deutsche Presse in der Wirtschaftskrise," *Zeitungswissenschaft*, 1931, No. 6, quoted in Koszyk, *Die Sozialdemokratische Presse*, p. 187.

[35] Kosyzk, pp. 186, 196, for specific details of revenue and subscription losses.

theless, the SPD printing and publishing establishments, with their buildings, machinery, equipment and stocks, which fell into Nazi hands in 1933, was a windfall of substantial proportions.

The political background of confiscation was provided by the chaotic and turbulent politics of 1932. As the Nazis continued their victorious sweep in state and national elections, the middle class press became less positive in combating the madness that seemed to grip the people and the SPD press was left alone to carry the message of opposition. As the clash became more furious, SPD journals were subject to suspension for attacks upon the ineffective policies and actions of the Weimar government. The Von Papen coup in Prussia was a heavy blow to the Socialist press, and as Nazis acquired key posts in state governments—Thuringia and Brunswick, for example—the SPD papers were repeatedly suspended. With Hitler's appointment as chancellor, in January 1933, and with Göring in power in Prussia, the number of suspensions increased. Few SPD papers were able to publish in Prussia after the Reichstag fire, and all ceased publication in the other states shortly after the March 5 elections. A wave of looting and destruction by bands of SA rowdies swept the country; SPD and KPD publishing establishments were principal targets. Appeals to the authorities for protection were useless and permission to publish non-political papers was refused by the new government. Finally, following the period of destruction, looting, and illegal seizures, the position was regularized by the "Law for the Confiscation of Communist Property," promulgated on May 26. It was extended on July 14 to SPD property by the act entitled, "Law for the Confiscation of Property of the Enemies of the State and People." These laws were expanded and interpreted by a further act of September 26. Altogether the measures conferred upon the state authorities power to confiscate all Communist and Socialist property and assets, including publishing enterprises, wherever located.[36]

Compared to the SPD we have little reliable information on the organization, extent, and value of Communist publishing enterprises in Germany. The only factually based work on the KPD press is by H. Girardet, son of the well-known newspaper publisher.[37] Girardet had access to the records of the seized publishing properties in the Ruhr region and interrogated leading figures in the KPD publishing apparatus.

The Communist press was "democratically centralized" in its publishing structure as well as in content and opinion. Its organization dated from the 1920's, when it was set up in three registered holding companies, one for buildings and land, one for machinery and inventory, and one—the Stern-Drückerei—for the actual publishing of the KPD papers. Rudolf Bernstein was the dominant figure in the Communist publishing organization. In 1932 there were fifty KPD newspapers in Germany of which fully half were sub-editions of larger papers. Girardet gives the following circulation figures for some of the more important journals:

| | |
|---|---|
| Rote Fahne (Berlin) | 130,000 |
| Ruhr-Echo (Essen) | 48,000 |
| Der Kämpfer (Chemnitz) | 46,500 |
| Thüringer Volksblatt | 43,000 |
| Hamburger Volkszeitung | 42,800 |
| Arbeiterzeitung für Schlesien | 42,000 |

Girardet estimates the average daily circulation for all KPD papers at around 658,000 copies. Economically the party

[36] *Reichsgesetzblatt* (1933), Pt. I, pp. 293, 497, 668. On the last days of the SPD press see Koszyk, pp. 202-18.

[37] H. Girardet, *Der wirtschaftliche Aufbau der kommunistischen Tagespresse in Deutschland von 1918 bis 1933.* (Leipzig diss., 1938.) Also W. Kaupert, *Die deutsche Tagespresse als Politicum,* pp. 112-18, gives a brief factual description of the Communist press.

publishing enterprises were in a seriously depressed condition by 1932. The Karl Liebknecht House in Berlin, and four additional important pieces of party-owned real estate, had been foreclosed by the mortgage banks early in 1933 and were advertised for sale. All KPD property was seized after the Reichstag fire and, following the looting and destruction, the properties and equipment were appropriated by the National Socialists or sold at distress prices.[38]

## Confiscation of the Marxist Press

As has been noted, with some exceptions Nazi party papers were printed by contract printers, and the ill-equipped editorial and business offices occupied the meanest of rented quarters. Who knew how long they would be in business? With the confiscation and transfer of SPD and KPD properties many of the Nazi journals acquired their own printing plants with adequate business and editorial offices. Hartmann's historical sketches indicate the scope of this action and what it meant to the economic shoring up of the Nazi press in the provinces. A typical example is afforded by events in the town of Heilbronn in Württemberg, which before 1933 was an SPD and KPD stronghold. The *Neckar-Echo* was a well-established and thriving SPD paper. The Nazi *Heilbronner Tagblatt* had appeared as a daily in March 1932 with most of its material supplied in stereotype by the *N-S Kurier* in Stuttgart. Serving a political purpose, it had no economic foundation whatsoever until the plant and office of the "Marxist Neckar-Echo" were confiscated, together with other properties belonging to "enemies of the state." In the words of the narrator, "the problem of moving into the new plant and quarters now became acute." Nor was this all. The middle class publisher, who served the area with four small papers,

[38] H. Girardet, pp. 35, 37, 42, 102-3. On the structure of the KPD press see Groth, *Die Zeitung*, II, 425-26.

was unable to compete with a politically potent rival and soon sold his papers to the Gau publishing concern.[39]

Confiscation was the order of the day. Where KPD or SPD quarters and plant were suitable, they were confiscated or requisitioned and the Nazi publisher moved in on a nominal lease basis. If the plant and quarters were too small, or otherwise unsuitable, the equipment—linotypes, presses, and office furniture—were seized and removed to the nearest Nazi publishing plant.[40] Typical is the history of the *Niedersächsische Tageszeitung* of Hanover, founded on February 1, 1932. Supported by party funds and contributions, it circulated 35-40,000 copies daily in the service of the party's propaganda effort. The acquisition of KPD and SPD property gave it the economic means needed to survive and become a legitimate newspaper. First, it acquired the printing plant of the Communist *Neue Arbeiter-Zeitung* and shortly thereafter the plant and offices of the SPD *Volkswille*. The *Niedersächsische Tageszeitung* then moved its entire operations into the commodious trade union building. In a short time its circulation exceeded 100,000 in the city and province; it published seven sub-editions in rural Lower Saxony and four dailies in Brunswick, Göttingen, Hildesheim, and Blankenburg.[41] Nearby in Westphalia the SPD printing and publishing plants in Minden and Bielefeld were taken over by the *Westfälische Neueste Nachrichten*. The *Niederschlesische Tageszeitung* of Breslau likewise acquired the plant and offices of the Social Democratic *Volkszeitung*.[42]

In the Cologne area, Robert Ley's *Westdeutscher Beobachter* took over, in May 1933, the offices and plant of the

---

[39] Hartmann, *N-S Presse*, pp. 387-88.

[40] This was done at Coblenz, where the loot was three linotypes and two rotary presses from the SPD *Rheinische Warte*. (Hartmann, p. 255.)

[41] Hartmann, pp. 335-37.

[42] Hartmann, pp. 300, 356.

thriving *Rheinische Zeitung*. By 1935, Ley's paper was publishing twelve local editions in the Cologne area and
claimed the largest circulation of any Nazi paper except the
V-B. In Magdeburg, the *Mitteldeutsche*, which together
with its sub-editions covered Gau Magdeburg-Anhalt, acquired the confiscated property of the Social Democratic
*Volksstimme*. All other publishing resources of the KPD
and the SPD were acquired by the Gau publishing company, the Mitteldeutsche Zeitungsblock.[43] In Lübeck, the
Nazi *Lübecker Beobachter*, which was in extreme financial
difficulties, fell heir to the property and facilities of the
SPD *Volksbote*, which had been edited since 1921 by Julius
Leber.[44] On June 8 the Bremer *N-S Zeitung* occupied the
establishment of the SPD Bremer *Volkszeitung*. Under the
heading "Changing Times," the editor, Kurt Thiele, a Nazi
Reichstag deputy, demonstrated the low level of taste which
was a persistent characteristic of Nazi journalism: "The
property of the SPD and the Social Democratic Press have
been seized and confiscated by the Reich. The party secretaries and editors are under arrest. Herr Faust, widely
known in Bremen for his swinish writings under the appropriate pseudonym 'Mephisto,' is now more suitably employed in cleaning toilets in a concentration camp."[45]

In Saxony, where the Nazi press had barely gained a foot-
hold before 1933, the *Freiheitskampf* of Dresden was one
of the principal beneficiaries of the wave of seizures and
confiscation. In May and July 1933, the extensive properties of the SPD and KPD press in Dresden, Chemnitz, and
Zwickau passed into its possession. In the Rhineland and
South Germany, where the Marxist parties were weaker

[43] Hartmann, pp. 154-55, 188, 190.

[44] Hartmann's correspondent describes this event as follows: "Am
10 Mai des Jahres 1933 wurden dann urplötzlich die Dinge andere,
als durch die Beschlagnahme und Gleichschaltung der Lübecker
Volksbote in Staats—und dann in Parteibesitz der NSDAP über-
ging." (Hartmann, p. 203.)

[45] Quoted in Koszyk, *Sozialdemokratische Presse*, p. 215.

than in Prussia and Saxony, there was less publishing property to be seized. The historian of the Nazi press in Gau Coblenz-Trier complained that "While in many cities well-equipped publishing offices and printing establishments could be made available after the confiscation of the Social Democratic papers, we in Gau Coblenz-Trier were forced to build and equip our plant from the ground up." In consequence, the *Nationalblatt* of Coblenz had to refuse new subscriptions and advertising for two months in the summer of 1933 until facilities could be expanded to take care of the new business. However, its circulation rose steadily from 24,000 in September, to 48,000 in December 1933, and to 64,000 by December 1934.[46]

Among other seizures and conversions in this area may be noted the occupation of the Karl Marx House in Trier by the *Nationalblatt* of Coblenz, the take-over of the *Volks-wacht* by *Der Alemanne* in Freiburg, and the acquisition by the *Oberbergische Bote* in Gau Cologne-Aachen of the building and plant of the *Volkszeitung* in Gummersbach.[47] In Mannheim, the *Hakenkreuzbanner* occupied the offices and plant of the *Volksstimme*, which the SA had seized on the pretext that a Nazi parade had been fired upon from the building.[48] Gauleiter Wagner had founded *Der Führer* in Karlsruhe in 1927 and converted it to a daily in January 1931. Like most Nazi papers it had no printing plant or permanent editorial and business office until it moved, in June 1933, into the establishment confiscated from the SPD *Volksfreund*.[49]

Since Hartmann's informants were beneficiaries of the liquidation of the Socialist and Communist press, the details of seizure and conversion by force are generally omitted. How the seizures were effected and subsequently

---

[46] Hartmann, pp. 254-56, 288-89.

[47] Hartmann, pp. 62, 152, 257.

[48] Hartmann, pp. 59-60; also Hauptarchiv der NSDAP, File 1024, BDC.

[49] Hauptarchiv, File 1014, BDC.

cloaked with legality is revealed in records of a series of restitution cases concerning the properties and assets of the KPD in Stuttgart. These consisted mainly of land and buildings, printing equipment, library, office furniture, and other property incidental to the party's publishing activities. On March 8, 1933, the central government, on the pretext that public order and security were threatened, appointed the SA leader, Dietrich von Jagow, Reich Police Commissioner and invested him with all police powers in the state of Württemberg. Protests of the state cabinet were rejected, as this was a planned step to remove all non-Nazi state governments and coordinate their affairs with the National Socialist central government.[50] On March 9 an auxiliary police (Hilfspolizei) was organized from elements of the SA, SS, and Stahlhelm. On the night of March 10-11, the Reich commissioner ordered the arrest of all KPD functionaries. At the same time the auxiliary police occupied the buildings and seized the property of the KPD publishing house. Similar action was taken against the SPD leaders and their property. Retroactively, on the basis of the Reich laws of May 26, and July 14, the state ministry of interior issued an ordinance confiscating all property of the KPD and SPD and their affiliated organizations. What the state of Württemberg actually sequestered was the KPD land and buildings; for the machinery, equipment, and other movables had already been looted, destroyed or dispersed. In May or June 1933, with the concurrence of the office of the state police, a Nazi publisher, Fritz Kiehn, hauled away on three trucks all printing machinery and other equipment and installed it in his own plant at Trossingen. After the formal sequestration ordinance was issued, Kiehn paid only a token sum for the looted machinery, some of which he subsequently sold at market prices to another publisher.[51]

[50] Waldemar Besson, *Württemberg und die Deutsche Staatskrise, 1928-1933*, pp. 344-52.

[51] These facts are extracted from the records of the Restitution Chamber of the Landgericht Stuttgart in the cases: Druckerei

One other example of how SPD publishing property was treated by the local Nazis will suffice. The *Münchener Post*, organ of the SPD in Munich and Upper Bavaria, was published by the Verlag Birk, whose shares were held by prominent members of the SPD in Bavaria. It had a circulation of approximately 15,000, which was not insignificant considering that Munich, in 1933, had seven daily papers. The property consisted of a substantial building and a well equipped printing plant, library, and editorial offices in the Altheimer Eck. When Hitler became Chancellor, on January 30, the paper was not affected and continued to publish until the Held-Schäffer cabinet was displaced and Ritter von Epp appointed Reich Commissioner. On the evening of March 9, when the state government fell, the publishing establishment was stormed by the Munich SA, the editorial offices and library plundered, and fixtures and equipment destroyed or thrown into the street. Likewise the stock of books and party literature was dumped into the courtyard and burned. In the printing plant the linotype machines were wrecked; the large rotary press was set going and iron bars thrust into the gearing, thoroughly wrecking this valuable machinery. Later the police locked the wrecked plant and placed it under the supervision of the building superintendent. An ordinance of the ministry of interior, similar to that issued in Württemberg, eventually effected transfer of the property to the state. Since the Nazi party in Munich had its own printing establishment in the Müller Verlag, it had no need of the SPD property, which was subsequently leased by the ministry of finance to a book publisher and contract printer.[52]

GmbH, Stuttgart vs. former State of Württemberg, June 8, 1953; State of Baden-Württemberg as assignee of the Druckerei GmbH, Stuttgart vs. the German Reich, Dec. 22, 1955; State of Baden-Württemberg as assignee of the Schwäbischer Verlag GmbH, Stuttgart vs. the German Reich, Sept. 30, 1957.

[52] Interview notes, Herr E. Goldshagg, Aug. 14, 1958. In 1933 Goldshagg was political editor of the *Münchener Post*. When the

Every SPD official concerned with the party's publishing activities before 1933 can testify to the willful destruction of property, theft, and dissipation of assets resulting from the Nazi suppression of the labor press in Germany. Gunther Rothe, a member of the SPD district committee in Leipzig and an official of the Leipzig Buchdrückerei, publisher of the prosperous *Volkszeitung*, described the general procedure as follows: "When the Nazis came to power and police protection of SPD property was withdrawn in many centers, the SA broke into the plants and plundered and destroyed. Oftentimes cash boxes and office equipment were stolen. All stocks of SPD books and other printed matter were destroyed outright. Sometimes the heavy equipment, such as linotype machines and rotary presses, were removed and converted to Nazi use or sold for what they would bring. When the plants were later confiscated by the state and their value appraised, a very great difference had developed between the original value and the appraiser's figure. The Nazi Gau enterprises then purchased the remaining assets at distress prices." [53]

Although less affected, middle class democratic papers were not spared entirely in the epidemic of seizures and confiscations during the spring and summer of 1933. Where a paper had distinguished itself as an opponent of National

SA mob stormed the printing plant, Goldshagg escaped through the back court and joined Erhard Auer, Otto Wels, Wilhelm Hoegner, and other SPD leaders, who had gathered at the Kunstlerhaus on Lenbachplatz.

[53] Interview notes, Bonn, Aug. 3, 1958. In Prussia the capital stock and assets of the Konzentration AG were confiscated by the Ministry of Finance and under its authority the "Konzentration im Liquidation" disposed of the SPD publishing properties. When the Hauptarchiv der NSDAP was established in 1934, the title to all files of SPD papers was vested in the Hauptarchiv. The director, Dr. Uetrecht, made a vigorous effort to have all extant files shipped to Munich from the twenty-six district offices of the Konzentration. Hundreds of these newspaper files were forwarded but their final disposition is unknown.

Socialism, the editorial staff was "coordinated," a trustee forced upon the publisher, and the property in effect taken over by the Nazi party. A notorious case was that of the *Dortmunder Generalanzeiger*, which was seized by the Nazis on April 23, 1933, and merged a year later with the local *Rote Erde*, an insignificant Nazi paper with 20,000 circulation. This forced merger produced a paper which in 1935 had a circulation of 178,000 and ranked as one of the ten largest dailies in Germany. It was reported, but unconfirmed, that the publisher received only 25,000 RM indemnity for the loss of his valuable publishing property.[54]

Under heavy pressure, or facing economic ruin, many small and middle-size publishers sold their newspaper properties to the Nazi competitor. *Der Führer* of Karlsruhe thus acquired the substantial publishing firm of Thiergarten; the *Mainzer Anzeiger* took over the liberal *Mainzer Tageszeitung*; the publisher of the *Zittauer Nachrichten* was forced to sell to the Nazi Gau publishing house; the Pommersche Zeitungsverlag, acquired thirty-six privately owned weeklies and small dailies in Gau Pomerania between 1933 and 1936. On May 1, 1934, the property and title of the *Ulmer Tagblatt*, a leading paper in the Upper Danube region, was confiscated and transferred to its Nazi competitor the *Ulmer Sturm*. The latter then merged and continued publication under the honored name of the old established *Tagblatt*.[55] Thus through outright confiscation, forced mergers, and distress sales a revolutionary transformation of the German newspaper publishing industry was begun.

[54] *New York Times*, letter to the editor, Aug. 9, 1948. The historian of this paper, quoted by Hartmann, simply states that "Am 23 April 1933 wurde der wegen seiner Tendenz berüchtigte Dortmunder Generalanzeiger durch die NSDAP übernommen." On Jan. 30, 1934, the name was changed to *Westfälische Landeszeitung— Rote Erde*.

[55] Hartmann, pp. 54, 142, 270-72, 289-90, 386.

One additional economic advantage that accrued to the Nazi press with the triumph of the party should be noted. As the various levels of administration came into the hands of the party leaders, government printing contracts and publication of official notices were switched to the party press. For small newspapers in many towns, cities, and counties, this resulted in a substantial shift in assured revenue from the established papers to the political newcomers. With confiscated property, official revenue, and a flood of new subscribers and advertisers, the Nazi party press by the end of 1933 had acquired, in part, the economic means for the transition from a political combat press to a competitive form of newspaper.

With the conquest of political power by the Nazis, the structure, ownership, and business of newspaper publishing were vitally affected. A new political party press had been created in an economic sector already overcrowded and disorganized by the business depression. The working class press—SPD and KPD—was wholly suppressed and its property and assets handed over to the Nazi party. For the Nazi press in the provinces this was its first substantial economic foundation. There remained on the scene, however, the broad array of the middle class press, an integral part of the nation's business structure. It was a spiritual and ideological force of great consequence, and was basically hostile or indifferent to National Socialism. These papers and their publishers had either opposed the Nazis in the Kampfzeit, taken a position of neutrality, or, in the case of the German Nationalist press, had strongly supported a competing program. For the totalitarian state, which Hitler and his supporters proceeded to establish, the middle class press presented a problem and a challenge of major proportions, and one for which Hitler and his lieutenants had no blueprinted solution when they came to power.

# III. The Organization of Total Control

## A Strait Jacket for Editors and Publishers

In the Nazi party leadership it was an accepted view that the new order would require establishment of a control system for the German press. In *Mein Kampf* Hitler dwelt at length upon the theme that the national interest required firm control of this instrument of guidance and education. The credulous masses easily fell under the influence of ignorant, stupid, and ill-disposed leaders; it was the duty of the state to prevent this. The press, he said, must be carefully supervised because it had a continuing and not an intermittent impact upon the masses. "The state therefore must proceed with ruthless determination and take control of this instrument of popular education and put it in the service of the state and nation." [1]

The first steps taken to realize this objective came within the general movement of Gleichschaltung, the coordination of all organizations with the new regime, which was ruthlessly pursued during 1933. Professional groups, business and trade associations, sports organizations, cultural and educational institutions, in short, the whole range of organized life was brought under Nazi party control. This was accomplished voluntarily or under pressure, and was usually signaled by the election or appointment of Nazis to the leadership positions and executive committees. Throughout the land the little as well as the big Nazis had their moments of triumph. The gloom of the depression, massive unemployment, and deep political unsettlement had a tiring, depressing effect. Many who disapproved fell into line because there appeared to be no other course. Each day the papers recorded actions of corporate bodies

[1] *Mein Kampf*, I, 264 (Volksausgabe, 1933).

and groups which had voluntarily reorganized and aligned themselves with the new regime. The foreign observer was reminded of lemmings rushing blindly toward the sea. But the Nazis hailed it as the work of "national reconstruction."

Among deeply troubled leaders in German public life were the members of the executive board of the German newspaper publishers' association. For these publishers of middle class papers who had sought to influence, enlighten, and lead the nation politically, the preceding three years had been a nightmare. The publishers were as dispirited, tired, and confused as the political party leaders. To many it appeared that the old established press had lost all influence with the German people. When the *Hannoverscher Kurier* headlined its November 1932 election story a "Triumph of Folly," it lost a fifth of its subscribers in a fortnight. Readers appeared to resent advice and counsel from a press which seemed to have nothing new to offer. Under these circumstances many publishers followed a neutral line, recording and observing but not opposing the Nazis. As the democratic forces became weaker and more confused, and a Nazi victory a distinct possibility, the future of the independent middle class press became the deepest concern of the leaders in the VDZV. Neither the democratic parties, the Reich president, nor the Reichswehr barred the road to Hitler's accession.

What could the press do under the circumstances? Pessimistically, the executive committee of the VDZV decided to explore the terrain upon which the country was entering with Hitler's appointment as chancellor. Dr. Walther Jänecke, board member and publisher of the *Hannoverscher Kurier*, was authorized to make the approach. His first attempt through the party directorate in Munich failed, but greater success was achieved through Wilhelm Keppler, Hitler's contact with business and industry. Keppler gave assurances of Hitler's moderation and urged that legal actions which the association had pending against the *Völkischer Beobachter* and *Der Angriff* be dropped. While Keppler was reassuring, it was evident that the Nazis would force the publishers into a state controlled organization. Keppler arranged a meeting between the leaders of the VDZV and the chancellor. Present at this meeting in the chancellery were Dr. Krumbhaar, chairman of the executive committee, A. Neven DuMont of the *Kölnische Zeitung*, and Dr. Jänecke. Hitler was affable, considerate, and reassuring. Of course, he said, he had to suppress the KPD and SPD press, but the independent publishers had nothing to fear. He could not establish his government and conduct the affairs of the country with only the support of his N-S "trumpet press." He needed "violins and other instruments in the national orchestra," and he needed especially those papers with prestige and contacts abroad. A meeting with Goebbels at the propaganda ministry on March 29 was less encouraging. Krumbhaar, Neven Du-Mont, Jänecke, and the executive director of the association, Von Boetticher, composed the delegation. Goebbels, who felt considerable antipathy toward the publishers' association, told them that the German press must not indulge in destructive criticism but cooperate positively in the work of reconstruction. Freedom to criticize, and anything resembling a coordinate power in shaping policies, would be denied them under the new regime.

At this juncture the alternatives as seen by the executive committee appeared to be: Either close their publishing enterprises or find some basis for cooperating with the Nazi leaders. In the executive board and in informal contacts with the members, it was agreed that they would not close down their enterprises. If they did, that would leave the field to the Nazi press and at one blow the titles of their papers, their plants, and their circulations would fall into the hands of Nazi rivals. They therefore decided to negotiate, to maneuver, to seek influence and support, and to resist at the local level the competition of the Nazi press.

Considerable encouragement as to their future was doubt-less derived from remarks made by Hitler in the interval between his appointment as chancellor and the elections of March 5. In statements to a delegation of publishers and in an informal talk to a meeting of N-S journalists, Hitler proclaimed his adherence to the principle of a free press, the right to criticize objectively officials and policies of the state, and a positive role for the press in the conduct of public affairs.[2] Goebbels' pronouncements, less reassuring than Hitler's, at least did not foretell earthquake and eclipse for the middle class press. Closer to reality and more indicative of the future was a blast set off by Otto Dietrich, the Reich press chief, in an address before a conference of the N-S Kulturbund in Berlin. In the sharpest terms he denounced the "downright mistaken orientation of the German press" during the preceding fourteen years. The middle class press, he declared, which was now supporting the "national revolution," had tolerated and collaborated with the Marxist parties, it had admitted representatives of the Marxist press to the publishers' association, and it had failed woefully to defend the national honor and interests. Until the last minute, the middle class press and its publishers had misrepresented and combated the National Socialist movement. He then rang the changes on capitalistic corruption of daily journalism and promised a thorough housecleaning by the new regime; they would eliminate the selfish publisher interests and the capitalistic interest groups and create a new press in Germany.[3]

[2] "Reichskanzler Hitler über die Aufgaben der Presse," *Zeitungs-Verlag*, No. 8, Feb. 25, 1933. For the posture of Hitler's cabinet and the atmosphere in Germany during the first weeks, see K. D. Bracher, *Die Nationalsozialistische Machtergreifung*, pp. 547-49. As a resident observer in Berlin at this time, the author can testify to the cautious optimism that prevailed even in non-Nazi circles.

[3] *Zeitungs-Verlag*, No. 17, April 29, 1933. In the same issue the publishers' trade journal reprinted from the *Deutsche Allgemeine Zeitung* a refutation of Dietrich's charges against the middle class

The decision of the executive committee of the VDZV to cooperate with the Hitler-Hugenberg government was manifested in the policy line pursued in the publishers' trade organ, *Zeitungs-Verlag*. Not a word of protest—not even an announcement—was uttered at the massive assault on freedom of the press resulting from the suppression of 150 Socialist and Communist newspapers. The executive committee also published a statement of solidarity with the government and the NSDAP in denouncing the "atrocity propaganda" directed by the foreign press against the new regime. For this demonstration of "national discipline" they were thanked by Goebbels.[4]

Another important step toward collaboration was taken when the executive committee decided to meet the wishes of the Nazi leaders in reorganizing the VDZV. During April and May negotiations were conducted with representatives of the Nazi party publishers. On June 28 at a full meeting of the executive committee, the association was reorganized. Krumbhaar, Von Boetticher, Neven Du-Mont, and others who were especially *persona non grata* with the Nazis, resigned and seven Nazi publishers were elected to the board. Amann was chosen chairman and Dr. Jänecke, first vice-chairman.[5] Hitler attended the formal reorganization meeting at Amann's invitation, repeated his assurances with regard to the future of the press, and

---

press. Shortly thereafter, in connection with another breach of discipline, DAZ was suspended for three months. While the suspension was canceled on June 16, the editor Fritz Klein was "furloughed" and replaced by the London correspondent Karl Silex. (*Zeitungs-Verlag*, Nos. 22, 25, June 3, 24, 1933.)

[4] *Zeitungs-Verlag*, No. 13, April 1, 1933.

[5] The Nazi members of the executive committee, all party Verlag directors or officials, were: Gerhard Kuhn, Neustadt a. Haardt (Palatinate); Edgar Brinkmann, Hamburg; Walther Marx, Cologne; Dr. Rudolf, Breslau; Otto Weiss, Stuttgart; Richard Jahr, Eher Verlag, Berlin; and Max Amann. *Zeitungs-Verlag*, No. 26, July 1, 1933.

congratulated the publishers on their display of patriotism and recognition of the new order that was being constructed.

At the first business meeting the vacant executive directorship—the key position—had to be filled. Amann's personal candidate was wholly unacceptable to Jänecke and the other board members representing the old association. They proposed Dr. Fritz Hertel, who had been Von Boetticher's chief assistant. A compromise was finally reached with the appointment of Hertel but with Rolf Rienhardt, a lawyer and Amann's adviser and confidant, appointed to the staff as the chairman's personal representative with extensive rights of control including access to all correspondence. The old members of the board felt that a catastrophe had been avoided. Rienhardt, upon whom Amann obviously depended, appeared to be the lawyer-type, reasonable, not a fanatic, and outwardly conciliatory. In fact, however, they had introduced a Trojan horse. As Amann's personal representative, Rienhardt soon had the affairs of the association completely in his hands and Hertel was shunted aside. For the next ten years, Rolf Rienhardt, cloaked with Amann's authority, was the most powerful figure in the German publishing industry.[6]

In much the same way, although the details are not so fully recorded, the association of editors and journalists was brought under Nazi control. Scarcely a Nazi journalist belonged to the Reich Association of the German Press (RVDP) as they had their own letterhead organization, the Reich Working Group of N-S Journalists. With less tact than had been shown in dealing with the powerful

[6] This account of the Gleichschaltung of the VDZV is based on interview notes, Dr. Walther Jänecke, Aug. 18, 1958; Walter, *Zeitung als Aufgabe*, pp. 158-64; Gerhard Baumann, *Die organisatorische Aufbau der deutschen Presse*, pp. 71-75; and *Zeitungs-Verlag*, Jan.-July 1933. The account in Fritz Schmidt, *Presse in Fesseln*, pp. 256-58, is factually garbled and highly colored.

publishers, the RVDP was taken over. On April 30 it was announced that Otto Dietrich, Hitler's press chief, had been elected chairman of the national association, and Wilhelm Weiss, chairman of the Berlin section. At the same meeting the constitution and by-laws were set aside and the executive committee instructed to draft and present a new constitution. What was more significant was a resolution on membership: "Jews and Marxists," so the resolution proclaimed, could no longer be members. The purging of the membership and the admission of new members was delegated to the executive committees of the provincial societies until the new press law, which was in preparation, could be published. In the future, Dietrich announced, membership in the association would be required of all working journalists, and everyone, old as well as new members, would be screened for "racial and political reliability."

The new constitution and by-laws of the reorganized RVDP gave the association the external form and appearance of a self-governing body or guild, with authority to establish conditions of admission, to maintain standards of professional conduct, to discipline members, and to represent the interests of the working members of the press. The association's principal function, as it turned out, was the maintenance of the professional list of accredited journalists. All those who had failed to maintain or acquire membership were excluded from the press. Employment as a journalist was declared a public function and observance of professional requirements was made a rigid condition for maintenance in good standing. A system of professional courts at the level of the provincial societies was established with power to investigate, render judgments, and punish infractions of the journalists' code. However, the special relationship in which the association stood to the ministry of propaganda made it in fact an agency of coercion and control. The minister of propaganda appointed the president (Leiter) of the association and the members of the professional courts; he had a veto over admission to the occupational list and could remove persons on his own authority when he held it to be "in the public interest." The Nazi party's claim to leadership insured that the principal officers at national and local levels were reliable party members. Thus coercive force was fully applied and the journalists became bondsmen of the state and party.

Party membership or declared adherence to N-S ideas could not at first be made a condition of enrollment on the lists of the provincial societies because few professional journalists in 1933 were outwardly or inwardly Nazis. But if they wanted to stay in the profession they had to conform. Wilhelm Weiss, who succeeded Otto Dietrich as president of the reorganized RVDP, consistently emphasized the moderation with which exclusions and admissions were effected. There is some justification for this as not all who might have been proscribed were driven into the wilderness. But Weiss also stated at a journalists' conference in Cologne, in 1935, that 1,300 "Jewish and Marxist" journalists had been purged from the profession.[7]

## The Editor's Law of October 4, 1933

For the reorganized publishers' association the first major crisis arose in the autumn of 1933 with the promulgation of Goebbels' Editor's Law, or *"Schriftleitergesetz,"* a measure which set the cornerstone of state and party control of the press. While it concerned primarily the working journalists, the law also struck a blow at proprietors and pub-

---

[7] Weiss, Spruchkammer file, No. 1, Doc. 184; also Walter Hagemann, *Publizistik im Dritten Reich*, pp. 38-39. On the Gleichschaltung of the journalists' association, see Gerhard Baumann, *Der organisatorische Aufbau der deutschen Presse*, pp. 46-48, 53-54, 66; and H. Schmidt-Leonhardt, *Das Schriftleitergesetz vom 4. Oktober 1933—Kommentar*, pp. 234-39, gives the constitution and by-laws of the reorganized Reichsverband der Deutschen Presse.

lishers of newspapers from which they never recovered. The law was framed as part of the process of establishing the responsibilities and defining the areas of competence of Goebbels' ministry of propaganda. This entailed transfer of many functions previously performed by other ministries to the new agency. The press bureau of the Reich government became a division of the new ministry; foreign news and press representation was transferred from the foreign ministry; from the Reich ministry of the interior came the supervisory powers over press, radio, films, and theater; and from the ministry of economics responsibility for economic propaganda such as fairs, exhibitions, and festivals. Amidst the turbulence created by this reorganization, the Editor's Law was drafted and presented to the cabinet.

While the policy requirements were undoubtedly defined by Goebbels and his principal advisers—mostly young Nazis active in party propaganda—the framing of the law was in the hands of Hans Schmidt-Leonhardt, chief of the legal division of the propaganda ministry, who had transferred from the ministry of interior together with the functions which had formerly been within the competence of that agency. The genesis of the law is clear: It combined a reworking of the rejected Journalists' Law of 1924, with the compulsory organization of editors and journalists modeled on the system developed by Mussolini in Fascist Italy.[8] When the first draft of the proposed law was cir-

[8] When promulgated on Oct. 4, 1933, with effective date January 1, 1934, the accompanying official commentary stated that the law had been under discussion for years in the legal division of the ministry of interior by experts and commissions, and that the "professional list for editors and journalists" was modeled on Italian Fascist decrees and laws of July 15, 1923, July 10, 1924, December 31, 1925, March 4, 1926, and February 26, 1928. (*Zeitungs-Verlag*, No. 40, Oct. 7, 1933.) Gerhard Schulz, a contributor to K. D. Bracher's *Die N-S Machtergreifung*, emphasizes (p. 551) the Italian Fascist origin when he states: "Die Prinzipien dieser Regelungen übernahmen die jungen nationalsozialistischen

culated to the interested ministries—interior, justice, and economics—it evoked considerable expert criticism of details as well as objections to the domination of the press by the new ministry. To counter these objections, some revisions were made without altering substantially the main provisions. It was then forwarded by Walther Funk, state secretary in the propaganda ministry, to the chancellor's office to be placed on the cabinet agenda for consideration on September 22. Since time for circulation and study was considered insufficient it was dropped from the agenda. Funk submitted the draft a second time with further changes made in the interim. It had been coordinated with the interested ministries at a special meeting on September 19 and the changes agreed upon had been incorporated, he wrote.[9] At the cabinet session on October 4, the draft law was presented by Goebbels and explained in detail. The discussion is not recorded but apparently Von Papen registered doubts and suggested additional changes. With minor alterations the measure was adopted. The only significant change made by the cabinet was an amendment to Paragraph 34 which gave the minister of propaganda authority to remove a journalist from the occupational list without recourse to the professional court.[10]

As enacted by the cabinet, the law broadly defined

Beamten, um eigene Originalität recht unbekummert, mechanisch aus dem italienischen Presserecht, um sie in eiligem und derbem Zugriff in Gesetzform zu bringen." This misplaces the emphasis and overlooks the "Made in Germany" aspects of the greater part of the law.

[9] Protocols of the German cabinet meetings, National Archives, Micro-copy T-120, R-1714; Funk to the State Secretary in the Reich chancellery, Sept. 30, 1933.

[10] Protocol of the cabinet meeting, Oct. 4, 1933. In a letter of the same date, Von Papen's office proposed a number of specific changes, one being that a person rejected or eliminated from the list be notified of the reasons in writing. NA Micro-copy T-120, R-1714.

"Schriftleiter" as any person who wrote, edited, or selected the text or illustrative material of serial publications (Pars. 1-4). Educational, racial, and experience qualifications for admission to the profession were stated in detail (Pars. 5-11), and the obligations, duties, and modes of conduct of a person engaged in the profession were likewise given legal definition (Pars. 12-21). Legal protection of the professional members through their association (RVDP) was firmly anchored in the law (Pars. 22-35), and the enforcement measures and penalties specified (Pars. 36-46).[11] Like all guild and corporative measures instituted by the Nazi regime this law appeared to give editors and journalists protected status in a self-governing body, with rights to admit, exclude, and discipline the members. But in operation it was something quite different. When journalists were required by law to "Regulate their work in accordance with National Socialism as a philosophy of life and as a conception of government," the professional independence of the journalist and freedom of the press were legally terminated.

With regard to the relations of editor and publisher, the law was even more destructive, stating flatly: "The chief editor is responsible for the total content and attitude of the textual part of the newspaper." When the law prescribed that he must follow the directives and instructions of the ministry of propaganda, the publisher was deprived of all rights in the determination of content and in estab-

[11] Text in *Zeitungs-Verlag*, No. 40, Oct. 7, 1933; also *Handbuch der deutschen Tagespresse*—1937, pp. 356-64; and H. Schmidt-Leonhardt, *Das Schriftleitergesetz*, pp. 34-196, with explanatory comment. Schmidt-Leonhardt, presumptive author of the law, was also the principal framer of the ordinances, laws, and decrees establishing the chambers of culture through which Goebbels' ministry controlled the cultural and intellectual life of the country. He was a state official in Saxony until 1926, when he transferred to the Reich ministry of interior, and thence to the propaganda ministry in March 1933.

lishing the policy of his paper. Indeed, even an attempt by the publisher to influence the editor by offering advantages or threatening disadvantages was defined as a crime punishable by fine and imprisonment, or withdrawal of the publisher's license. Moreover, a publisher could not terminate an editor's contract without the concurrence of the professional association. As defined in the law, the editor became the equivalent of a state official, exercising the functions of a "public educator," and therefore responsible to the Hitler state rather than his employer. In effect, the Editor's Law interposed an iron curtain between editor and publisher and restricted the latter to the role of a business agent concerned with his technical plant and business organization. Thus the publisher was excluded from his former position of authority and influence in the press, a position which was now legally assumed by the ministry of propaganda. It should be noted that on the surface this measure was responsive to a current of opinion in Germany, formed and influenced for decades by economic determinism, which interpreted the editor-publisher relationship as one in which "capitalistic corruption" could flourish, and through which unclean forces were introduced into the shaping of public opinion. However, as the law emerged from the cabinet it was a cunning device to achieve the Hitler-Goebbels Pressepolitik, placing the entire middle class press in its news dissemination and opinion forming functions at the disposal of the Nazi state.

In the leadership of the publishers' association the draft law aroused the greatest apprehension and hostility. From the standpoint of the publishers it was catastrophic. The editor's responsibility toward an agency of the state now took precedence over his employment contract with the publisher; the latter could no longer give guidance and direction, even make suggestions, to his editorial staff without risking serious violation of the law. It remained to the publisher to make his good name, the prestige of his paper, and his economic resources available for the broadcasting of the news and views that emanated from the propaganda apparatus of the state and party. In the words of the embittered publishers it degraded them from Rittmeister to Zahlmeister.

At the installation of the new chairman and board members of the publishers' association, on June 28, which Hitler had attended on Amann's invitation, the officers of the organization had taken their position with regard to changes in the press law which they knew were in prospect. At the meeting, Amann had spoken sensibly and objectively about the tasks of the association and promised that the publishers' interests and views would be represented. The association's position was then expressed in a resolution which was delivered to Hitler, Goebbels, and Frick. It was an emphatic reaffirmation of the publisher's rights over the editors and editorial staff, stating unequivocally that the publisher alone could represent his paper's obligations and duties toward the public and the state. This responsibility was total and indivisible, and "the VDZV requests the government, in revising the press laws, to make this principle its point of departure." [12] The Editor's Law as it came from the propaganda ministry was a stunning defeat for the publishers.

Action outside the bureaucratic ministries to block adoption of the law was taken as soon as a draft of the measure came into the hands of the leaders in the publishers' association. Dr. Jänecke took the initiative and had no difficulty convincing Rienhardt and Amann that the law would cut deeply into the rights and responsibilities of the publisher of the *Völkischer Beobachter* as well as those of the private publishers. The Jänecke group prepared counterproposals that would have preserved their rights and prerogatives. There then ensued a power struggle in which Goebbels' ministry and the Reich press chief, Otto

[12] *Zeitungs-Verlag*, No. 26, July 1, 1933.

Dietrich, were pitted against Amann and the publishers' association. Hitler had the ministry's law removed from the agenda when first it came before the cabinet, saying that he wanted to discuss it with Amann. At this critical juncture the publishers, through Rienhardt, tried to get Amann to come to Berlin for a personal conference with Hitler, but Amann was hunting in the Bavarian mountains and could not be reached. Goebbels and Dietrich won by default and at the next cabinet meeting the measure became law.[13]

Amann's account of the Editor's Law varies considerably from Jänecke's, and the two cannot be wholly reconciled. According to Amann, Dietrich was the driving force behind the law and exerted more influence in the reorganization of the press, and subsequently in disciplinary matters, than the propaganda minister. Briefed by Rienhardt, Amann personally presented the publishers' counter-proposals to Hitler, who said he would accept them if Goebbels and the ministry of justice concurred. Goebbels reluctantly agreed, but then Hitler told Amann his draft proposals were too long and complicated and that he would work them over himself! To Dietrich, Amann allegedly said: "That is a one-sided measure and the ruin of the publisher," and to Wilhelm Weiss, "Dietrich wants to put us all in his pocket." Amann asked Hitler when he might expect a decision and Hitler replied that he would let him know. Later Amann heard that Dietrich's objections to the counter-proposals had prevailed and that the original

[13] Interview notes, Dr. Walther Jänecke, Aug. 18, 1958. Also Walter, *Zeitung als Aufgabe*, pp. 164-65. At this point Jänecke withdrew from his leading position in the VDZV, partly because of the Editor's Law, but partly because of the excesses committed by the party against local publishers. He reorganized the *Hannoverscher Kurier*, vested the shares with his wife and sisters, and gave up active participation in the enterprise—he could not "mitmachen." He left Hanover and went to Berlin for a few months, but as it turned out, for ten years.

draft had been accepted and enacted.[14] This marks the beginning of one of the standing feuds within the leadership of the Nazi party over control of the press. Dietrich in his position as Reich press chief, and later state secretary in the propaganda ministry, controlled the regimented editors and journalists, while Max Amann commanded the publishing field. Continuous friction was the result. Despite Rolf Rienhardt's efforts to amend or replace the Editor's Law, it remained in force to the end of the Reich. The raising of a wall between editor and publisher probably appealed to Hitler. At least Hitler's statement, quoted by Amann, points to such a conclusion: "The editors are rendered powerless and the publishers can do as they please."

## Organization and Powers of the Reich Press Chamber

Nazi domination of the publishing industry was exerted through the Reich Press Chamber, one of the seven chambers comprising the Reich Chamber of Culture established by the law of September 22, 1933. This measure authorized the propaganda minister to organize the various branches of the arts and cultural professions, with which his ministry was concerned, as public corporations. Seven fields were organized as separate chambers: Literature, radio, theater, music, films, fine arts, and the press. An implementing ordinance, specifying the organization and powers of these bodies, was issued on November 1, 1933. The minister for propaganda was designated president of the Reich Chamber of Culture with power to appoint the presidents of the subordinate chambers. These were formed by incorporating the existing professional and vocational groups—actors, musicians, film producers, publishers, etc. —into their respective chambers, for which were specified

[14] Interrogation report, Nürnberg, Oct. 30, 1947, Spruchkammer München I, Amann file.

uniform administrative structure, powers, and subordinate officers. Grouped in the Reich Press Chamber, of which Amann became president, were the two most important organizations, the Association of German Newspaper Publishers and the Reich Association of the German Press, together with eleven other trade and professional organizations concerned with the production, sale, and distribution of published materials—books, periodicals, and newspapers.

On the surface the chamber organization appeared to invest the Fachverbände (the constituent trade and professional organizations) with broad powers of self-government and administration, but in fact they became captive organizations through which the state and party controlled all reportorial and creative writing, all publishing, and the dissemination of printed materials throughout Germany. Specifically, with regard to publishing, a closer examination of the implementing ordinances reveals the dictatorial powers conferred upon the chamber president and his subordinates. Paragraph 4 specified compulsory membership for persons engaged in all fields of the press and publishing business. Paragraph 10 provided for the exclusion of any person from membership who was deemed unreliable or unfit for the exercise of the vocation or profession. Paragraph 25 empowered the Reich Press Chamber, through the subordinate trade groups, to establish the conditions for opening and closing enterprises and to promulgate ordinances for the regulation of all important matters in the field of their competence. Significantly, Paragraph 26 specified that measures initiated under the preceding provision could not give rise to claims for damages on the grounds of expropriation.[15] Applied ruth-

---

[15] *Reichsgesetzblatt* (1933), I, 661-62, 797-800, with effective date Nov. 15, 1933; also *Handbuch der deutschen Tagespresse—1937*, pp. 351-55. The authoritative Nazi work on the organization and direction of the cultural chambers is Hans Hinkel, *Handbuch der Reichskulturkammer* (Berlin, 1937), and for the Reichspresse-

lessly in the publishing field by Amann and Rienhardt, the ordinance became in effect an instrument of unlimited expropriation and despoilment.

With the announcement by Goebbels of the chamber organization on November 15, Amann was appointed president of the Reich Press Chamber, Dietrich, vice-president, and a former lawyer on the staff of the publishers' association, Ildephons Richter, executive director. The advisory council was loaded with such Nazi figures as Wilhelm Weiss, Schwarz van Berk, Gunter d'Alquen, and Rolf Rienhardt, with a sprinkling of officials from the propaganda ministry and the N-S party directorate. Concurrently, the publishers' association was reorganized and given a new constitution as the Reichsverband der Deutschen Zeitungsverleger. The previously semi-autonomous provincial associations became subordinate agencies of the Reichsverband, in most instances with a Nazi publisher as president and an executive director acceptable to the central office and the local Gauleiter. When Amann became president of the Reich Press Chamber, Edgar Brinkmann, publisher of the Eher-owned *Hamburger Tageblatt*, was appointed president of the reorganized Reichsverband. Brinkmann was a nonentity and the affairs of the association rested chiefly in the hands of Rolf Rienhardt, who held the post of permanent deputy director.

Materially and politically the most important constituent group in the RPK was the publishers' association. Its functions were described officially as "guaranteeing that German newspaper publishers meet the personal requirements and fulfill the tasks and responsibilities assigned to them by the party and state as the molders of a press

---

kammer especially, pp. 21-22, 28, 209-10, 212, 234-37. Hinkel began his propaganda career in the party as an associate of Gregor Strasser in the Kampfverlag but he switched his allegiance to Goebbels and served as chief of the Gau Presseamt in Berlin in 1932. Later he occupied several posts in the propaganda ministry.

committed to National Socialism"; and second, that "conditions and standards required for effective publishing work be maintained within the press as well as externally." The foundation of its power lay, however, in the provision that "Within the limits of its competence, the RVDZV is responsible for the preparation of appropriate ordinances for the Reich Press Chamber and supervises their execution." [16] In this provision and in the ordinance-making authority of the Reich Press Chamber were lodged the unlimited power which the Nazi party leaders henceforth wielded over the German publishing business and upon which their eventual monopoly was based.

In contrast to the office of the RVDZV, the Reich Press Chamber was a small organization with limited duties and functions. The office was in Berlin; Amann, the president, resided in Munich. The executive officer, Ildephons Richter, was a sincere Catholic and a moderate man. Richter did not become a party member until 1937. He was a tool rather than a creative person, and while he executed Amann's orders, he showed restraint in dealing with publishers. The principal function of the RPK was to promulgate the ordinances and regulations which were formulated by the subordinate trade groups. The staff was small—eight employees and assistants in 1934—with a personnel budget of 57,240 RM.[17] Partly for prestige but principally to counteract the Gau propaganda offices of the Goebbels-Dietrich apparatus, Amann and Rienhardt set up in 1935 a system of Gau advisers (Vertrauensmänner) to the RPK. These were selected from the ranks of party publishers and

[16] Hinkel, *Handbuch*, p. 212; also important is the article—probably prepared by Rienhardt's staff—published under Amann's name, "Die deutsche Presse im neuen Recht," in *Zeitungs-Verlag*, No. 28, July 14, 1934.

[17] Propaganda ministry, "Budget File Reichskulturkammer, 1934-40," BDC. Also a descriptive statement prepared in Berlin, September 1945, by Dr. Rudolf Vincentz, former office manager of the RPK; file marked "RPK Feststellungen," BDC.

functionaries of the RVDZV. A vassal list, it included Wilhelm Baur (Berlin), Georg Schemm (Bayreuth), Edgar Brinkmann (Hamburg), Konrad Goebbels (Hesse-Nassau), Gerhard Kuhn (Saar-Pfalz), Alfred Gutbrod (Württemberg), Max Fink (Franconia), and Wolfgang Müller-Clemm (Essen).[18] This does not appear to have been—as originally intended—an effective means of balancing the propaganda ministry control of provincial editors and journalists.

Through the Reich Press Chamber, the reorganized Reichsverband of the publishers' association, and the Editor's Law, the Nazi leadership developed the essential controls for the management of the press. However, centralization and mastery did not stop with the middle class press. To complete the structure, in 1933-1934, the Nazi papers were taken from the Gauleiters and subjected to the authority and financial management of the Eher Verlag.

## Centralization of the Nazi Party Press

When the Nazi party came to power its "trumpet press" was loaded with debt, its business organization a makeshift structure, its economic survival uncertain, and its new ideological role undefined. The importance of the confiscated publishing resources of the SPD and KPD to the survival of the party press has been noted. Substantial as were these assets, their appropriation by the Gau press did not by any means assure a sound economic foundation. As an integral part of the party's apparatus and the principal bearer of its ideology, the Gau press could not be thrown entirely on its own resources in the overcrowded, fiercely competitive, and depressed field of newspaper publishing. The greatest pressures bore upon the Gauleiters, and among the more radical or primitive, the view was strongly expressed that suppression and confiscation should not halt

[18] Complete listing in Hinkel, *Handbuch*, pp. 234-37.

with the Marxist press, but should be extended to the enterprises of their middle class opponents. They proposed that the party take over the entire press. Hitler certainly heard these voices even if he could not heed them. In one of their private discussions on the future of the German press, Hitler said to Amann: "We must confiscate all private press enterprises." To which Amann replied that "Germany was not a Bolshevik country—owners should be compensated for their property." [19] In the long run both Hitler's proposal and Amann's condition were substantially realized. But the more immediate and pressing problem was the deplorable financial condition of the Gau press and the absence of a uniform structure and publishing policy for the official organs of the party. While it sufficed as a political weapon in the struggle for power, the Gau press lacked the resources, publishing experience, and trained personnel to convert to salable mass circulation newspapers. It was, in short, utterly incapable in its existing condition of carrying the will and wisdom of the N-S party to the masses of the German population.

Ownership of the Gau press was as complicated as a Chinese puzzle. Many of the Gauleiters, local party leaders, friends of the party, and local financial institutions had invested in the establishment of these papers. Gauleiter Schemm owned the Kulturverlag, which published the official party paper in Bayreuth; Bernhard Rust owned 85 per cent of the capital stock of the *Neidersächsischer Beobachter*, Gauleiter Koch was a participant in the Gauverlag in East Prussia, as was Terboven in Essen, Mutschmann in Saxony, Bürckel in Saar-Pfalz, and Ley in Cologne. Kreisleiters and other party officials of less exalted rank were also shareholders in party papers. Aside from political and ideological considerations, the possibility of deriving substantial income from these properties, if they could be converted and rehabilitated financially, cannot be disre-

[19] Interview notes, Max Amann, Aug. 22, 1945.

garded in speculating on the motives and maneuvers of the Gauleiters in 1933. Hitler and Amann, as heads of the only large and financially sound publishing concern in the party, were besieged with requests for financial assistance. Amann was not inclined to jeopardize the financial position of the Eher Verlag to salvage or build up the Gau press. In fact, his attitude as a successful publisher was one of scorn and disapproval of these poorly founded, ill-financed, and slipshod publishing ventures. His was the disdain of a successful entrepreneur for a sloppy amateur. What was more—and he was certainly not mistaken—he smelled corruption. The Gau press was such a swamp of insufficiencies and insecurity that he preferred to have nothing to do with it. The picture of Amann, presented by Fritz Schmidt, in *Presse in Fesseln*, as an insatiable conqueror and trustifier of the Gau press is wholly imaginary. Hitler, Hess, Schwarz, and other members of the Reichsleitung shared Amann's pessimism with regard to the future of the party's papers. All were agreed, however, that thoroughgoing reorganization and reform would have to be undertaken.

According to Amann, in the summer of 1933 the Gauleiters began to badger Hitler for financial support for their papers. He referred them to Amann with a request that a searching examination be made of the financial and operational accounts of their publishing ventures. Amann's examiners found some bad situations and serious irregularities, which were reported to Hitler. The latter then told the Gauleiters he would not give them subventions and that the Eher Verlag had no reserves it could draw on. He ordered that henceforth their business accounts and records be regularly audited by the Eher representatives in place of the routine reports submitted to the Reich party treasurer. The next step was an order from Hitler prohibiting the personal participation of party functionaries in the ownership of official papers and publishing enterprises.

This was followed on January 31, 1934, by a party decree defining and extending Amann's powers as Reich Leader for the Press and bringing the Gau papers under the immediate control of the party central directorate. According to Amann, this reflected Hitler's strong desire to centralize party publishing and to keep the Gauleiters on the leash. To meet acute problems of property control and finance, to insure uniformity in policies and practices, and to give effective guidance in developing the party press, Amann was now invested with the broadest authority. Under the ordinance of January 1934, he was empowered to give or withhold the party imprimatur for all official publications; to authorize the establishment of official periodicals and papers; to issue general regulations binding upon all party publishers; to make policy decisions in all publishing questions; to give orders to any Verlag director; to investigate any Verlag director, and to remove a director and appoint a trustee if circumstances warranted.[20]

To discharge his new duties and responsibilities, Amann established in Berlin the Administrative Office of the Reich Leader for the Press, with Edgar Brinkmann as titular head (Leiter), but with Rolf Rienhardt as staff director (Stabsleiter). This placed Rienhardt in two commanding positions with regard to the German publishing industry— permanent deputy of the president of the RVDZV, with broad powers over the privately owned press, and staff director of Amann's office for the administration of the Gau

[20] *Verordnungsblatt der NSDAP*, Jan. 31, 1934, No. 64; also in altered form in *Organisationsbuch der NSDAP*, pp. 308-9. The appointment authority was conferred under a supplementary regulation, signed by Hess, April 10, 1934. The decree served a second purpose in clarifying the jurisdictional areas of Amann as Reich Leader for the Press and of Otto Dietrich as Reich Press Chief of the NSDAP. The latter's authority was defined in a party directive issued by Hitler on Feb. 28, 1934. The clarification of powers, however, did not remove the friction or banish the personal ill will that Amann and Dietrich bore toward one another.

enterprises. Examination of the business and financial position of the Gau papers was carried out for Amann by the Cura staff of auditors and examiners, made available by Max Winkler. What these accountants and experts in the publishing business discovered we do not know in detail, as the records of the Cura staff were in large part destroyed. We can assume that the financial examination of the Gau enterprises revealed shocking weaknesses and irregularities.

To give the Gau press a new structure required about six months. After the Cura reports were received, one Gauleiter after another came in for negotiations with Rienhardt. The pattern was simple. All personal participation of party officials—Gauleiter, Kreisleiter, Verlag director—must be canceled and ownership rights surrendered to an incorporated Gauverlag, which became the sole owner of all official party papers. If shares were in private hands they were recovered at the earliest opportunity. To hold the shares of the Gau publishing companies, control their finances, and direct their operations, the Standarte GmbH was organized by Rienhardt, who became its managing director in addition to his other duties. Its modest capital was held by the Eher Verlag. To the Standarte company the Gau firms surrendered fifty per cent of their stock, the remaining fifty per cent being held in most instances by the Gauleiter as "trustee of the NSDAP." The trustee instruments, however, specified that Amann could call these shares at will, so the Gauleiter was legally a trustee of the Eher Verlag.[21]

Through the Standarte company financial support was rendered the Gau papers when needed. The Gau publishers were kept under continuous pressure by the central office to make their papers self-supporting. Their financial needs were considerable until 1936, and substantial sums—the amounts are not known—were borrowed from the confis-

[21] W. R. Beyer, "Die gesellschaftsrechtliche Geschichte des Eher-Verlages," pp. 8-9, 10, 30, File 3820-b, Gutachten im Pressesachen, BWB.

cated resources of the German trade unions through the German Labor Bank (Bank Deutscher Arbeit). Profits from the Gau press flowed to the treasury of the Standarte, and were employed either to finance the weaker publishing enterprises of the Gau or returned to the Gauleitung for party purposes. As an incentive, Standarte profits and surpluses were distributed to the Gau directorates in proportion to income derived from the publishing enterprises of each Gau. Besides financial support the Standarte rendered management services to the Gau press—appointing able business managers, recruiting journalists and editors, providing centralized purchasing, operating training courses, and helping in the procurement of national advertising. Detailed periodic reports were required by the central office and the books of the establishments were subject to the closest scrutiny by the Cura auditors. By 1936 the enterprises administered by the Standarte trust were, in the main, in fair financial position and yielding profits.

Amann was not loved by the Gauleiters and the procedures and regulations of the Standarte holding company made some of them visibly unhappy. The strongest resistance to the reorganization came from Gauleiters Koch, Bürckel, and Ley. But the Führer's will prevailed with two exceptions. Concessions were made to Koch and Bürckel who vested their Gau publishing interests each in a foundation and thus kept control of profits in their own hands. The terminal date of these concessions was optimistically set by Amann for 1964! [22]

[22] In the absence of records this account of the reorganization of the Gau press is based mainly on interview material: Max Amann, Aug. 22, 1945; Wilhelm Weiss, Aug. 31, 1945; Rolf Rienhardt, July 8, 1958; Willy Imhof, July 9, 1958; also *Max Amann: Ein Leben*, pp. 56-57; and Fritz Schmidt, *Presse in Fesseln*, pp. 83-94. Establishment of the Verwaltungsamt and the appointment of Brinkmann and Rienhardt was announced in March 1934. The offices were in the Columbushaus on Potsdamerplatz. *Zeitungs-Verlag*, No. 9, March 3, 1934.

The description of the institutions and controls established by the Hitler regime in the publishing sector of national life would be incomplete without a brief reference to one of its most efficient and effective economic management instruments. The Cura Auditing and Trustee Company (Cura—Revisions und Treuhand GmbH) was established by Max Winkler, a West Prussian emigré, during the Weimar period to manage and audit the Reich-supported newspapers in the German ethnic territories lost under the treaty of Versailles—Schleswig, Saar, Memel, Danzig, West Prussia, and Upper Silesia. Through the Cura, with headquarters in Berlin, Winkler administered approximately a dozen German minority newspapers. Over the years was built up a small staff of able, experienced, and expert management consultants and examiners, thoroughly acquainted with all aspects of newspaper publishing—commercial, technical, and financial. Precisely when the Cura became attached to the Eher concern cannot be determined, but one of the first assignments given it by Amann was the examination of the Gau press in 1933-1934. Thereafter the Cura company worked exclusively for the Verwaltungsamt and the RVDZV under the direction of Rolf Rienhardt. It functioned not only as an auditing bureau for the Eher subsidiaries but also as an instrument for exploring the financial and business position of the entire press in Germany. Cura was capitalized for a modest 50,000 RM, the shares being held by the business director, Julius Mundhenke, and the banker Papenberg.

Cura operated with a staff of 50-60 persons, mostly auditors, accountants, and management specialists. Amann was correct in stating that when the Cura staff entered his service it had not a single National Socialist in the organization. Key members of the organization only joined the party in 1937 when nominal membership was required of those holding official or semi-official positions. The record of Julius Mundhenke, head of the Cura staff, is significant in this connection. Born in Hanover, October 3, 1891, he joined Max Winkler's organization at an early date. He remained as chief of Cura when it was transferred to Amann's service and he became a party member in March 1937. On Amann's recommendation, Mundhenke was awarded the party's Golden Honor Badge on the occasion of the tenth anniversary of the Nazi accession to power.

By the end of 1934 the corporate reorganization of the Gau press was completed. It had received a rational business structure. Each Gau had its incorporated Verlag, which owned and controlled all official party newspapers. The Gau publishing companies, in turn, were grouped financially and administratively under the Standarte concern, which functioned also as a holding company for the parent Eher Verlag. Paralleling and reinforcing this centralized corporate structure were the expanded powers conferred upon Amann by the party constitution. The authority and instrumentalities for exercising these controls were established in the Verwaltungsamt, in Berlin, with its subordinate staff of management experts and auditors in the Cura offices. The Gau press, although loaded with debt, was now in a better position to compete with the independent provincial press for a larger share of the newspaper business.

# IV. The Party and the Publishing Industry, 1933-1934

## The Gauleiters and the Provincial Press

For the independent publishers in the provinces, the first two years of Nazi rule was a time of grave uncertainty and continual harassment. Added to the political uncertainty was the strained economic position produced by the business depression. Both politically and economically hundreds of private publishers stood in grave danger of foreclosure. Among the radicals in the party, including many of the Gauleiters, the view was strongly held that the party should monopolize the provincial press. This would have entailed expropriation on a wholesale scale. The endorsement by the party leadership of a privately owned press coexisting with the party press blocked achievement for the moment of this more radical objective. However, the reorganized Gau press had still to acquire a sufficient share of circulation and advertising from the middle class publishers to bring it out of a deficit position, to cover the large investments in machinery and equipment, and to pay for the skilled professional and technical personnel required to produce a standard newspaper. Advertising revenue was as important as circulation revenue. While many business concerns cynically advertised in Nazi papers as a precaution—like fire and theft insurance—the large national advertisers demanded certified circulation. On this level the stronger private publishers were prepared to wage a bitter struggle for every subscriber. Hence, the first year of Nazi power was marked by circulation wars which broke out all over Germany.

The Gau papers were usually the aggressors. Much of the zeal for the National Socialist revolution in 1933 worked itself out at the local level in subscription canvassing by party members and SA men on behalf of the party paper. Local leaders would organize subscription drives and a plague of canvassers would descend upon a community. The techniques employed were not those that would be sanctioned by a "Better Business Bureau." The canvassers in ringing doorbells often wore their SA uniforms and practiced a mild form of intimidation. Slander and disparagement of competing papers and publishers was common, and if a privately owned paper accepted Jewish advertising this was harped on as a violation of the new order. Threats of business and professional boycott, the black list, and other actions violating Reich laws against unfair competition in business were regularly employed. Such a shower of complaints reached the central office of the VDZV from injured publishers that the executive committee issued a statement sharply condemning the unsavory methods employed.[1] That two of the authors were Nazis—Amann and Jahr— suggests that the situation was bad indeed.

Conditions were far from uniform during the Nazi seizure of power, but in some of the party districts the leadership waged an intensive campaign against the middle class press. In Silesia the Gauleiter's office issued a circular directive to party officials, including blockleaders, calling for special efforts on behalf of their press. They were instructed to form a "Press Action Group" to support the party papers and combat the non-party press, using placards, handbills, and demonstrations. Party officials were forbidden to associate with non-Nazi press representatives, to give them information, or invite them to meetings. Party discipline was invoked to insure that party members subscribed to the Nazi papers. All party members of city and county councils were instructed to introduce motions to cancel publication contracts for legal notices in papers that published Jewish

[1] *Zeitungs-Verlag*, No. 22, June 3, 1933.

advertising, and to secure the assignment for Nazi papers.[2] Undoubtedly, the large circulation gains made by the Gau papers in 1933 were due in part to the coercive tactics of party leaders on behalf of their newspapers.

Public officials and state employees were placed under especially heavy pressure to subscribe to the local Nazi paper. While compulsory subscription was never ordered officially by the central government or party directorate, the Gauleiters favored it as a policy and some enforced it in their districts. At the top level of Reich administration, Frick issued an order to all Reich agencies and bureaus specifying that officials had an obligation to subscribe to the V-B.[3] In Gau Rheinland-Pfalz a report form was issued by the Party Office for Officials (NSDAP-Amt für Beamte) to all Reich, state, and local officials. They were required to give their name, position and address, to give the name of the paper to which they regularly subscribed, to state whether they took a N-S paper ("Yes or No"), and if not to give full reasons for not subscribing.[4] In a land of officials and numerous state enterprises the loss of these subscribers by the middle class press was a serious economic blow. Despite published appeals, the VDZV in 1933 was quite unable to police the subscription canvassing business, suppress Nazi abuses, and enforce fair practices in the solicitation of subscribers and advertisers. Nor were those central party leaders responsible for the press able to deal effectively with the Gau and local officials. Not until 1934 was the

[2] The document is reproduced in Hortlof Biesenberger, *Der Schwarzwälder Bote*, pp. 33-34.

[3] *Zeitungs-Verlag*, No. 50, Dec. 16, 1933.

[4] Kurt Liesenberg, *Der N-S Verlagskonzern Saarpfalz*, p. 25, reproduces the form. Counter action was taken by one Hamburg publisher who issued a full-page "Appeal to Our Readers!—No Compulsion to Subscribe to Party Papers." Readers were urged to retain their subscriptions and not to yield to pressure and threats. (Handbill, Archive of the Institut für Zeitungswissenschaft, Munich.)

Reich Press Chamber in a position to establish regulations requiring licensing of all canvassers, prohibiting the wearing of uniforms while making calls, and forbidding compulsory subscriptions for members of organizations or occupational groups. Even these regulations were difficult to enforce uniformly and complaints continued to come into the central office of the VDZV.[5]

Another uncertainty visited upon the non-party publishers was the practice of official suspension of papers for infractions of the press policies established by the propaganda ministry. In several pronouncements during the first year of power, Goebbels piped the tune of cooperation and confidence between government and press and deplored the practice of newspaper suspensions as punishment for infractions of the rules. Nevertheless the instances of suspension increased rather than diminished. During the summer and autumn of 1933, the *Zeitungs-Verlag,* organ of the newspaper publishers, carried a special rubric listing "Suspensions Imposed" and "Suspensions Lifted." Later the rubric was dropped but the listings continued. When the Berlin *Tägliche Rundschau* was suspended for four months there was nothing for the publisher to do but discontinue the paper. Police action was sometimes taken; when the *Essener Allgemeine Zeitung* was suspended for four days, Dr. Girardet, one of Germany's leading publishers, together with the editor-in-chief and the managing editor, was taken

[5] The RPK order was published by Amann on Dec. 13, 1933. Hess issued a circular order to all party officials on Jan. 10, 1934, which stated in part: "Any kind of pressure to subscribe to papers of the NSDAP is prohibited. Further, it is not permissible to use subscription receipts to check on party members who do, or do not, subscribe to a particular paper and to make this a basis for expulsion from the NSDAP. It is the will of the Führer that the N-S press be read by our fellow Germans because of its qualities and that they not be *forced* to subscribe." (National Archives, World War II Records Center, German Documents, EAP 99/293.)

into protective custody.[6] The power to suspend a paper for violations of the presidential emergency ordinances of February 4 and 28, gave the Nazi authorities the ultimate weapon in dealing with recalcitrant publishers. Under the economic conditions then prevailing a thirty-day suspension could ruin any paper.

In many districts, depending on the attitude of the Gauleiter and his press advisers, severe pressure was put on private publishers to get out of business or to surrender control of their papers to the Gau Verlag. In fact, something resembling a drive-hunt against the independent publishers was staged in many party districts. While the big publishers were under pressure from Berlin, the little publisher had even a worse time with the local N-S officials. The views of the hard core dedicated Nazi at the grass roots level were expressed by a writer in the *Mainfrankische Zeitung* of April 7, 1934: "In the years of struggle, as we were engaged in heavy combat with a world of enemies, there was scarcely a single newspaper in all Germany that gave assistance in spreading National Socialist ideology. . . . The so-called 'bürgerliche' press left us deplorably in the lurch, either because it was not capable of grasping the demands of the new age, or because of economic self-interest. They did not want to risk losing subscribers because only a part of the German people was on our side and there appeared to be little prospect of our winning the others. . . . But in a single day we destroyed the whole rickety structure and with it the disintegrating political party system, which was represented by a pack of irresponsible press hounds. The one disappeared but the other transformed itself quickly and now considers that it has done us a favor by conforming. But this Gleichschaltung, which took place with the marvelous mimicry of a chameleon cannot satisfy us. We must have a press that can transmit the substance of National Socialist ideas, sound and unadulterated, and not a press

[6] *Zeitungs-Verlag*, Nos. 41, 42, Oct. 14, 21, 1933.

which in clumsy word-for-word repetition reports all events and speeches, and if once it assumes a positive attitude, falls into a laughable Byzantinism. No confidence is or can be placed in people who twist and turn with the wind like a weather vane on a signal mast. For this reason it is essential that we create a new press, one that will function in the spirit of the new state."

The move launched by some Gauleiters to liquidate the independent press and establish a party monopoly was vigorously pursued in East Prussia, Pomerania, Hesse-Nassau, Rhineland-Palatinate, and Württemberg. The greatest excesses were perpetrated in the Rhineland-Palatinate by Gerhard Kuhn, in Württemberg by Dr. Otto Weiss, in Hesse-Nassau by Konrad Goebbels, and in East Prussia by Gauleiter Koch. The details of Konrad Goebbels' operations have not been reconstructed, but after the war the denazification tribunal classified him as an "activist" on the proven charges that he had "conducted a large number of unwarranted negotiations involving middle class publishing undertakings in a manner so disadvantageous to them as to have led to their economic ruin." [7] Gerhard Kuhn was an East Prussian who appeared in the Saar shortly before 1932 as Max Winkler's representative with funds for the support of the "notleidende Grenzlandpresse." From this position as Winkler's agent he moved into the Palatinate, where he became the publisher of the *NSZ-Rheinfront*—official organ of the Gauleitung—and special deputy to Gauleiter Bürckel for all press matters. Kuhn used this as a special hunting license and by 1938 he was calling himself the largest publisher in Germany and boasting that he had brought under the control of the Gauverlag almost all the private publishing properties in the Palatinate. Kuhn and Bürckel were personal participants in these enterprises, and Bürckel was able to keep their profitable empire out of the party's Standarte holding company. Kurt Liesenberg, one of

[7] Liesenberg, *Der N-S Verlagskonzern Saarpfalz*, p. 16.

Kuhn's victims, has given an account of his experience with the Gau publisher. Liesenberg, principal owner of the *Pfälzische Verlagsanstalt* in Neustadt a.d. Haardt, resisted vigorously the pressures and approaches to acquire control of his business in 1933. The coercive methods used were those which the Nazis found most effective: Withdrawal of paid official notices, a party boycott of advertisers, pressure on public employees to cancel subscriptions, whispering campaigns, and the circulation of flysheets denouncing the publisher and his paper. Liesenberg held on for some time but was finally forced into bankruptcy and his creditors turned the business over to Gerhard Kuhn.[8]

Weiss's operations in Württemberg were equally disastrous for the private publishers. With the support of the Gauleiter, Weiss forced almost the entire local and provincial press of Württemberg into the Gauverlag combine. The treatment which publishers received is illustrated by the case history of the *Schwarzwälder Bote*, a paper circulating about 30,000 copies daily in southern Württemberg. The business was organized as a stock company with one principal owner and several local minority stockholders. Threats and pressure were directed at the paper and publisher when the Nazis came to power. In June the publisher had an interview in Stuttgart with a representative of the Gau publishing interests. This person, presumably speaking for Weiss, told the publisher that the N-S press authorities had the following plans and objectives: First, to destroy the "bürgerliche" press within three months, using any means and tactics necessary to accomplish this goal; second, all officials and state employees would be required to subscribe to N-S papers under threat of dismissal; third, all innkeepers and merchants would be boycotted if they continued to subscribe to non-Nazi papers; fourth, mayors and community council chairmen would be made personally responsible for insuring that only N-S papers were

[8] Liesenberg, pp. 1-8, 25-26.

read in their communities; fifth, all non-Nazi papers would be deprived of official advertising and prohibited from publishing such announcements even without compensation. To effect all this they need not issue written orders, he said. Secret orders would suffice and they had for circulation activity the entire SA and SS at their disposition. Protests by private publishers would be useless as they would be disregarded or taken care of in "a way which you can easily imagine." Furthermore, any paper that attempted to be colorless and neutral would be suspended on some pretext for a period of one year. Concluding his exposé, the plain speaking representative declared: "Public opinion must be formed and dominated one hundred per cent by the NSDAP."

After this briefing on the future of the independent press, Weiss's representative made his proposal with regard to the *Schwarzwälder Bote.* He demanded that fifty-one per cent of its shares be surrendered to the N-S Presse Württemberg without compensation—as the party had no immediate funds! The representative's brother would become the general manager; all employees would be retained in their positions and profits would be paid to the shareholders. All this he was prepared to put into a contract which would be strictly observed for "we live now in a state where law is respected" (*wir leben ja in einem Rechtsstaat*). After serious and agitated discussion the owners in a special meeting in Stuttgart, on August 5, voted unanimously to reject any merger or connection with the Gau Verlag. The Nazi threats were not unrealized. In September the paper lost its position as the official paper in the Kreis. Boycott and intimidation followed and intensive canvassing was carried on to take subscribers from the stubborn publisher. One device used by the Nazi agents was a perforated subscription form, one part for the N-S paper, the other half a cancellation notice for the *Schwarzwälder Bote.* Despite threats and unfair competition the paper managed to survive as one of the few independently owned papers in Württemberg.[9]

The attempt to despoil the owners of the *Schwarzwälder Bote* was not an isolated case. All over Germany in 1933 similar threats and pressures were used against private publishers. In Württemberg, Otto Weiss waged a veritable war of extermination against the non-Nazi press. Biesenberger estimates that by November 1933 over seventy per cent of the middle class local newspapers had reorganized as stock companies and surrendered their majority shares to the N-S Presse Württemberg. "Most of the private publishers were moved to take this step because they did not want to lose the official status of their papers. Moreover, in consequence of the economic depression of the 1930's, they lacked the financial reserves necessary to meet with any prospect of success the unscrupulous competition of the N-S press." [10]

Amann and Rienhardt disapproved of the actions of Gerhard Kuhn, Otto Weiss, and other Gau Verlag directors who terrorized local publishers, but they could not take disciplinary action as long as these men had the support of their Gau chiefs. Werner Stephan, a responsible official in the press division of the propaganda ministry, has testified that "public scandal resulted from the methods of force and coercion employed by the Gauleiters in Pomerania, Rhineland-Palatinate, and Württemberg to acquire for the

---

[9] H. Biesenberger, *Der Schwarzwälder Bote in den Jahren 1930-1950*, pp. 26-32, 36-37. This is an unusual study by the son of the former editor and present publisher. The author used the business papers of the firm, minutes of stockholders' meetings, local records, and material provided by the former director of the Landesverband Württemberg of the RVDZV. It is more than the history of one paper, giving a good picture of publishing conditions in Württemberg during the Third Reich.

[10] Biesenberger, p. 38. Loss of official legal notices was frequently sufficient to ruin a local paper. When the V-B in Munich became the official journal for legal notices the old *Bayerischer Staatszeitung* ceased publication. (*Zeitungs-Verlag*, No. 25, June 23, 1934.)

Gau publishing companies almost all the local and county newspapers. . . . Repeatedly I brought to the attention of the propaganda ministry, the Reich Press Chamber, and the newspaper publishers' association the measures that were employed in these territories. All representations were in vain. I was always told that the Gauleiters were not authorized to proceed in this manner but that they were conforming in general to the wishes of the Führer, who desired to strengthen for political reasons the power position of the party in the field of the press." [11]

Corrupt and malign, Weiss was detested by his associates in Württemberg, and to Amann and Rienhardt he was a thorn in the flesh. Both received numerous complaints of his methods and actions but they were powerless to remove him as long as he enjoyed the support of Gauleiter Murr. In September 1933, he was sharply reprimanded by Amann, who closed his letter with a declaration of impatience: "I am completely fed up with receiving every day complaints from Gau Württemberg." [12] Amann and Rienhardt were not able to effect Weiss's removal until 1936. Meanwhile, he had come near to his goal of an N-S press monopoly in Württemberg.

## Regimentation of the Publishers— Reichsverband and Landesverband

Ordinarily publishers placed under extreme pressure by officials of state or party would look to their trade organization for defense of their interests. In the institution of the old Verein Deutscher Zeitungsverleger were many powers

[11] Werner Stephan, Gutachten, March 28, 1949, Institut für Zeitungswissenschaft, Munich.

[12] Amann's letter and the testimony of witnesses—Rienhardt, Amann, Winkler, and Richter—are reproduced or summarized in the case of Ilse Pielenz vs. Baden-Württemberg, Sept. 28, 1953, pp. 72-75. A former Kreisleiter testified that Weiss had employed "a sharp elbow policy" and had not hesitated to "put the pistol to their breasts."

of self-government and regulation, including local agreements on advertising and subscription rates, uniform contracts with editors, standards of practice in soliciting subscribers, and arbitration boards for the settlement within
the industry of complaints and charges. The VDZV also
vigorously represented the newspaper publishers in their
relations with government agencies and officials. With the
Hitler dictatorship all this went by the boards. Gradually
during 1933 the central office and the provincial associations were converted to agencies for the control and discipline of the publishers. With the Gleichschaltung of the
national organization a similar turnover occurred in the regional associations. Here the Nazi Gau Verlag director
was usually chosen president, the executive committee reorganized, and the former executive director replaced or
retained depending upon the personal and local factors involved. The independent publisher subjected to pressure or
unfair competition by the Gau press authorities found no
support in his Landesverband or in the central office in
Berlin. If he appealed to the president of the Landesverband he would be appealing to the Gau Verlag director,
who in all probability was his oppressor or unscrupulous
competitor. If he appealed to the Reichsverband in Berlin
his complaint went to Rienhardt who was also the head of
the Standarte organization of the Gau press. It was this position of isolation and helplessness that led many small publishers to yield to the lightest pressure and to salvage what
they could from their business by selling or leasing to the
Gau Verlag.

While the records of the central office of the publishers'
association were destroyed, the surviving files of the executive director of the Landesverband Northwest Germany
give a detailed picture of a provincial office during the transition period from October 1933 to June 1934.[13] A. D. Latt-

[13] The area covered by the Landesverband Northwest Germany
included Brunswick, Hanover, Oldenburg, and Bremen.

mann, a former publisher in Goslar, had suffered business reverses and the executive committee of the Landesverband generously aided him with an appointment as business manager of the provincial association. Lattmann became an enthusiastic Nazi and made himself acceptable to the new regime in Berlin, which led a former publisher associate to describe him as "einer schlimmer Kerrl." Helmuth Raabe, Verlag director of one of the Leonhardt papers in Brunswick, was president of the regional association. From Lattmann's reports to Raabe and the central office in Berlin the political and economic conditions of the industry at the local level are starkly revealed. Much of Lattmann's correspondence dealt with ordinary complaints concerning infractions of agreements and regulations by members. But it also reflected the turmoil created by the political revolution in Germany. Most numerous were communications about acceptance of advertising from Jewish firms, the shortage of editors acceptable to the new regime, and the wearing of uniforms by party members working as advertising and subscription agents. Lattmann was also much concerned about collecting the membership dues owed by the suppressed Social Democratic papers in his district. When he applied to the Konzentration AG in Berlin for payment from the sequestered property he was referred to the minister president of Prussia as the competent authority. The correspondence does not reveal the disposition of this claim which Lattmann pressed as "a matter of equity." [14]

In November the executive directors of the regional associations were called to a conference in Berlin. Schmidt-Leonhardt of the propaganda ministry briefed them on the Editor's Law, leaving Lattmann more optimistic as to the retention of publisher's rights than the law and its application subsequently justified. Erwin Finkenzeller, advertising manager of the Eher Verlag, recently appointed executive

[14] Lattmann File No. 1, RVDZV collection, BDC.

director of the newly created Advertising Council for the German Economy (Werberat der deutschen Wirtschaft), spoke to them at length on advertising and the press. The substance of his remarks was that the German advertising business had declined by more than forty per cent owing to the economic depression. Private enterprise and the trade organizations had failed to restore the advertising business to a healthy condition; now the National Socialist state was going to take positive action. To that end the Advertising Council had been created with power to "cleanse and organize" the advertising business.

At the regular district conference, held in Hanover in early December, the principal speaker was Dr. Kurt Jahncke, director of the press division in the ministry of propaganda. Jahncke, an educated man and former financial editor of the *Oldenburger Nachrichten*, spoke reassuringly of the position of the private publisher. "You all know what difficult months lie behind us. . . . The party papers of the old system have had to transform themselves. On the other hand we have experienced the powerful upsurge of the N-S press. The Führer himself and the heads of other high government agencies have repeatedly emphasized that the old press shall retain its right of existence. Happily we can say that the embittered battle to win readers is assuming quieter aspects. It speaks for a great ethical consciousness that the Führer has declared that in the German newspaper industry the principle of performance must prevail." Closer to the truth was Jahncke's candid appraisal of the business situation of the press: "The position of the newspaper trade in the current year, to speak frankly, is catastrophic." [15] This appraisal was fully confirmed by Lattmann in his report to the executive committee in Bremen on March 18. He reported that advertising revenue, so far in 1934, was approximately fifty per cent below the same period in 1932. This was the average for small papers and the larger enter-

[15] Conference report, Dec. 8, 1933, Lattmann File No. 1, BDC.

prises were not doing much better. Lattmann presented a gloomy picture of the publishing business and he saw no signs of revival. Nor did developments support Jahncke's assertion that the worst aspects of the subscription war had disappeared. In January Lattmann wrote to Raabe that in the area of the Landesverband "The competitive subscription battle has flared up again and is carried on in a manner reminiscent of the worst months of the preceding year." [16]

A structural change of major significance in the organization of the publishers' association occurred in February 1934. At a membership meeting in Berlin, on February 18, the old VDZV was dissolved and reconstituted as the Reichsverband der Deutschen Zeitungsverleger, with a new constitution and by-laws. Established as one of the trade groups of the Reich Press Chamber, the RVDZ was no longer a voluntary self-governing trade association, but a compulsory membership organization subject to the policies, ordinances, and directives of the Reich Press Chamber. The provincial associations became subordinate agencies of the central organization and the executive directors became paid employees of the Reichsverband. While externally some of the trappings of an autonomous trade group were retained, the reorganized publishers' association functioned internally on strict bureaucratic principles.[17]

Uniformity and centralized direction were the principal features of the new association. From the central office came a stream of bureaucratic directives, instructions, notices, conference reports, and memoranda. Routine directives dealt with execution of the new advertising regulations, certification of newspaper circulation, labor relations,

[16] Lattmann to Raabe, Jan. 24, and report of the executive committee meeting, March 18, 1934; Lattmann File No. 1.

[17] The constitution and by-laws were published in *Zeitungs-Verlag*, No. 8, Feb. 24, 1934. The Landesverband Northwest Germany had a membership of two hundred. All non-members were notified by Lattmann that to continue in the trade they must join the association.

publicity for party organizations, requests for specific reports, and problems of subscription canvassing. The actions started through most of these administrative directives were designed to bring order out of chaos in a depressed and disorganized industry. The stringent regulations established for subscription agents were justified, and the industry as a whole was probably benefited by other regulatory actions covering free copies, advertising rebates, and obligatory subscriptions for members of organizations.[18]

More important than these matters, however, are the directives and instructions of a political nature for the purging of the publishing industry of all elements regarded as unreliable, discordant, or inimical to National Socialist ideas and programs. It will be recalled that Paragraph 10 of the implementing ordinance of the Reich Chamber of Culture law specified the terms under which a publisher could be denied membership in the Reich Press Chamber or expelled therefrom. This applied the rubber yardstick of "political reliability" and "suitable qualifications" for activity as a publisher of newspapers or periodicals. The determination of "political reliability" was made by the central office of the Reichsverband, while the Reich Press Chamber took the official action.[19] In February 1934, when the new organization was established, the authorities of the association began the examination essential to membership certification under Paragraph 10. Instead of being completed in a few months, as first anticipated, the inquiry, which was sev-

[18] Copies of these important directives survived the destructive bombing and are now in the Berlin Document Center. Designated "RVDZV, LV Rundschreiben," they cover the critical years 1934-1936 and fill two large Leitz binders.

[19] Paragraph 10 of the implementing ordinance of the law establishing the Reich Chamber of Culture stated: "The admission to an individual chamber can be denied, or a member expelled, if facts are presented which lead to the conclusion that the person in question does not possess the necessary reliability and qualifications for the exercise of his profession or vocation."

eral times expanded and deepened, was not concluded until June 1936.

Action under Paragraph 10 began with the issuance of an official questionnaire distributed to all publishers on April 25, 1934. This was the first document that went into the rapidly growing file which was developed for every publisher remaining in the industry. On August 1, the Landesverband directors were instructed to visit each publisher in their district, to check with all local party and state agencies, including the Gestapo, and to render a detailed report on the publisher and the condition of his business. Specifically, the following subjects were to be included: Personal impression of the publisher; his past and present political attitudes; previous political or Masonic affiliations; and relations to local party officials. Some of the searching questions to be answered were: Was the publisher a former anti-Nazi, has he changed his mind, and if so, is this change shown in the conduct of his enterprise? Does he have children of an age to inherit and carry on the business? Is the heir being brought up as a National Socialist and does he belong to N-S groups and organizations? What is the publisher's competitive position in the district? In arriving at a political estimate it was suggested that the director consult the political police, the Gestapo, and the Kreisleiter. The detailed character of the report required is indicated by the fact that a ten-page directive was developed for the guidance of the Landesverband investigators. The reports were wanted by the central office so that a comprehensive view of the publishing trade could be prepared by the end of September. This was an optimistic deadline. Lattmann, for example, in the Landesverband Northwest Germany, had approximately 200 publishers to investigate. In fact the personal visitation and reporting dragged on for eighteen months.

The questionnaire and the probing interviews conducted by the Landesverband directors understandably created alarm and apprehension in publishing circles. At the Berlin conference of field directors in September, Rienhardt addressed himself to the problems of the visitation program. He reminded the directors that the RVDZV was a corporate trade organization and that their principal mission was to help and support the members and develop confidence in the association. He underscored one organizational difficulty—that the Landesverband chairmen were in almost all instances directors of the party's Gau Verlag, and therefore regarded by private publishers as their principal competitor. The information which the executive directors secured about individual business enterprises must therefore be held in strict confidence. The impression prevailed in publishing circles that the work of the Reichsverband was directed toward the destruction of part of the press, but he wanted to emphasize that the mission of the Reichsverband was not to destroy but to build up a sound and healthy publishing industry. If some enterprises had to be excluded from the field to assure an "organic development of the press," this was not the task of the directors or Landesverband presidents but of the central office and the Reich Press Chamber.[20]

The visitation reports were not completed when an additional burden was placed on the regional staffs. In March 1935, to supplement the personal investigations, a comprehensive instruction was sent to the district directors requiring them to analyze the files of each newspaper with a view to determining its ideological position in relation to National Socialism. In this examination special attention was to be given to reporting and editorial treatment of political events. In the files for 1933 they were instructed to check reactions to the following events: Suppression of the SPD press, storming of the city halls, dissolution of the political parties, and the dismissal of Duesterberg, leader of the

[20] Conference protocol, Sept. 25-27, 1934, LV Rundschreiben, File 1.

Stahlhelm. In the 1934 files special attention was to be given to the "Röhm revolt" and the party congress; and in 1935 to Hitler's proclamation of "defense sovereignty," Goebbels' speech on cultural policy, and the speeches of Rosenberg and Frick on the church issue at the Gau conference in Münster on July 8. A special section of the instructions was devoted to the former Center party press. Especially to be noted was: Whether the paper published the schedule of services for both confessions; whether a Catholic event was given greater publicity than a N-S event; and whether notices of pilgrimages in a Catholic community were placed in a framework of editorial persuasion. Finally the examiners were given a slogan for their work: "Tact, sensitivity and generosity, but without being flabby!" [21]

As the Paragraph 10 action was being completed in early 1936, some especially difficult cases were subjected to a final test on specific instruction from Rienhardt to the Landesverband directors. Where doubts existed because the information was conflicting, or when adverse opinions had been recorded but not supported by specific facts, the publisher was to be sent a special letter. The text of this brusque communication informed the publisher that the certification of his Verlag was pending and in conformity with the policies laid down by the president of the RPK he must return, within five days, complete answers to the following questions: In what relationship he and his family and the leading employees in his Verlag stood to the N-S Weltanschauung and to the party; whether he, or members of his family, and principal employees were members of the party or of its affiliated organizations—SA, SS, N-S-Frauenschaft, etc. If the answers were negative the recipient was requested to explain why he and members of his family,

[21] LV Rundschreiben No. 84, March 7, 1935; and supplementary directive No. 98, Dec. 23, 1935.

and principal employees, had not joined the party or its affiliated organizations.[22] We may assume that this interrogatory represented a final check in doubtful cases to measure the publisher's adjustment to the regime and his progress in National Socialist education.

Action on the Paragraph 10 cases was finally completed in March 1936 and in early June the lists of publishers in each Landesverband, who were granted certificates of reliability, were dispatched to the district directors. Unfortunately these lists have been ripped from the Leitz binders now in the record collections of the Berlin Document Center.

It was to be expected that there would be repercussions from publishers who were denied certification and excluded from the Reich Press Chamber. An echo of this comes in a communication from Amann, president of the RPK, warning the Landesverband directors that information given by the secret state police and the party offices had been made available on a confidential basis. "Under no circumstances may the person concerned be informed that an evaluation (Beurteilung) by the secret state police or the party was submitted. This does not mean that the person cannot be questioned about reported incidents or derogatory information. But this is to be carried out in a manner that will not reveal how the derogatory information reached the Reich Press Chamber." [23]

How many newspaper and periodical publishers failed to qualify for membership in the RPK under this microscopic examination extending in some instances over a two year period? Fritz Schmidt's unqualified assertion that in 1933-

[22] LV Rundschreiben No. 15, Feb. 4, 1936.
[23] LV Rundschreiben No. 172, Nov. 17, 1936; marked "Geheim zu bleiben." At the conference of Landesverband directors in April 1935, Rienhardt said that the visitation reports had been of great help but "for the final decision we depend on information from the party and the secret state police. . . ."

1934, under Paragraph 10, altogether 1,473 publishers were disqualified, and "robbed" of their publishing rights, is a gross exaggeration. Rolf Rienhardt's statement in one of the post-war restitution cases that less than 100 publishers were denied certification may be too low but it is probably closer to the correct number. Since the records presumably were destroyed, the exact number cannot be determined. This can be said with certainty: Greater inroads were made upon private rights in the publishing industry by the Amann ordinances of April 1935 than by the political screening under Paragraph 10. The scope, significance, and impact of these ordinances, and their relationship to the Paragraph 10 action, will be treated in the following chapter.

While the private publishers who remained in business outwardly conformed to Nazi policies and requirements, the press in Germany at the end of 1934 was far from being a National Socialist press. Barely twenty-five per cent of the circulation of daily newspapers was produced by party-owned publishing houses. Neither were the indications convincing that the old publishers who still dominated the field had been born again and were now convinced National Socialists. As the Paragraph 10 investigations proceeded, Rienhardt and his associates concluded that action more radical than Gleichschaltung and purging of the industry would be required to satisfy the demand of the party leadership that the German press be a National Socialist press. The methods pursued by the Gauleiters and their Verlag directors in Rhineland-Palatinate, Pomerania, and Württemberg, could not be employed uniformly throughout the Reich, nor would they be effective against the large, well-established newspaper publishers. These methods brought the party into great disrepute locally. Furthermore, economic conditions in newspaper publishing worsened perceptibly during 1934 despite measures taken to stimulate the advertising business and the intensive campaigns conducted by publishers to increase circulation. Least affected by the depression were those publications most obnoxious to the Nazis—the popular Generalanzeiger papers, with their highly rationalized production, department store advertising, and connections with influential industrial and financial circles. The raging competition between the Gau press and the middle-sized provincial papers would bring many of the latter to the bankruptcy court, with the possible collapse of the entire newspaper publishing business as a further prospect. These were the two major problems— the political and the economic—that engaged Rienhardt's attention during 1934 as he worked deeper into the details of the publishing industry. From the Nazi standpoint, any acceptable solution must deal with the two basic and urgent problems—a rationalization of the industry through the elimination of uneconomic enterprises, and transfer of ownership of large or important papers from private to party hands. The Amann ordinances of April 1935 were designed to produce the "final solution" in the matter of private ownership and ultimate control of the newspaper publishing industry.

## Amann, Rienhardt, and Winkler

In the liquidation of the middle class press and the building of a giant party trust in the newspaper field, which evolved as the N-S press policy, three men played major roles—Amann, Rienhardt, and Max Winkler. Amann, in his state and party positions and his relationship to Hitler, provided the reality as well as symbols of authority; Rienhardt contributed high intelligence, ingenuity, and undeviating purpose; Winkler provided unrivaled knowledge of the publishing industry, great skill as a business negotiator, and a flair for corporate finance and management.

With his appointment as president of the Reich Press Chamber and undisputed master of the party press, Amann's field of operations and responsibilities was vastly extended. Some men grow in the positions which they acquire and disclose unexpected reserves of talent and ability. This formula does not fit Max Amann. He did not move to Berlin as did other party leaders. He was not seized with the Nazi frenzy for bigness and avoided building a large and imposing Verlagshaus for the Eher company—as he might well have done. Instead he remained in the dumpy quarters in the Thierschstrasse and despite the loss of his arm continued to spend much time in the hunting field. In 1945, Amann represented himself to Allied interrogators as a simple business man, a publisher who had achieved great success. This was not entirely a pose. Amann was not ideologically motivated and he had only modest intellectual endowments. He could not prepare a speech or participate effectively in free discussion and debate. He was intellectually primitive, and yet in managing an enterprise like the Eher Verlag and its subsidiaries he was direct, dedicated, and enterprising—just as he had been in the early days of the V-B. In this sense he was a simple businessman. The Eher Verlag, the V-B, and their interests, were almost the boundaries of his world. Within these boundaries he operated effectively and efficiently. Shrewd and ruthless, Amann had certain principles which derived, as with most practical men, from his experience. These he projected to the larger field in which he found himself after 1933. One of these was: "Where there is no competition there is no performance." This he thought had been the secret of his success with the Eher Verlag and the V-B. Where his simple principles, or obsessions, came into play he was not easily diverted or deterred. His loyalty to Hitler was unswerving, but he would oppose like a bull the Gauleiters, the Reichsleitung, and any competing or poaching rival in the field of his competence. Because of his unique influence with Hitler his position was almost unassailable. It is probably owing to Amann's personality and preconceptions that the total publishing business was not turned over to the party in 1933—in this instance to the Gauleiters—and all private ownership of newspapers and periodicals liquidated.

In December 1933, when Amann formally assumed the presidency of the Reich Press Chamber, he made an important policy address—probably prepared by Rienhardt—which embodied his ideas on N-S publishing policy. He endorsed private ownership of the local press and the national dailies under conditions of positive cooperation with the regime; he sharply condemned the principles of the Generalanzeiger press whose policies were directed toward the highest circulation and advertising revenue; and he warned that the political dailies must abandon their confessional ties and leave these interests to confessional periodicals. For the welfare of the industry he promised vigorous action to eliminate the chaos in subscription canvassing and advertising. If not wholly reassuring to all branches of the publishing trade, Amann's pronouncements were far from radical. They echoed, in general, public statements by Hitler and Goebbels on the press and its role in the new state. Among the Gauleiters, whose visions oftentimes substituted for plans, Amann's address was much disliked for its endorsement of private ownership and competition in the important field of the press. In subsequent pronouncements Amann added the "performance principle" (Leistungsprinzip) as the yardstick for measuring the worthiness of publishing enterprises, an idea that was hammered home by Rienhardt in frequent conferences with publishers. We may credit Amann with some degree of sincerity in presenting his policies, even though they were not in accord with subsequent developments. Amann was in fact opposed to radical action, but probably for tactical reasons. In 1933-1934 he had his hands full salvaging and reorganizing the Gau press, and he was not at that time in a position to force the issue with the middle class publishers. In the end, however, Hitler's desires and objectives prevailed. Asked, in

1945, about the principle underlying the Eher acquisitions of publishing concerns and newspapers, Amann tersely replied: "Hitler regarded the press as an instrument of government and wanted it taken entirely out of private hands." [24] And it might be added: If an acquisition promised profit, Amann was prepared to deal.

Rolf Rienhardt, who became the most powerful figure in the German publishing industry, was of a wholly different order than his chief. Born in 1903, he was considerably younger than Amann, and could be classified with the idealists in the party. Son of a Lutheran pastor, well educated in law at Berlin and Munich, highly intelligent, forceful, and a prodigious worker, Rienhardt devoted the best ten years of his life to the National Socialist state and party. Rienhardt was typical of many young men that a visitor belonging to the same generation encountered in the German universities in the late 1920's and early 1930's. Their complete devotion to the N-S cause was incomprehensible to the outsider. With excellent family backgrounds, high personal standards of ethics and conduct, still they could close their ears to the immoral and irrational clamorings of the party demagogues and their eyes to the brutalities displayed or inherent in the movement. One could compile a long list of such university educated men, who were in no wise opportunists but who served the Nazi cause loyally and enthusiastically.

Rienhardt was drawn to National Socialism through his acquaintance with Gregor Strasser who introduced him to the party leaders. In 1928 he became legal counsel to the Eher Verlag. At Strasser's suggestion and with his support, he was elected on the party list in the Reichstag elections of July 1932 and reelected in November. In 1932 he became a division chief in Strasser's Reich Organization Office, but in December he was purged together with other Strasser followers. He was also dropped from the party's Reichstag list

[24] Interview notes, Max Amann, Aug. 22, 1945.

in the March elections. With Hess's somewhat nervous approval, Amann appointed Rienhardt his personal representative in the executive committee of the VDZV in April 1933. At this juncture talented and educated persons to fill a multitude of vacant positions were scarce. From this post Rienhardt moved into two strategic positions—staff director in Amann's administrative office for the party press, and deputy director of the newspaper publisher's association. Rienhardt was the brains as well as the motor of the Amann system. He was responsible for the planning, implementing, and application of the policies which revolutionalized the German press. With extraordinary talent for organization, fertile in ideas, and flexible but persistent in negotiations, he supplied Amann with those qualifications which the little Verlag director utterly lacked. He wrote the articles that appeared under Amann's name in the trade journal *Zeitungs-Verlag*, prepared his major speeches, and drafted all important papers and directives. The speech which Rienhardt wrote for delivery by Amann at the Nürnberg party rally in 1936, was pitched on such a level that poor Amann could scarcely deliver it, and so out of character that it amused his associates in the party leadership. In the conduct of his important offices Rienhardt followed the general lines set by Amann and faithfully reported on all matters of policy and operations. Final decisions, particularly in business and personnel matters, rested with Amann who in turn was guided by Hitler's expressed desires and views. Rienhardt never sought the limelight, and never "howled with the wolves." His speeches were limited strictly to the areas of his responsibility. Characteristically he kept his party uniform in his office wardrobe and wore it only on official occasions.

The staff in Rienhardt's office was small—not over twenty persons, including secretarial and clerical personnel. But the amount of work performed was impressive. He directed a clean operation; no suggestion of graft or corruption, for which great opportunities existed, was ever made by his many enemies and critics. When he was dismissed summarily by Amann in November 1943, he left his office without severance pay, pension rights, or a substantial bank account.

In the early years of the Third Reich the mystery man of the publishing business was Dr. h. c. Max Winkler, former mayor of Graudenz in West Prussia, and "Reich Trustee for Everything," including the German film industry and, after 1939, confiscated property in the annexed districts of Poland. Winkler was a self-made man. Born September 7, 1875, in Kreis Rosemberg, West Prussia, he attended the common schools and a postal training school, and entered the postal service at age sixteen. In 1914 he took a paid position with the city of Graudenz where he had been for some time a member of the city council. He was elected vice-mayor of the town and delegate to the Prussian state constitutional assembly in 1919 on the Democratic ticket. When his West Prussian homeland was incorporated into Poland, he moved to Berlin where he lobbied effectively for economic and cultural support for the German minorities which had been separated from the Reich. In 1920 he was appointed Reich Trustee and Economic Adviser for the separated territories, a position which he held until 1933. He operated in Danzig, Eupen-Malmedy, Schleswig, West Prussia, Upper Silesia, and the Saar. The aid rendered first by Prussia then by the Reich, took a variety of forms—credits to prevent foreclosures on German farms, support of social and cultural organizations, and assistance to German banks and cooperatives. In 1933 Winkler was acting as trustee for nineteen enterprises under the authority of the Reich finance ministry and the Reich central accounting office. To provide proper cover, and to receive and disburse funds provided by the Reich government, Winkler organized in 1929 the Cautio GmbH of which he was the business director and sole shareholder.

Later in his newspaper and film industry operations he used the Cautio company as a purchasing and transfer agency.

One of Winkler's important operations was founding and supporting German newspapers in the minority areas. Altogether some dozen papers were under his control and it was for their management and direction that he established the Cura Trustee and Auditing Company (Cura Treuhand und Prüfung GmbH). In his work with the press Winkler gained a thorough knowledge of the publishing business and made wide contacts in the industry. Winkler was also politically active in the interest of his operations, alertly cultivating all accessible influential circles in Berlin. An adaptable man, he moved politically with the times and by 1932 he was well over toward the right. In the re-election of Hindenburg in 1932 he acted as collector and paymaster for the coalition parties, including the Social Democrats. In that election, Winkler received from industrial and financial circles seven million marks which he disbursed to the parties for campaign purposes.

Since Winkler's services to the anti-Nazi parties was well known in Hitler's circle, the termination of his position as trustee for operations in the minority districts became a distinct possibility in 1933. Later an unfriendly witness commented that during the February-March turnover in Berlin, Winkler could be seen waiting patiently in the antechamber of every Naxi 'big-shot' who had gained high rank in the new government. The right contact was eventually made through State Secretary Lammers and Walther Funk, who had been named press chief of the Reich government and state secretary in the newly organized propaganda ministry. Funk introduced Winkler to Goebbels, Amann, and Rienhardt, and also facilitated his continuance as Reich trustee for the press in the German minority districts. Soon his contacts, his knowledge of the newspaper business, and his skill as a negotiator and financial organizer were being utilized by the new regime. He worked first for Goebbels

and Funk in purchasing the Telegraph Union from Hugenberg and merging it with the Wolff Telegraph Bureau to
form the DNB news agency, which became a cornerstone
in the news and information monopoly established under
the ministry of propaganda. But his first major coup was the
purchase of the Ullstein Verlag on behalf of Goebbels and
Amann in March 1934. Thereafter his experience and
knowledge were regularly drawn on by Rienhardt and
Amann in all matters concerning the press. He briefed
Amann on conditions in the Berlin publishing industry and
his knowledge of provincial publishing was useful to Rienhardt in the reorganization of the Gau press. His Cura auditing and management staff was made available to the new
publishing chiefs. Without this staff their work would have
been more difficult if not impossible. Winkler's greatest
period of activity in the publishing field came in 1935-
1937, when as Amann's agent he purchased for the Eher
Verlag a large part of the Generalanzeiger press and numerous provincial dailies, grouping these under the Vera holding and management company which he directed.

In 1935 Winkler appeared with the official designation
"Reich Plenipotentiary for the German Film Industry," operating on behalf of the propaganda and finance ministries
but working closely with Goebbels and Funk. In a remarkably short time the nationalization of the film industry was
accomplished. Most of the firms were acquired at bargain
prices, only Hugenberg realizing somewhere near actual
value for the UFA company. In these acquisitions for the
Reich government, Winkler used his Cautio company as a
trustee agency for the shares of the film companies. Henceforth Winkler controlled the budgetary and financial affairs of the German film industry. Next to Goebbels, who
made the motion picture field his empire, Winkler was the
most potent figure in the business. This was not the end of
his service to the Hitler Reich. In October 1939, he was appointed director of the Central Trustee Office East (Haupt-

treuhandstelle Ost), under Göring's Four Year Plan administration, to effect the seizure and administration of Polish state property, Jewish property, and the property of enemy Poles in the occupied and annexed areas of Poland. He held this position until the end of the war.

Winkler never became active in the Nazi party although he joined in 1937. At his denazification hearing in August 1949, in Lüneburg, he was exonerated and placed in Category Five. In the proceedings his operations in Poland as head of the HTO were passed over quickly and the derogatory information on his press and film operations was washed away in a flood of "Ivory soap" testimony. The witnesses on his behalf included some of the most important German newspaper publishers who had been his victims. What the prosecutors failed to prove was that he had personally employed political force, threats, or pressure in concluding his deals; or that he had enriched himself during his service to the party. Before the denazification chamber, Winkler presented himself as the savior of the German newspaper press, claiming that he kept the enterprises out of the hands of the Gauleiters and local fanatics by purchasing the papers at reasonable prices for the Eher trust. Within a month following his clearance by the denazification court, British authorities reported that Winkler was negotiating to recover the UFA film concern for its former private stockholders. In 1958 a German publisher formerly active in Berlin was asked if he knew Max Winkler. He replied: "Winkler! What a figure! No, not a figure—he was a Kuriosum!" [25]

[25] Reliable information on Winkler is scarce. The records of his *Grenzland* operations were destroyed as were also the records of his various companies. The BDC holds a single but valuable file on the Cautio corporation when it served as the holding company for the nationalized film industry. Winkler's interrogations, reports, and depositions, made at Nürnberg, are the principal sources for this sketch. These are interrogations, Aug. 7, and 13, and Sept. 28,

## Early Acquisitions—Ullstein and the Ala Advertising Agency

Amann's first major publishing acquisition, which provided the pattern for subsequent deals, was his purchase in the spring of 1934 of the Ullstein publishing company, Germany's largest newspaper, periodical, and book publishing house. Founded and developed by Leopold Ullstein, the enterprise was owned and managed in 1933 by his three sons. Besides its world-famous book publishing department, Ullstein issued a large variety of popular magazines, trade and technical journals, and several popular newspapers. The *Berliner Morgenpost* circulated over a half-million, the *B-Z am Mittag*, 200,000, the *Montagspost* over a half-million, the *Berliner Illustrierte* nearly two million, and the weekly family paper, *Grüne Post*, nearly a million. Ullstein also published the old established *Vossische Zeitung*, a quality newspaper with a sturdy democratic tradition. The commanding position which the firm enjoyed depended upon mass production and circulation and a large volume of advertising. Being Jewish owned, liberal, and a product of capitalistic enterprise and initiative, Ullstein was a target for concentrated Nazi hate. Trouble began immediately after January 1933: There were threats from the party leadership conveyed to the Ullsteins through intermediaries; the proclamation of anti-Semitic policies which would make it impossible for them to continue in the publishing business; intimidation of their subscription canvassers and subscribers by Nazi block wardens and SA men; and severe pressure on advertisers. Suffering from the depression, as were all other publishers, the Ullsteins made defensive moves designed to counter or conciliate their enemies. First, they reorganized the company and appointed a non-Jewish

---

1947; and a long deposition, Sept. 12, 1947. Winkler's denazification hearing is reported in *Die Welt*, No. 113, Aug. 8, 1949.

son-in-law, Fritz Ross, as manager.[26] As the pressure increased, Fritz Ross, brother of the well-known journalist Colin Ross, arranged an interview with Rudolf Hess through a mutual friend, Prof. Karl Haushofer. Hess brushed aside the board reorganization as a clumsy subterfuge and "in a threatening manner demanded that the Verlag be really Aryanized in the shortest time; otherwise the party would resort to the various means at its disposal to end the unsatisfactory situation which had developed with respect to this important Jewish Verlag." [27] What these "various means" were had already been demonstrated by a three months' suspension imposed by Goebbels on the *Grüne Post* for an infraction of the press rules. Since the probable outcome of further Nazi persecution would be bankruptcy and the total loss of the properties, the Ullsteins decided to sell if a buyer could be found.

On the Nazi side, the most detailed account of the purchase is Winkler's statement prepared at Nürnberg in 1947. Toward the end of January 1934 he had a meeting with Amann in Berlin. In the course of their conversation Amann referred to the *Grüne Post* suspension and the further economic blows that appeared to be impending. Winkler expressed concern lest such an important enterprise be economically crippled or forced into bankruptcy. Conditions were bad enough in the publishing industry. Amann agreed and then called Goebbels and asked him to see Winkler. The latter told Goebbels what he had said to Amann and in the course of the discussion suggested it would be better to buy the Ullstein Verlag than to destroy

[26] The company was reorganized on Nov. 2, 1933, with a new board and management committee. The new board included such public figures as Karl Haushofer, Martin Spahn, Heinrich Pferdemenges, and Fritz Ross. Ferdinand Bausback became chairman of the board. *Zeitungs-Verlag*, No. 45, Nov. 11, 1933.

[27] Statement by Dr. Fritz E. Kock, legal counsel to Ullstein in 1934; Handakten des Generalanklagers, Max Amann, Spruchkammer file.

it. Goebbels asked if he thought it possible and Winkler replied that he could try. Goebbels then said he would report on the matter and let Winkler know the result. Winkler was led to make his suggestion to Goebbels because of hints dropped by Frau Ullstein and another family intermediary. The day following their conversation, Goebbels called Winkler and commissioned him to enter into negotiations with the Ullsteins. Over a period of several weeks Winkler negotiated with a team composed of Ferdinand Bausback, chairman of the board, Fritz Ross, and the Ullstein lawyers, Ludwig Ruge, Dr. Tinner, and Fritz E. Kock. The business directors estimated the total value of the enterprise, including good will and reputation, at between fifty and sixty million marks. But Winkler could only offer six million for the shares, four million for the non-voting stock, and two million for the publishing rights and titles. All efforts to get a better price failed, so the family, fearing worse if they did not agree, accepted the offer. With the deductions and twenty-five per cent capital transfer tax, which the Third Reich imposed upon emigrés, what the Ullsteins received was a pittance in relation to the real value of their property. That the Ullsteins were persecuted for political and racial reasons and despoiled of their property is apparent. This was the finding of the restitution court after the war.

The deal was closed on June 30, 1934, and the Ullstein shares were deposited to Winkler's Cautio account in the Deutsche Bank. When he requested Goebbels to notify the ministry of finance to cover the first payment, Goebbels informed him that Hitler had decided the Eher Verlag was the purchaser and Amann would make the funds available. Where Amann got the money has already been noted— a loan of thirty million marks from the former trade union institution, Bank Deutscher Arbeit, which covered the Ullstein purchase and some of the subsequent major acquisitions by Eher. While Winkler thought he was negotiating for the propaganda ministry, Amann had intervened with

Hitler, advancing the claims of the party publishing house and arguing that a government agency, as a matter of policy, should not own and operate a large publishing business. Amann prevailed and Goebbels withdrew from the scene.[28]

After the war Amann represented his role in the Ullstein case as that of a philanthropist. The Verlag, like all the others he purchased, was "run down and losing money"; Hitler and Goebbels would have closed the enterprise and thrown all the employees on the street, a heavy blow to the industry and the profession. By taking it over and supplying it with contracts, he saved the business from liquidation. Amann always stressed the point that Ullstein had operated with a deficit of three million marks during the year prior to its purchase. (Actually it was 2.1 million.)

On the condition of Ullstein's business and the true value of the property opinions varied widely, but that its basic difficulties stemmed from political persecution and unfair trade practices cannot be doubted. Probably the fairest appraisal was given in a sworn deposition by Gustav Willner, a former director of Ullstein and chief of the accounting and finance department from 1921 to 1945. Willner shows that the company produced a good profit until 1929. Nazi anti-Semitism did not affect the business until 1930. Thereafter it was felt in sales and advertising and reached serious proportions in 1934. To tide over their difficulties a loan of four million marks was raised with the Deutsche

[28] This account is based on sworn and unsworn statements by participants: Winkler's deposition, Sept. 12, 1947; letter of Rudolf Ullstein to the Munich Spruchkammer, Dec. 17, 1948, and enclosed deposition by Fritz E. Kock; sworn statement by Ludwig Ruge (undated); all in the Handakten, Amann's Spruchkammer file, except Winkler's deposition. For his services as negotiator Winkler received no commission or honorarium. In 1937 Walther Funk proposed to Amann that Winkler be paid a monthly stipend of 2,000 RM as compensation for services to the Eher Verlag since 1933. This was approved and paid until the end of 1943. Winkler, unlike Amann, does not appear to have been corrupt or avaricious. His vanity, however, was boundless.

Bank and the Berliner Handelsgesellschaft. With this support it was thought they could withstand the Nazi propaganda action and the unfair competition for subscribers. But in the spring of 1934 direct action to ruin the firm was taken in the suspension, first of the *Berliner Illustrierte* and then the *Grüne Post*. In Willner's opinion, despite the company's obligations, it was in a sound financial position and could have survived the depression if the Nazis had not marked it for destruction. Willner supported his conclusions by citing circulation statistics for the principal Ullstein publications from 1928 to 1934. They all show the same curve—a circulation peak in 1928, and moderate declines in the years 1930-1932. In 1933-1934, with the Nazi boycott and anti-Semitic propaganda campaign, the losses were heavy. The *Berliner Morgenpost* had an average daily circulation of 576,000 in 1928, but dropped to 323,000 in 1934. The *Berliner Illustrierte*, Germany's most popular illustrated weekly, dropped from 1,808,000 in 1928 to 1,080,-000 in 1934. Other Ullstein publications showed similar losses. According to Willner advertising contracts for the various publications showed the same trends as circulation —a high in 1928, followed by decline in 1931-1932, resulting from the depression, and an intensified downward trend in 1932-1933, reaching its lowest point in the first half of 1934.[29] It is significant that during the next two years, under Eher ownership, the principal publications showed a slight but encouraging recovery.

With the exclusion of the Ullstein brothers from the concern, Dr. Bausback remained as board chairman and Max Wiessner, a partner of Broschek in Hamburg, was appointed Verlag director. Wiessner and Bausback purged the Verlag of its Jewish editors, although Winkler states that they acted generously in the matter of severance pay and pension rights. In 1936 the concern was reorganized

[29] Deposition by Gustav Willner, Berlin, Feb. 1949; Handakten, Max Amann, Spruchkammer file.

and a new management board was created with Rienhardt as chairman. Other members were Wilhelm Baur, of the Eher Verlag, Mundhenke of the Cura, Wiessner, and Winkler.

Under the new management a slight improvement in the business position of the Verlag and its publications was immediately achieved. Amann diverted a number of party printing contracts to the new firm, beginning with sports publications—*Reichsportblatt, Sport der Jugend, N-S Sport*. Other party sponsored periodicals followed—*Motorwelt, Sirene*, and *Der Volksdeutsche*. A considerable volume of contract printing for the Reichsleitung was also diverted to the new party enterprise. In 1936 the *12 Uhr Blatt* was acquired and teamed with the *B-Z am Mittag*, and in 1939 the *Deutsche Allgemeine Zeitung* was taken over as a replacement for the old *Vossische Zeitung*, which had been discontinued in 1934. This gave the Verlag an important national daily. The book publishing division, which was starved for contracts in 1933, showed considerable recovery although its products were scarcely of Ullstein quality. Further, the Verlag's sales and distribution system was integrated and considerably extended. The business volume rose from 47,730,000 RM in 1934 to 109,705,000 RM in 1940. The following statistics, showing gross income from circulation and advertising for all newspapers and periodicals, illustrate the record of recovery:

| CIRCULATION INCOME | | | | ADVERTISING INCOME | | | |
|---|---|---|---|---|---|---|---|
| 1934 | 29.6 | million | RM | 1934 | 11. | million | RM |
| 1935 | 30.3 | " | " | 1935 | 12.35 | " | " |
| 1936 | 33.5 | " | " | 1936 | 14. | " | " |
| 1937 | 37.7 | " | " | 1937 | 15. | " | " |
| 1938 | 44.3 | " | " | 1938 | 17.5 | " | " |
| 1939 | 56.4 | " | " | 1939 | 20. | " | " |

In 1935 Amann made a highly publicized visit to the Verlag, which in effect announced and advertised the new ownership. In January 1938, in recognition of its recovery and achievements, Amann bestowed upon the enterprise the name Deutscher Verlag. With the subsequent additions to its publishing list and the large volume of contract printing funneled to the company, the Deutscher Verlag became, next to the parent Eher Verlag, the largest and most profitable unit in the party trust.[30] Shortly after the Ullsteins had been bullied out of their property, Amann is reported to have boasted: "Now we have bought the largest German publishing house and it has not cost us as much as a pencil." [31]

In the fields of news dissemination and advertising, the Nazis made two notable gains during the first year of power. With regard to news services the reeducation of the German people required the establishment of a monopoly, through which all domestic and foreign news could be centrally controlled and filtered. Two major news agencies, supplying foreign and domestic news services to the German press, competed with one another in 1933— the semi-official Wolff Telegraph Bureau and the Hugenberg Telegraph Union. Wolff maintained forty-two branch offices in Germany and employed over 1,300 persons; the Telegraph Union was an energetic rival with 1,600 German newspapers as subscribers. We do not know what arguments, pressures and inducements were employed to move Hugenberg and his associates to surrender control of the Telegraph Union. Max Winkler conducted the negotiations on behalf of the propaganda ministry; and the merger of the Wolff Bureau and the Telegraph Union to form the

---

[30] The factual and statistical information on the Ullstein Verlag after 1934 is derived from the publication, *Deutscher Verlag— 1934-1941*, pp. 1-10, 14-16, 23-25, 29. Rich in details and statistics, this book lacks only one significant item—a statement of annual profits.

[31] Wilhelm Baur reported the statement to Gustav Willner; and Winkler quoted Amann to the same effect.

Deutsches Nachrichten Büro (DNB) was announced on December 5, 1933. The DNB was state owned, through the propaganda ministry, and not a part of the Eher trust. Goebbels and the ministry controlled it absolutely and kept its affairs entirely to themselves. Reminiscing after the war, Amann said: "Since the Eher Verlag was the largest customer and major source of income, I insisted on getting a seat on the board of DNB so I could learn what they were doing with the revenue I paid them. I told Goebbels jokingly one day that his DNB rates were too high and that I was considering establishing my own news service, since I was about the only customer. The next day an old Generaldirektor called on me and said that he understood I had complained of the DNB rates! Of course, Eher could not have started its own news and press service." [32]

While news and information control in the Nazi state were clearly within the competence of the propaganda ministry, advertising belonged in the publishing sphere. That the advertising business in 1933 was in a deeply depressed condition is an undeniable fact. It was apparent, too, that the business suffered from serious abuses and unfair competition. Whether state intervention was justified is debatable. Nonetheless on September 12, 1933, a "Law on Business Advertising" was issued, followed by the creation of an Advertising Council for the German Economy (Werberat der deutschen Wirtschaft), with authority to establish standards and norms, regulate tariffs, certify circulations, and in general to reorganize and police the advertising business. Two concerns dominated the national advertising field in Germany—the Annoncen-Expedition Rudolf Mosse, an old established firm with branches

[32] Interview notes, Max Amann, Aug. 22, 1945. The new DNB board included Wilhelm Weiss, Rienhardt, and the Munich publisher Hugo Bruckmann. (*Zeitungs-Verlag*, No. 48, Dec. 2, 1933.) Fritz Schmidt in his *Presse in Fesseln*, p. 229, is in error in attributing a major role in DNB to the Amann interests.

throughout Europe as well as in Germany, and the Hugenberg Allgemeine Anzeigen (Ala), which after the war had developed a powerful position in the field. Three adverse developments brought the Mosse company into the bankruptcy court—collapse of the advertising business, the competition of Hugenberg's Ala company, and the Nazi boycott of Jewish-owned enterprises. In 1933 the Mosse company was placed in the hands of receivers and the company was dropped from the VDZV's list of recognized advertising agencies.[33] This left the Ala company in a dominant position in the national field. A year later, however, it was acquired by the Eher Verlag from the Hugenberg interests. The public announcement made at the time had many of the qualities of fiction. Under the heading "Centralization of the Advertising Business," it was stated: "The serious abuses which exist in the advertising business make necessary, under the National Socialist state, sharp intervention in this field. It seems essential to create a central advertising agency under state and Party control. To this end the Ala Anzeigen AG, which has had years of experience and commands a tested organization, has been acquired with public and Party funds. In addition to the Ala firm, only agencies will be allowed in the advertising field which can guarantee observance of orderly business practices as defined and required by the Advertising Council for the German Economy. It should be stated that the Ala company is not to be regarded by the other authorized firms as a competing enterprise, since its revenue will not be used for private economic purposes but simply for tasks in the public interest. Every advertising agency will be obligated to cooperate with the Ala company. To supervise its affairs and to insure the proper use of its revenue, the president of the Advertising Council will serve as chairman of the board and his

[33] *Zeitungs-Verlag*, No. 30, July 29, 1933. A number of Mosse's regional branches continued as local agencies under new management.

deputy will be the president of the Reich Press Chamber [Amann]. These men and the other members of the board receive no compensation so that an objective position with regard to the whole advertising business is fully assured." [34]

In recruiting other public figures for the board, it was explained that Ala would have "political as well as economic tasks."

The statement is a transparent fraud and could not have deceived experienced persons in the newspaper and advertising fields. Hugenberg's agency was acquired by the Eher Verlag and it was used in the interest of the party press. The ownership, management, and methods employed in securing large accounts are more exactly clarified in a personal letter from Amann to Hess shortly after conclusion of the purchase. Amann began with a statement of regret that his efforts to arrange an appointment for a briefing on the various transactions concluded by the party publishing house during the preceding quarter had been of no avail. He asked that a definite date be set for this purpose, and then continued: "Among the new business acquisitions of the Zentral-Verlag is the Ala Anzeigen AG, acquired by me for the Party publishing house through the purchase of seventy per cent of the shares from the Scherl-Verlag. The remaining thirty per cent of the stock is held by the Werberat der Deutschen Wirtschaft, represented by the president, [Ernst] Reichard. The Ala Anzeigen AG was previously a losing enterprise for the Hugenberg concern. After a thorough examination of its business affairs, made at the request of the propaganda ministry, it has been merged with the N.A.Z. (Nationalsozialistischen Anzeigen-Zentrale), founded by me two years ago, with the result that out of a losing enterprise has been created a sound business undertaking which in the first quarter of its operations has shown a substantial increase in business volume. Among the large firms whose accounts are being solicited by party

[34] *Zeitungs-Verlag*, No. 31, Aug. 4, 1934.

member [Erwin] Finkenzeller, who was appointed by me as general manager of Ala, is the company Heinrich Franck and Sons. Through one of the sons of Herr Franck, Senior, a very large advertising contract is in prospect, subject to the condition that Herr Franck, Junior, wishes to inquire directly of you, my dear Herr Hess, about the Ala company. It will suffice, if such an inquiry is made of you, simply to confirm from your own knowledge the fact that the Ala agency is owned seventy per cent by the party publishing house and thirty percent by the Advertising Council for the German Economy." [35]

One does not have to be suspicious by nature to detect in this communication a strong odor of political blackmail. That the Ala agency should have increased its business and flourished mightily under conditions prevailing in the Third Reich is not surprising. There is no need to stress further the importance of the acquisition of the Ala agency for the N-S Gau press and the central publishing house. While Eher did not acquire a national monopoly of advertising the Ala Anzeigen was the unchallenged giant in the field. Political considerations, too, were not lacking in its acquisition. Hugenberg had used the agency as a club over newspaper publishers and the Nazi party leadership wanted to eliminate his influence completely. The purchase of the agency, with its quasi-monopolistic position, was especially advantageous to the economically insecure party press. Party papers now received national advertising in increasing volume.

[35] Amann to Hess, July 10, 1934; NA, Nürnberg Docs. PS-3753, pp. 49-50. Erwin Finkenzeller headed the advertising division of the Eher Verlag prior to appointment as manager of Ala. In 1945 Amann explained the purchase as follows: "It was all run down and losing money when we bought it. Hugenberg always had too many old *Generaldirektoren* in his enterprises. I threw them all out and appointed one director to run it on my principles—that is, 'If we lose money we close down, if we make money you share in the profits.'" (Interview notes, Aug. 22, 1945.)

After eighteen months of power the Nazi leadership in the area of the press had introduced notable innovations. A monopoly of news and opinion had been established through the ministry of propaganda and the formation of DNB; the most potent position in advertising had been gained in the purchase of the Ala company; and, in negotiating under extreme political pressure the purchase of the Ullstein house, a road had been opened leading to the liquidation of the middle class press in Germany.

# V. The Final Solution—
# The Amann Ordinances

## The Depression in the Publishing Industry

Reduction of the number of newspapers by merger or closure, with a view to restoring the industry to a healthy economic condition, was one of the stated objectives of the Amann ordinances. The many papers that were insufficiently supported by advertising and subscription sales depressed the entire industry and deprived the stronger papers of that margin of income which would have made them economically viable. Too many papers for the number of readers and advertisers—this was the conclusion reached by the Nazi leaders of the Reich Press Chamber and the publishers' association. Was this view correct?

By the standards of other western countries Germany had an excessive number of newspapers. She had more daily papers than the United States and more than the combined total for France, England, and Italy. Overcrowding was a fact, but the condition antedated the Nazi period. Between 1924 and 1929—a period of expansion and prosperity—many weekly and bi-weekly papers converted to daily circulation without adequate economic justification. The multiple party system during the Weimar period likewise resulted in the founding of many party papers which lived on subventions. When the political parties disappeared in 1933, these papers withered on the vine. An extreme but significant example of conditions prevailing in the smaller German cities is the case of Ingolstadt on the Danube in northern Bavaria. With barely 30,000 population the town had supported two papers since the end of the nineteenth century. Politically one was non-partisan, the other represented the dominant Bavarian People's party. In 1923 a

Generalanzeiger type of paper was established and a local edition of an SPD paper also circulated in the area. In 1927 a Nazi daily was established by a party enthusiast. Thus five daily newspapers competed for a limited amount of circulation and advertising. Then came the depression and all were in serious financial straits. The condition of the publishing business in Ingolstadt was duplicated in other provincial towns and cities.

In the Kreis towns and rural districts where the smallest papers existed, the situation was equally critical. Here social and technological forces were operating which in a matter of time would eliminate the local papers. Public demand and habits were changing. With the motorization of distribution, speed in communication, and the influence of urban habits, the small towns and rural areas were being served by papers from larger cities. Broadcasting of news by radio was also a factor producing change. Village and rural people were no longer satisfied with a small local paper containing news which they had already heard on the radio or read in the city newspaper now serving the region. The depression increased the difficulties of the small-town press. In time these papers would have failed and disappeared regardless of National Socialism. A trend toward concentration and rationalization was operating in the press before the Nazis devised and imposed their publishing policies.

However, as we shall observe later, the Amann ordinance for the elimination of unhealthy competitive conditions was not directed so much at the small-town papers as it was at the provincial city press. Here the excess of papers was greatest. Zwickau with a population of 83,000 had four daily papers; Kassel (pop. 175,000) had six; Würzburg (98,000) had four; Halle (194,000) had five; Darmstadt (89,000) had five; Brunswick (150,000) had four; Coburg (25,000) had three; Mannheim (255,000) had six; Stuttgart (400,000) had nine; Bayreuth (37,000) had two; Stettin (254,000) had five; Essen (650,000) had six. The situation in Essen was typical of many German industrial cities. A popular non-partisan Generalanzeiger, with the largest circulation, was flanked by two nationalist dailies, a Catholic Center organ, an SPD paper, a Communist journal, and a Nazi paper. When the Marxist publications were suppressed subscribers did not switch to the Nazi paper, but went over to the Generalanzeiger, or the Catholic paper, or took no newspaper at all. Into this situation the Nazi political press injected itself in 1933, claiming and seeking predominance by winning circulation and sales from the established middle class papers. To the fanatics and doctrinaires in the movement it appeared self-evident that since the party now monopolized the political life of the country it should also monopolize the press. This invasion of the field by approximately 100 Nazi dailies at a time when circulation and advertising were sharply declining made the competitive battle the more bitter. In 1933 the pressure tactics employed by party volunteers in the first wave of enthusiasm for the new regime brought spectacular increases in the circulation of the N-S papers, but sharp losses were registered in 1934 and the issue remained undecided. Only intervention by the party and state could give the party press the position of predominance demanded for it in the National Socialist state.

The ills that beset the industry were the subject of reports and discussions at the conference of the Landesverband directors in Berlin in April 1935. Rienhardt acknowledged that relations between the official party press and the independent publishers had worsened considerably in recent months. Dr. Schott (Baden-Pfalz) confirmed this, saying that many publishers had cooperated enthusiastically with the regime at first but had since been alienated by the relentless competition of the N-S press. Publishers of Generalanzeiger and confessionally oriented papers had originally cooperated, but they too had since drawn closer to those forces basically opposed to National Socialism. On the economic side, most of the directors gloomily reported further decline in circulation and advertising in the area of their Landesverband. They estimated losses of 60 to 80 per cent for advertising and 10 to 20 per cent for subscribers as compared to the figures for 1931. One director reported—and this seemed to be general—that in his district the Generalanzeiger press was doing best of all, but the confessional and the official party papers were in serious straits, the latter being heavily indebted for machinery and equipment. It was the middle-sized papers that were the Sorgenkinder. These were the journals hardest hit by N-S press competition and many of their publishers were formerly strong supporters or sympathizers with the party.

Continuing the dismal reports, the director of the Bavarian Landesverband stated that advertising had declined from 60 to 70 per cent in Bavaria and there were no signs of improvement. The director of the Landesverband Lower Rhine-Westphalia, a heavily industrialized area, reported that owing to unemployment only 40 per cent of the households were regular newspaper subscribers. In the large workers' apartment buildings one or two families subscribed to a paper and then circulated it to the other families in the building.[1] Reports of these field representatives produce the impression of a distressed and deeply divided industry, its future made uncertain by the political upheaval, and showing no signs of the economic revival beginning to appear in other sectors of the economy. Rolf Rienhardt, who had the soundest statistical and financial reports at hand, also took a gloomy view of the economic position of the industry. In a memorandum justifying the Amann ordinances he pointed out that in 1934 certified circulation had declined by one million subscribers and advertising volume had declined from an estimated 400 million RM in 1932 to approximately 190-195 million in 1934. The latter figure rep-

[1] Conference report, April 9, 1935; LV Rundschreiben, File 2.

resented a further decline of 25 per cent from the 1933 level. Referring to the bitter battle waged for circulation he commented: "To general economic conditions, which have produced a serious depression in the publishing trade, has now been added during the past two years this additional heavy mortgage of a competitive struggle for existence, which is waged with all available means and which in the long run can only be disastrous in its consequences." [2]

The loss of a million in circulation by the German press in 1934 cannot be attributed solely to economic conditions, bad as these were. An important contributing factor, not mentioned by Rienhardt, was the dullness and uniformity in the press which led many readers to cancel subscriptions and resist street sales. This aspect of the industry's difficulties was examined in a remarkably frank article in the publishers' trade journal, *Zeitungs-Verlag*.[3] In the correspondent's opinion, enforced uniformity of content and viewpoint, resulting in a solid monotone in the press, was the reason why many persons ceased to read the papers. One newspaper was just like another since complete articles were delivered by the state and party news apparatus with specific instructions to print. Party officials and agencies at all levels had appointed press respresentatives and these gentlemen expected their "new releases" to be printed in full in the local press. Every tiresome crank in the party now demanded that his views be aired. To be sure, Goebbels had condemned dullness and uniformity and had challenged the editors to be creative and original. But what editor, cautioned by his publisher, would run the risk of antagonizing a powerful local party official by consigning his releases and announcements to the wastebasket, where most of them properly belonged? While not stated so bluntly, this was the import of the author's remarks, and this was

[2] "Explanation of the Draft Ordinances," photostat copy from the files of the RVDZV, in the BDC.

[3] No. 15, April 15, 1934, "Die Flucht aus der Zeitung."

why he heard people say on every hand: "Oh, I don't read newspapers much any more."

## The Amann Ordinances of April 1935

The liquidation of the Marxist press in 1933 was accomplished by seizure and expropriation; the liquidation of the greater part of the middle class press was effected behind a screen of legalism provided by the Amann ordinances of April 1935. These decrees, three is number, were issued by Amann under the authority of Paragraph 25 of the Reich Chamber of Culture implementing decree. This decree invested a Chamber president with power to establish the requirements for participation in one of the cultural occupations, to fix the conditions for opening, closing, and conducting enterprises in the field, and to issue general regulations for the conduct of business by those participating. A principal enforcement power in the hands of the Chamber president was Paragraph 10 which invested him with authority to admit and exclude persons from the trade or occupation.

The Reich Chamber of Culture law and its implementing decrees applied principally to the professional fields of journalism, radio, theater, film, literature, and the creative arts. But Amann and Rienhardt used these powers under Paragraph 25 to confiscate and reconstruct an entire industry, one that was interwoven with every important segment of economic life. Issuance of a general Reich law to achieve the party's goals with regard to the press, similar to the law of 1933 confiscating Marxist property, was considered and rejected as impracticable. Such a law would have required the concurrence in the cabinet of the ministries of justice, economics, interior, and propaganda. Schacht's strenuous objections could be anticipated, Gürtner might be stirred to opposition by experts in the ministry of justice, and there was no predicting what modifications and amendments to a draft law might be forthcoming from the ministries of interior and propaganda. Moreover such a law would be so transparently confiscatory as to make a mockery of the Nazi claim that they were defenders of private property. This avenue was plainly closed. But under the ordinances devised by Rienhardt, the goal was achieved by operating within the area of Amann's jurisdiction and powers as president of the Reich Press Chamber.

Before exploring the genesis of the Amann ordinances, they should be briefly summarized. Dated and effective April 24, 1935, they had the outward appearance of a radical code for the regulation of a quasi-public industry, incorporating some provisions that were obviously National Socialist, some that had been a matter of public debate in pre-Nazi days, and some that appeared responsive to the current economic depression in the publishing business. The first ordinance was brief and in the nature of a poor joke. It provided for the withdrawal of publishing rights from any publisher whose papers by sensationalism, or offenses against public taste or morals, cast reflection on the publishing business and the honor of the press. That the ordinance was never enforced against the worst offender—Julius Streicher and *Der Stürmer*—clearly reveals its sham ethical character. The second ordinance, "On the Closing of Newspaper Enterprises to Eliminate Unhealthy Competitive Conditions," was also brief but more serious, as it asserted Amann's power to close publishing enterprises where the number of competing newspapers created unsound economic conditions for publishing. The ordinance specified that the RVDZ would indicate the places where overcrowding existed, and the Cura auditing and management staff would examine the financial and business position of each enterprise and render a report as a basis for action by the president of the Chamber. Mergers might be authorized by

Amann as an alternative to closing down one or more newspapers.[4]

More complex and detailed, with multiple objectives, avowed and concealed, was the third ordinance, "For Insuring the Independence of the Newspaper Publishing Industry." Article I of this ordinance required full disclosure to the Reichsverband of the capital and ownership relations of all publishing firms, whether personal or corporate, and the furnishing by the owners of proof of German or German-related ancestry since the year 1800. The same proof of ancestry was required for wives, and board members of corporate enterprises. Owners or responsible publishers were required, further, to state if subventions were regularly received from individuals or organizations, and the amount of such subsidies. Indirect subsidization through sale of papers in wholesale lots to other than newspaper distributors also had to be reported. In the future receipt of such support or indirect subsidy would require approval by the RPK.

While Article I was designed to reveal the ownership of all publishing firms in private hands, Article II struck a heavy blow at private enterprise in the press. Specifically excluded from present or future participation in the trade were legally registered societies, organizations, public or private foundations, or trustee representatives. But this was not all, for the ordinance went on to prohibit the corporate form of business enterprise—the AG and GmbH forms—in newspaper publishing. Likewise prohibited was multiple ownership or newspaper chains. In other words: one newspaper, one responsible owner-publisher, and not a joint stock company, was henceforth the law. Finally, the indus-

---

[4] This ordinance had been foreshadowed in an important article prepared by Rienhardt but published under Amann's name on the second anniversary of Hitler's appointment as Chancellor. Entitled "The Press in the Second Year of the National Socialist State," it highlighted overcrowding in the newspaper business and the necessity for drastic action. *Zeitungs-Verlag*, No. 6, Feb. 9, 1935.

trial and banking interests actively participating in newspaper publishing were practically pushed out of the field. The ordinance specified that persons or corporations whose major economic interests were outside the publishing industry, but who published newspapers or held stock in such enterprises, would require the approval of the president of the RPK for continued participation. This provision was designed to exclude the sinister influence of anonymous industrial capital. "Money-bags shouldn't be allowed to make public opinion," was Amann's breezy interpretation of Rienhardt's devious legal phraseology. A calculated knock-out blow was struck at the former Catholic Center papers in Article IV, which prohibited the continued publication of newspapers which through their content and general tone were designed to appeal to "confessional, vocational, or special interest groups." In specifying compliance dates, the ordinance allowed from six months to one year for the liquidation of multiple ownership, joint stock enterprises, and trustee relationships; but only three months were allowed the confessional press for compliance, or liquidation. Responsibility for the application of the ordinances, from which the Nazi party and its authorized representatives were exempt, was conferred upon the RVDZV, that is to say, primarily upon Rolf Rienhardt, the author of the ordinances.[5]

The application of the ordinances during the next eighteen months produced a wave of closures, consolidations, and distress sales of large and small publishing houses. Between 500 and 600 newspapers, among them some of the choicest properties in Germany, disappeared, merged, or were purchased by the Eher Verlag or one of its subsidiaries.

[5] The official text of the ordinances is in *Völkischer Beobachter*, April 25, 1935; also *Zeitungs-Verlag*, No. 17, April 27; *Handbuch der deutschen Tagespresse—1937*, pp. 394-400; Schmidt, *Presse in Fesseln*, apps. 5, 6, 7; and a full summary in *Max Amann: Ein Leben*, pp. 67-69.

## Rienhardt's Commentaries

It is reasonable to ask why the Nazis waited over two years before taking decisive action against the independent publishers. Perhaps in the bloom of party optimism, following January 1933, the leaders thought all the newspaper proprietors would become convinced National Socialists. However, in 1935, Rienhardt commented that it might have been better if more papers had been suppressed during the 1933 revolution instead of waiting for two years. Many publishers, basically hostile to National Socialism, had drawn the wrong conclusions from the delay.[6] The course of events also suggests that Amann and Rienhardt required time to explore the terrain of the German publishing industry and to define the problems in terms of National Socialist policy. Moreover, until the regime had consolidated its power, it could not take radical action against the well-established provincial press and the Generalanzeiger papers. Party objectives had to be achieved without creating a major crisis or a public scandal; that is, achieved with apparent legality on grounds that could be defended. This was Rienhardt's contribution; he devised the means to do it quietly. It was the method of the legal "freeze out" and the "business deal."

Throughout 1934 Rienhardt devoted much of his time, thought, and energy to the exploration of this basic party problem. He used the office and field staffs of the RVDZV to collect information and lay the groundwork for action; only Amann was taken into his confidence. He worked alone without help of committees or staff conferences, he did his own legal drafting, and wrote the supporting memoranda. His masterpiece was the Amann ordinances.

Much of the information required for framing the ordi-

[6] Conference report LV directors, Nov. 13, 1935; LV Rundschreiben, File 1, BDC.

nances was collected in connection with the Paragraph 10 program. The three principal targets of the ordinances were indicated by a request sent to all Landesverband directors in December 1934. They were directed to forward to Berlin twelve consecutive copies of each paper published in their jurisdiction which seemed to correspond to one or more of the following types: 1) papers that had confessional characteristics or had such characteristics before the N-S revolution; 2) papers that were sensational in their content and makeup; and 3) papers that were patently of the Generalanzeiger type.[7] In Berlin the papers were reviewed by members of Rienhardt's staff working with analysis directives which for detail and guile would have been a credit to Matthew Hopkins, the self-styled "Witch-finder General" of seventeenth century England.

At the Landesverband conference in Berlin, early in April 1935, Rienhardt commented on some of the problems encountered in the work of analysis. It had been difficult, for example, to establish criteria for classifying Generalanzeiger papers. From the ensuing discussion one gets the impression that a Generalanzeiger was a paper in a strong capital position, with large circulation and advertising revenue, which had successfully resisted attempts of the party press to take away its readers and advertisers! A special problem was presented by the large number of small local papers, Rienhardt told the Landesverband directors. Today in Germany, he said, there were approximately 13.4 million subscribers to papers of less than 3,000 circulation. Among the publishers in this class were many "old party members" whose economic existence would be destroyed if their papers were suspended, and the party and the state would be blamed. "For the time being," he concluded, "but not for eternity, this problem can be postponed." The other problems of creating an "organic" publishing industry

[7] LV Rundschreiben, No. 67, December 1934, File 1, BDC.

would be solved by the application of the forthcoming ordinances, he confidently asserted.[8]

Two memoranda prepared by Rienhardt and his staff enable us to penetrate the legal formulations of the ordinances and determine their real objective—the establishment of party ownership and control of the greater part of the press. The first of these papers was prepared for the party leadership, the council of the RPK, and the higher officials of the propaganda ministry. The memorandum takes a broad view of the publishing trade in relation to party interests and objectives, the economic conditions in the newspaper business, and the position of the party press in relation to its privately owned competitors. Free of legalisms and euphemisms, it set forth the considerations which underpinned the specific terms and defined the objectives sought. Entitled "Brief Explanation," the document runs fourteen typewritten pages.[9] Its principal divisions and emphases were: 1) National Socialist requirements in the newspaper press and publishing trade; 2) the inability of the Gau press to compete successfully with the provincial Generalanzeiger papers; 3) the necessity for ending the competitive struggle which threatened to ruin the industry; 4) the liquidation of the confessionally oriented press; and 5) the specific terms of the ordinances in relation to their anticipated effects.

Since it is basic to the "final solution" of the publishing issue in Nazi Germany, the first paragraph on ideology should be quoted: "The National Socialist Weltanschauung sees in the press a means of educating the people for National Socialism. In consequence, the press is an instrument

[8] Conference report, April 9, 1935; LV Rundschreiben, File 2.
[9] The full title was: "Brief Explanation of the Drafts of the Ordinance for Insuring the Independence of the Newspaper Publishing Industry, and the Ordinance on Closing Publishing Firms for the Elimination of Unhealthy Competitive Conditions." (Photostat copy from the BDC.)

of the National Socialist state. The National Socialist Welt-anschauung demands total acceptance and does not tolerate the propagation of other basic political ideas. On this basis a state whose foundation is the National Socialist movement recognizes only a National Socialist press. To achieve and give legal expression to these principles the National Socialist state formulated and published the Editor's law and the Reich Chamber of Culture Law. Both laws enroll, on the basis of character and attitudes, all German citizens crea-tively employed in the press. Anyone who on professional or personal grounds is unsuitable for the fulfilment of the high demands of the press, loses all opportunity for activity in these callings by exclusion from the journalist's register or, if a publisher, by expulsion from the Reich Press Cham-ber."

In Part 2 it was explained how the newspaper press be-came divided into a party and a non-party press and how these two had been at war for two years to the detriment of the whole industry. "The National Socialist revolution renounced the use of political force to suppress the entire non-National Socialist press, limiting its action to the sup-pression of the Marxist-Communist press. In consequence thereof, after seizure of power, fewer than 100 National Socialist papers confronted about 3,000 papers, which be-fore January 30, 1933 took it to be their duty to represent other viewpoints, parties, and groups opposed to National Socialism, and to hinder the movement and prevent its coming to power." This had never been forgotten by the party organization and the rank and file members in the provinces. "As a result they saw, and still see, it as their duty to combat this press with all means at their disposal." This had been going on for two years and it had not been possible to end the strife. "The whole German press suffers economically to an extraordinary degree from this condi-tion. . . . While previously, twice yearly in spring and au-tumn, subscription salesmen were employed, today it is necessary to employ them throughout the year, and in numbers never before used. It appears to be their business to enroll for their paper subscribers to another paper. . . . [This] makes the canvasser the only gainer at the expense of the shrinking capital resources of the publishing industry."

The private publishers, the memorandum continued, also had a moral and legal right to demand clarification of their status, a final determination of the structure of the press, and a limitation of competition in proportion to the means and performance of the individual paper. On the other hand, the party rank and file would continue to demand that those local publishers whom they deemed unsuitable and unreliable be excluded from the publishing field. "The repeated pronouncements by the highest authorities of party and state, in agreement with the N-S program, that 'There is only a National Socialist Press', stand in sharp contrast to the facts, namely, that today a large number of publishing firms still exist of which no one could say they were National Socialist, for the men who own and direct them are everything but National Socialists." These publishers must be excluded from the field if a pacification and organic reconstruction of the publishing industry was to be achieved. Those publishers with a good conscience, who remained in the industry after meeting the highest requirements as to reliability, would no longer be subjected to party animosity and the strife and agitation would cease.

Part 3 of the memorandum designated the areas of competition, identified the type of publisher to be eliminated, and showed how the ordinance to eliminate unhealthy competition would contribute to the solution of the industry's problems. Analyzing the structure of the German press, the staff memorandum pointed out that of approximately 2,800 papers, 2,432 had average circulations of 15,-000 copies or less. These small papers were owned by local persons rooted in their communities who understood how

to establish connection with the N-S movement and therefore presented no serious political problem. "The publisher
personalities, whose political reliability and qualifications
for activity in the publishing industry . . . must be denied,
and against whom the struggle of the party is directed, are
mainly the proprietors of those newspapers possessing the
largest circulations." Newspapers with a daily circulation
of over 15,000 copies constituted only 7.6 per cent of the
German press (191 papers), but their share of the total
national circulation amounted to 60.3 per cent, while the
official party papers had only a scant 25 per cent of total
circulation. In this group of papers, whose power had been
acquired under the former political system, were found the
principal competitors of the Gau press. The Generalanzeiger class, whose principal concern had been "to continue
publishing Jewish advertising," produced the papers with
the largest sales and circulation. "The urgent need is to
draw from an appreciation of these conditions the only
possible conclusion, that the publishers of the Generalanzeiger press must give up the ownership of these properties.
These are the gentlemen least affected by previous developments, who operate on the assumption that the Reich
Chamber of Culture Law affords no basis for putting an
end to their position of predominance. To do just that is
the aim of the ordinance for the closing of newspaper firms
for the elimination of unhealthy competitive conditions."

The ordinance for insuring the independence of the German press was explained in Part 4, which emphasized the
elimination of Jewish and all confessional interests, the ban-
ning of newspaper chains and trusts, the prohibition of
anonymous capitalistic enterprises (AG and GmbH forms),
the exclusion of non-publishing interests from the newspaper industry, and the elimination of trustee relationships. Referring to the staff examination of those papers previously
connected with the Center and Bavarian People's party, the
memorandum described the results as "shocking." "This

group of papers withdraws itself more and more from the task of binding its circle of readers to the National Socialist state and, because of its present ownership, serves exclusively a church policy which is directed against the N-S state." Previous political and confessional connections also facilitated the ownership position of a number of the large publishing firms in the provinces. "The power of these publishing firms . . . assures them in competition with the official party press a position of superiority, and consigns the latter to a role of absolute subordination if the party press is solely dependent upon its own competitive strength." The dissolution of these connections and ownership relations would make it possible to remedy the unequal competitive situation.

In Part 5 the memorandum dealt with the anticipated consequences of the application of the ordinances. The former confessional daily press, it was stated, would be brought into the service of the National Socialist state by the exclusion of "irresponsible capitalistic ownership and special interests opposed to National Socialism." It should not be difficult to find purchasers for these papers among party members or in other reliable circles. Unsuitable editors could be removed and those elements of the population which were kept stirred up over confessional issues would be freed from this agitation.

For the large Generalanzeiger papers the memorandum specified a different solution. "In cleaning up overcrowded conditions it will have to be accomplished so that the party (as in the case of Ullstein) acquires the publishing enterprise and, operating it as a non-party concern, exercises influence in this way over the great masses of people." Once this change in ownership was made, relations between the Generalanzeiger press and the official party press would be placed on a different footing and the continued existence of the two groups would be assured. Moreover, the elimination of this unhealthy condition would give the remaining privately owned papers, which were so adversely affected by costly competition, a chance to survive. Only in this way could the Führer's demand for the preservation of diversity in the press be fulfilled. "It would be basically false to conclude that the application of these ordinances will produce eventually a situation in which there will be only official party newspapers and papers owned or controlled by the party. . . . On the contrary, it is the determination of the President of the Reich Press Chamber to create through these ordinances the circumstances necessary for continued existence of a worthy political press in private hands."

In conclusion, the memorandum returned to the central feature of the problem—the political and economic conflict between the party press and the non-party press and the methods employed in waging the struggle. As a result of this conflict, "a deep resignation pervades the German newspaper publishing industry. The publishers are no longer in a position to make capital investments, and thereby support the Führer's work-creating policy, since they are completely uncertain of their future and their right of existence." The ordinances offered the only solution. The private publishers who met the tests would be assured of their right to exist and find relief from the competitive pressure; and the party press could plan for the future, discharge its special tasks of publicity, and achieve economic health. If the ordinances were not adopted, "the future of the entire German press would be brought seriously into question, and consequences could develop within the next few months for which it would be hard to accept responsibility."

A second memorandum, prepared by Rienhardt, accompanied the first draft of the decrees submitted to Amann.[10]

---

[10] "Erläuterungen des Entwurfs für Herrn Präsidenten A." This document, also fourteen pages, has an interesting history. Through an unidentified intermediary, a copy came into the hands of Rüdiger Graf von der Goltz, a prominent lawyer in Stettin, son of General von der Goltz. He had served as defense counsel in a

It also served as a briefing paper in Amann's discussion of the ordinances with Hitler. Lacking the ideological generalizations and the deep concern for the publishing trade, which found expression in the staff memorandum, it stated baldly what the decrees would accomplish and specified by name the publishers and publishing groups whose positions in the field would be weakened or eliminated. To make the ordinances intelligible to Amann's practical mind they had to be explained in terms of anticipated concrete results. Special emphasis, therefore, was given to the advantages that would accrue to the party papers by eliminating competitors in those centers where the Gau press had not made satisfactory progress. There was little ideology in the "Elucidations" but a great deal of the robber baron.

In brief numbered statements the memorandum specified the purpose of each article and paragraph of the ordinance on the independence of the press—elimination of Jews, and all confessional, class, or special economic interests, and the prohibition of corporate enterprises, trustees, and organized interest groups. The major targets of the ordinance were sharply defined as the Catholic press, the newspaper chains and trusts, and the Generalanzeiger press. The requirement of ownership disclosure and the prior approval of the RPK for all transfers of properties or stockholdings, it was pointed out, would prevent the further development of undesirable interest groups in the industry.

---

number of political cases involving German nationalists in crimes of violence and was retained by Huck and Girardet, owners of Generalanzeiger chains, to defend their interests as affected by the Amann decrees. Von der Goltz submitted a brief to Minister Gürtner, seeking intervention of the ministry of justice, and enclosed a copy of the "Elucidations" and other documents as appendices. Copies of the correspondence and documents are a part of Amann's Spruchkammer file. In a publisher's restitution case after the war, Rienhardt acknowledged that he had prepared "Erläuterungen" for Amann but avoided specific admission of authorship.

This would effectively block the Catholic publishers and financiers—Hackelsberger, Fassbänder, and Pötz—who were endeavoring to extend their control over former Center party papers. The prohibition of the corporate forms of business organization would bring many Catholic publishers under heavy pressure, and numerous company reorganizations would be required. In the German publishing field there were 376 companies with the GmbH form and 48 with the AG form. The confessional press was represented by 73 GmbH's and 21 AG's, the latter form being preferred by the Catholic press so that shares could be widely distributed among supporters and subscribers. These papers would have to reorganize and reform, or suspend.

Examination of the Catholic papers had revealed that in addition to the joint stock companies were many enterprises that were family owned or simple partnerships. These would not be affected by the business reorganization requirements although they came under the ban of papers having a "confessional character." The drafters of the ordinance had been unable to devise a valid legal definition of "confessional character." However, these cases could be handled by publication of an article in *Zeitungs-Verlag*— a draft of which was appended—setting forth what these publishers must do to re-orient and reform their papers. Failure to meet the requirements set forth in the article could be treated as evidence of unreliability and lack of qualifications, and handled under Paragraph 10.

Another predictable effect of the ordinances, as set forth in Rienhardt's memorandum, was the breaking up of the newspaper chains. Since all these combinations used the corporate business form, they would be required to reorganize and the principal owner would have to assume direct responsibility for one of his enterprises. These requirements, Rienhardt asserted, would break up the concentrations of publishing power represented by the newspaper concerns of Huck, Girardet, Leonhardt, and Kausche, as well as the Catholic cooperative groups in Württemberg and Westphalia. More specifically, the writer predicted, "The destruction of the trusts and the requirement of prior approval for sales of stock and transfer of ownership, as well as the prohibition of anonymous capital forms, will bring the publishers of these business papers into a situation of great embarrassment and incline them in given situations to capitulate to the Party. The Huck concern will be brought into a more serious position than the Girardet group. Girardet will be able to separate into its four main elements and retain possession of the important papers. Nevertheless, Paragraphs 1 and 2 afford the means of exerting strong pressure upon these combinations, whose papers stand prominently in the way of the advancement of the *Hamburger Tageblatt*, the *National-Zeitung* (Essen), and the *Volksparole* (Düsseldorf)."

Not directly affected by the provisions of the ordinance to insure the independence of the press were the publishers of Generalanzeiger papers who were independent of the combines—for example those in Frankfurt, Lübeck, Rostock, Magdeburg, Leipzig, and Stuttgart. In these and other cities of the Reich the business press blocked the advancement of the party papers. All conceivable solutions to this problem had been explored, according to Rienhardt. If these publishers were declared "unsuitable" and excluded from the RPK under Paragraph 10, their papers might come into the hands of other persons less vulnerable than they. An amendment to the Reich Chamber of Culture law had been considered and rejected because it would require the concurrence of the minister of economics (Schacht). This concurrence would be difficult to secure as, more and more, those publishers affected by developments in the press regarded Schacht as their protector. In order to reach these proprietors and achieve the desired goal, a separate ordinance "On the Closing of Newspaper Enterprises to Eliminate Unhealthy Economic Conditions" had been prepared.[11] This ordinance, Rienhardt stated, would give the RPK a legal position with regard to those publishers who were not affected by the ordinance on the independence of the press. Since the ordinance on over-crowding in the publishing field was based on sensible economic principles, the memorandum concluded, it could be assumed that opposition by affected publishing companies would have slight prospects of success.

This loosely drafted decree conceived almost as an afterthought, placed every newspaper proprietor in Germany at the mercy of the party demagogues and the president of the Reich Press Chamber.

## Appeal to the Ministry of Justice

Although the publishing industry anticipated drastic action, foreshadowed by Amann's admonitory article in *Zeitungs-Verlag*, "The German Press in the Second Year of the N-S State," the newspaper proprietors were stunned by the scope and harshness of the ordinances. In his commentary on the draft decrees, Rienhardt predicted that the most determined attempts at evasion must be expected from the publishers of confessionally oriented papers. But the first reaction came not from Catholic publishers but from the owners of the Generalanzeiger chains, Huck and Girardet. Identifying his clients as owners of Generalanzeiger papers, the lawyer Von der Goltz submitted a forceful

[11] The briefest of the ordinances, the main paragraph read: "If in a place several newspaper publishing companies exist, whose capacity for sales and circulation exceed the local demand to the point of violating sound publishing principles, individual papers can be closed in order to bring about healthier economic conditions. To determine the facts as a basis for decision, these publishing companies will be subjected to an examination of their business affairs, and they are hereby required to cooperate with the agency designated to make the examination." The Cura Auditing company, part of the Eher concern, was designated by Amann as the examining authority.

brief to the minister of justice, Gürtner, challenging the legal and ethical bases of the ordinances and urging the minister to protect the property rights of the newspaper owners. In his argument Von der Goltz did not challenge the legality of the ordinances under the constitution of the Reich Chamber of Culture, but took vigorous exception to the forced disclosure of business secrets, the prohibition of multiple ownership of newspapers, and the authority given to the president of the RPK to close newspapers on the grounds of unhealthy competition. The last provision, he declared, could be invoked to close non-party papers that were in competition with the N-S party press. "If . . . only a National Socialist press is to be tolerated in Germany and, with a few exceptions, the remaining newspapers are to be suppressed, then this should be done by means of a Reich law and not by these roundabout measures, which must of necessity create doubts and unrest, to say nothing of their more serious consequences." He then described the economic difficulties and repercussions that must result from enforcement of the ordinances, and their effects in other sectors of the economy. The last part of his brief concerned Rienhardt's "Elucidations," of which he enclosed a copy. From this document he quoted the passages which stated that one of the main purposes of the ordinances was to smash the Generalanzeiger chains and convert the papers to party ownership. The Amann decrees, he concluded, did not relate to the broad interests of the public and the industry but were in fact directed against named persons and were designed to despoil them of their property and their legal rights.[12]

Two weeks later Von der Goltz addressed a second letter to Gürtner, enclosing a copy of the questionnaire which had been sent to all publishers by the Cura staff, requiring disclosure of the minutest details of their business affairs.

---

[12] Rüdiger Graf von der Goltz to Dr. Franz Gürtner, Berlin, May 15, 1935; Amann, Spruchkammer file.

Again he emphasized the basically unjust nature of this procedure, pointing out that the Cura staff was a known Eher Verlag apparatus and that the most intimate business details and secrets were now being revealed to a competing publishing concern. He dwelt further on the unrest that publication of the decrees and the Cura procedure had produced among newspaper owners and their employees. Alarm had also spread to the newsprint industry and to producers of printing equipment and machinery. Bank loans had been called in some instances. The association of newsprint producers had appealed to Dr. Schacht, and Von der Goltz enclosed a statement from the executive secretary of the organization. All this, he said, confirmed the fears that he had expressed in his previous letter. Prompt action was necessary and he appealed again for the minister's intervention. "Certainly the newspaper publishers may have to give way under this pressure if no one comes to their aid; but such a result will not confirm the justice of the ordinances but exactly the opposite." [13]

In a state guaranteeing individual rights and due process, the courts would have been available for the defense of the publishers' interests, but in Hitler's Reich this door was closed. Paragraphs 25 and 26 of the ordinance implementing the Reich Chamber of Culture law made it impossible for an injured person to initiate a civil suit for compensation or damages. Intervention by the ministry of justice was a still-born hope; Gürtner, as usual, remained passive and events took their predetermined course.

The questionnaire, to which Von der Goltz took strong

[13] Von der Goltz to Gürtner, May 28, 1935. We do not have Gürtner's reply. In 1958 a search was made of the ministry records in Bonn to determine whether the ministry took a stand, but with negative results. Rienhardt has stated that an advisory opinion was obtained from the ministry upholding the legality of the ordinances under the powers granted the Chamber presidents by the Reich Chamber of Culture Law.

objection, was a model of foresight and thoroughness. Dispatched with a covering letter from Julius Mundhenke, the director of Cura, it went to all publishers affected by the ordinances. The recipient was informed that Cura had been authorized by the president of the RPK to investigate the financial and business position of all publishing companies. The enclosed forms were to be completed, "umfassend und lückenlos," and returned by June 7, under penalty specified for non-compliance by the ordinances of April 24. The questionnaire contained forty-five parts beginning with the names of papers issued and the circulation of each for the years 1933, 1934, and the first three months of 1935. The number of editions, the average number of pages, and full details of printing costs were also specified. The publisher was required to state the cost of subscription advertising for 1934 and the first quarter of 1935, also whether any subventions were received and the source thereof, whether he had any club or wholesale subscriptions and to whom delivered, and whether he received any stereotyped service or news service and at what cost. The required financial statement covered current debts, interest rates, mortgages, and by whom held; also valuation of plant and publishing rights, the names of all owners and shareholders and the value of their holdings; finally, wages and salaries of all employees, and the advertising and circulation revenue for the first six months of 1935. A full profit and loss statement for 1934 was also required. When this inquest was completed the publisher stood stark naked before the auditors and management specialists of Mundhenke's staff.

In applying the ordinance for the closing of enterprises because of unhealthy competitive conditions, the Landesverband directors played an important supporting role. They were instructed to locate in their districts the areas where overcrowding existed and to prepare recommendations on closings and possible mergers. After conferences with the publishers concerned, they were instructed to report their findings and recommendations to Mundhenke at the Cura office.[14] After all information was collected a final report on the enterprise was made to the office of the RVDZV where the findings were measured against the requirements of the ordinances. Compliance notices were then dispatched, conferences were held in important cases with owners or their representatives, and over a period of eighteen months the fate of each publishing house was decided.

In a police state no major action in an important sector of public life is taken without concurrent action by the control authorities. It is not surprising therefore that the reorganization of the press took place under the vigilant eyes of the secret police. In Bavaria—and we may assume similar action in other states—all district and city police offices were alerted by Gestapo headquarters in Munich to establish surveillance of publishers and publishing firms affected by the Amann ordinances. "It is to be anticipated," the order stated, "that publishers and publishing establishments will reorganize their business in such a way as to appear outwardly in compliance with the ordinances but which will in reality afford an opportunity to maintain the former conditions in a concealed manner." The agencies were instructed to be especially watchful of those persons and firms known to be unsympathetic toward the regime and to take appropriate measures—control of post, telephone, and telegraph services—to detect attempts at evasion of the ordinances. All suspicious occurrences were to be reported promptly to the central office in Munich.[15]

[14] A reporting conference with Mundhenke was scheduled for each director between May 16 and 31. LV Rundschreiben, No. 16, May 9, 1935; File 1, BDC.

[15] Bavarian political police order, July 1, 1935. Attention was directed to the official text of the ordinances in V-B, April 25, 1935. This order is found in a miscellaneous and unnumbered file in the BDC, which appears to have come from the Bezirksamt in Neu-Ulm.

The text of the Amann decrees and the explanatory memoranda, which have been summarized at some length, clearly reveal the objectives of the planners. All the statements after the war by Amann, Rienhardt, Richter, and Winkler, as to the justification and purpose of the measures can only be regarded as so much dust in the air. That only a National Socialist press could be allowed to exist was doubtless a logical expression of the principle of totalitarianism, but neither Hitler nor his lieutenants were prepared openly to suppress the non-party publishing enterprises. They chose instead the indirect way of sham reforms and spurious legality. To free the road for the advance of the party press, and to achieve the party demand—"there is only a German National Socialist Press"—required the elimination of numerous privately owned newspapers or their transfer to party ownership. These were the unqualified objectives of the Amann ordinances which threw over the private publishers a legal net with a mesh so fine that their chances of escape were slight indeed.

# VI. The Political and Economic Cleansing of the Press

## The Purge of the Confessional Press

Concurrently with the application of the Amann ordinances, the screening of the Reichsverband membership under Paragraph 10 was pushed forward. Indeed, the two actions merged in 1935-1936 and became intermeshed mechanisms for the achievement of party domination in the press. By using one or the other, the Nazi overlords could eliminate any publisher or major stockholder in a publishing enterprise, who, in their judgment, blocked party objectives. Oftentimes it was only necessary for the Reichsverband officials to remind a publisher that his Paragraph 10 clearance was pending to make him willing to hand over fifty-one per cent of the shares of his newspaper enterprise to one of the party holding companies.

The Amann ordinances, with the Paragraph 10 procedure as a reserve weapon, had three main targets—the Catholic press, the Generalanzeiger papers, and the independent political press in the provinces. The shortest compliance period under the ordinances was specified for the confessional press, and it was to this section of the publishing field that the officials of the RPK and the Reichsverband gave first priority during the summer and autumn of 1935.

At a special meeting of the leaders and directors of the regional associations held in Berlin on April 29, one of the principal addresses was made by Ildephons Richter, executive director of the RPK. The purport of his remarks was the serious spirit of the ordinances and how they must be interpreted and applied. Referring to the critical reception of the ordinances by the foreign press, he remarked that this was anticipated but it would have no effect. He was aware that in the past contracts had been made to place a publishing enterprise in the hands of trustees for five years, with the expectation that all would blow over within that period. But his listeners must know and carry the conviction to their Landesverband members that the reforms required by the ordinances would be effected. They would re-shape the industry, proceeding reasonably but firmly. The extended compliance periods were a measure of this reasonableness, but it must be understood that the ordinances would be applied so that one day they could go before the Führer and say: "Now the German press is actually the instrument that you and your advisers require, an instrument upon which you can play with complete harmony." The Landesverband officials were instructed to discourage attempts to play Dietrich off against Amann or to use influence with the president of the RPK.[1]

Of immediate concern to the regional directors was the Catholic press. A confessionally oriented paper might be vulnerable on one or more of several counts under the ordinance for the independence of the press—if it were organized as a joint stock company, if it received any kind of subvention from a confessional organization, or if it belonged to a newspaper chain or combination. But what affected all confessional papers immediately was Article IV of the ordinance. This article stated: "Newspapers are prohibited which through the selection and shaping of their content are oriented toward a designated or definable circle of persons representing confessional, vocational, or other special interests." We may dismiss "vocational" and "other special interests," for the provision was aimed at the Catholic press. This provision had the shortest compliance time—three months. Within ninety days these papers must cleanse themselves of all signs of a special

---

[1] Conference protocol, April 29, 1935; LV Rundschreiben, File 1, BDC.

interest press and develop a positive and cooperative attitude toward the ideology and practices of the National Socialist state.

Rienhardt in his "Elucidations" had stressed the difficulty of defining "confessional character" in an ordinance, and had proposed the publication under Amann's name of an article which would establish guide lines and lay down principles to which this section of the press would have to conform.[2] Amann's article was followed shortly by one prepared by J. Wilkens, staff member of the RVDZV, who had presumably participated in the December analysis of the confessional press. Wilkens specified in detail what they had found to be objectionable from the party standpoint and what the publishers and editors would have to do to place themselves in a state of grace with the regime.[3] Catholic publishers were invited by the executive director of the RPK to submit copies of their revised make-up and editorial directives. But judging from a second appeal by Richter, the response must have been meager.

Special meetings for Catholic publishers were scheduled in the Landesverband districts where the confessional press was strongly represented. Richter, who was more optimistic than Rienhardt about converting the Catholic publishers, represented the RPK at a number of these meetings. In speaking to the publishers he endeavored to clarify the ordinances, reassure them as to their future if they conformed, and win them to positive cooperation with the regime. Since his remarks reflected official policy and demands, we may summarize and quote at some length from his address at Münster on June 18.

[2] The article, "Es gibt nur eine deutsche Presse," was published simultaneously with the ordinances. *Zeitungs-Verlag*, No. 17, April 27, 1935.

[3] "Was heisst konfessionelle Gestaltung des Inhalts?—Winke für die Aufstellung von Richtlinien." *Zeitungs-Verlag*, No. 20, May 18, 1935.

He began by saying that his hearers should not draw
wrong conclusions from his presence at the meeting. The
ordinances and the government's intentions did not center
alone on the issue of the Catholic daily press, or to put it
more bluntly, "the liquidation of the Catholic daily press."
The objective of the ordinances was to give the final form
to the press which was required by the National Socialist
state. "Based on the will of the Führer it can only be an
instrument in his hand through which he can educate and
lead every fellow-German as a member of the national
community. . . . The positive task of every single newspaper can only be that of bringing the fund of ideas of
National Socialism to the reader, to clarify for him the
National Socialist Weltanschauung, and all to the single
end of educating him to National Socialism." Richter then
specified some of the non-cooperative attitudes of Catholic
publishers, which would have to be abandoned. First, there
was the publisher who said: "I recognize the facts, but I
am bound by my faith and must take a position of reserve
toward actual events and not contribute to their further
development." This position, Richter declared, was untenable. Second, there was the publisher who said: "My paper
has so-and-so many thousand readers who are confessionally oriented. I bring them what the government has to
say, but I can only do this by emphasizing the difference
between my paper and the official party newspaper. If I
were more positive in supporting National Socialism, my
readers would desert me and probably subscribe to no
newspaper at all." This position Richter described as "un-
worthy." The publisher, he continued, is also mistaken,
who out of timidity says: "This regime will not last—I
must maintain reserve until the next page is turned." Then
he advised his hearers that if they could not cooperate from
sincere conviction, they should withdraw from the publishing field. Following a historical review of the Kulturkampf
and the origin of the Catholic press, he assured them that

this chapter was now closed, and that National Socialism had overcome this national division. "The Catholic daily press must recognize this and merge itself with the national press for the good of the whole community and the state."

For the Generalanzeiger type of confessional paper Richter entertained little hope of satisfactory reform because of the basic nature of these journals, devoted as they were to one objective—to observe a certain "Catholic etiquette" because the owner believed that in so doing he could monopolize a selected circle of readers and advertisers and make a good profit. Such papers, he said, must be completely eliminated. Any Catholic paper, not of the Generalanzeiger type, which developed a "positive attitude" toward National Socialism, had nothing to fear. One thing above all others was to be avoided: "A journalistic make-up and orientation for the express purpose of being Catholic and in so doing to cut out and reserve a Catholic circle of readers to the exclusion of all other elements of the national community." What then, he asked, is the final solution for a Catholic publisher? "To cooperate, not with an air of resignation by filling columns with government and party speeches and announcements, but by reworking this material and infusing the whole paper with a positive National Socialist spirit." In conclusion Richter solemnly warned his hearers that the ordinances had been issued by the president of the RPK after long and serious reflection, with full appreciation of the consequences of their uncompromising application. But every publisher would be given the opportunity once more to determine his own fate. He could decide freely what that fate would be.[4]

While Richter tried to reason with the Catholic publishers, direct pressure was applied through the RVDZV and the regional associations. In a six-page directive, signed by Rienhardt and marked "strictly confidential," the directors

[4] LV Rundschreiben, File 1, BDC.

were instructed how to proceed in measuring compliance. "The article by the president of the RPK, 'Es gibt nur eine deutsche Presse', requires of the Reichsverband and its provincial associations a certain work of assistance and control with regard to that part of the daily press which was formerly associated with the Center and Bavarian People's parties. This work is of special significance with regard to the enforcement of Article IV of the 'Ordinance for Insuring the Independence of the German Newspaper Publishing Industry'. Doubtless on the part of many of the papers in this category there is lacking the good will to observe the directives set forth in that article. Another part of the identifiable confessional press possesses the good will and inclination to function in a National Socialist sense but lacks perhaps internally the necessary feeling of unity with the movement and externally all contact with the competent party authorities and local agencies." The Landesverband authorities were instructed to call a meeting of publishers affected by the ordinance and to explain to them the principles enunciated by the president of the RPK. Those papers which after such instruction continued to follow a confessional line were to be reported and adequate issues of the paper forwarded to the central office for examination.

The directive then stated: "The examination of the whole of the confessionally oriented press, carried out previously in the central office, reveals certain factual attributes and formulations which distinguish these papers and which under the principles enunciated in the above-mentioned article can no longer be tolerated." What follows might well be headlined: "How to Sniff Out a Catholic Paper!" Under nine main headings and thirty-nine subheadings the field representatives were told what to look for as the signs, qualities, and characteristics of a confessionally oriented newspaper. The clearest indications could be derived from news content as it pertained to international, national, state, and local events. Reports of Catholic youth organizations or a conference of the Kolping association should be carefully compared with the amount of space given to meetings of party organizations such as the SA, Hitler Youth, and Labor Front. It should be noted whether the political and local reporting and the entertainment sections were directed toward an obviously confessional rather than a general circle of readers; and whether its advertising was exclusively Catholic—religious books, rosaries, votive candles, and religious pictures. It should also be noted whether the paper sought to isolate its readers by omitting or under-reporting political news of the Gau and the community, or whether it reported only those political and public developments which were acceptable to the Catholic Church, such as measures to promote social and national welfare, but ignoring the Hitler Youth program, the National Socialist Cultural Community, and the racial issue. It should be noted, too, whether publicity was given to those state and party leaders who were acceptable to a Catholic community while unacceptable leaders were ignored.

Further it should be noted that the Catholic press in its religious columns did not always speak of "The God of all nations," but frequently today used the expression, "The God of all men, nations, and races." It was also not acceptable that a paper publish a statement by a bishop, priest, or Catholic professor which conflicted with the National Socialist Weltanschauung and then defend the action on the grounds that it was performing only a reportorial function. The Catholic paper might also sensationalize news events unfavorable to the party and state, such as difficulties arising between the Evangelical church and the government, or by tendentiously reporting church-state conflicts in Mexico, Spain, Russia, or Turkey. In its subscription advertising the paper might openly identify itself as a journal for Catholic readers, or cite the implied or stated approval of the paper by church leaders, as for example: "The Holy Father blesses especially the paid-up subscribers of the German Catholic press, as well as readers of our National Socialist papers!" The supplements published also frequently provided a clue to the paper's position, i.e., "Our St. Quirinus Supplement is Included." Whether publisher and editor were formerly active in the Center Party, and whether behind the paper were religious organizations or functionaries, must also be taken into consideration in determining the character of the paper. In conclusion, the document stated that these were only some of the signs and indications that would serve to identify Catholic oriented papers and measure their compliance with the Amann ordinances.[5]

What would be an appropriate comment upon this document the author is scarcely prepared to say. The pedantry and inquisitorial spirit are so pronounced on the face of it that any emphasis would be misplaced or redundant. If the document were introduced as a political burlesque, it could best be appreciated on that level, but issued as it was in deadly earnest, it set in motion the whole machinery of meddlesome prying and intimidation so characteristic of the Nazi regime.

At the Landesverband directors' conference, held in Berlin in late July, the progress in reeducating the Catholic publishers was an important topic on the agenda. After a thorough discussion, the general opinion seemed to be that conversion and reform had not been fully achieved. Speaking for the RPK, Richter counseled moderation and patience. In considering the individual cases, he said that a clear line of demarcation must be made between the Catholic faith and "political Catholicism." Also they must

[5] LV Rundschreiben, No. 7, April 25, 1935. For the convenience of the Landesverband directors a supplementary circular giving the points in outline, with examples, was issued on the same date. (LV Rundschreiben, No. 8.)

consider the economic consequences of closing up a firm
and the resulting employment prospects of the employees.
"You cannot just close an enterprise, but must endeavor
by patient negotiation to carry out the ordinance. We must
proceed cautiously in applying the enforcement measures
so that later we shall not be overwhelmed with re-
proaches." [6] After the 90-day period allowed for compliance
with Article IV had expired, a new reading was taken on
the Catholic press in the Reichsverband headquarters. The
Landesverband directors were instructed to examine thoroughly each daily issue of former confessional papers published in their district and to report each infraction of
Article IV or departure from the principles established by
the RPK for the newspaper publishing industry. [7]

It is evident that in those parts of Germany where the
Center and Bavarian People's party had held majority positions a great many publishers and papers flunked the test.
In a communication marked "Personal and Strictly Confidential," addressed to the leaders and directors of the
regional associations, Rienhardt expressed serious concern
over the application of the Paragraph 10 penalty to those
publishers who had failed to conform. "I ask myself," he
wrote, "whether we shall reach the right solution in certain
Landesverband areas if we exclude publishers by the dozen

[6] Conference protocol, July 25, 1935; LV Rundschreiben, File 1,
BDC. For the record, the names of those present at this interesting
session should be listed: Boegner (Augsburg), Buschmann and
Henrici (Stettin), Claren and Jahr (Cologne), Gutbrod and Hoffmann (Frankfurt), Hornauer, Müller, and Werner (Dresden),
Jester and Strowig (Berlin), Dr. Kessler (Essen), Dr. Koeltsch
(Königsberg), Lattmann and Wittenberg (Hanover), Von Laur
and Dr. Rudolph (Breslau), Meyer-Imboldt and Schmidt (Hamburg), Michahelles and Dr. Weiss (Stuttgart), Dr. Schott (Karlsruhe), Stenzel (Magdeburg). From the RPK: Ildephons Richter;
and from the RVDZV: Rienhardt, Dr. Spies, Von Zweck, Anders,
Sturm, Wilkens, and Hossbach.

[7] LV Rundschreiben, No. 49, Aug. 17, 1935; File 1, BDC.

from the industry. The social and economic consequences
of such action would be far-reaching and serious. Moreover,
the danger arises that a great number of the subscribers will
not substitute another newspaper, especially since the
former paper is, in many cases, the home town journal,
which was the principal reason for subscribing to it in the
first place." As a solution, which he wanted the Landesverband directors to consider with reference to local conditions, he proposed that selected regional publishing firms
be acquired, including some of the larger Center party
enterprises, and that through them a stereotype agency
service be provided for the middle-size, small, and smallest
papers in the area. In this way they could insure the political attitude of these papers and they would only have to
apply the Paragraph 10 solution in those cases where "com-
pelling necessity" required it. Their experience with the
"black newspapers" had shown that the local columns
could be effectively controlled by local means. As an additional safeguard they might consider the transfer of publishing rights of small newspapers to the larger regional
enterprises that would be acquired. The Landesverband
directors were requested to examine these proposals and
give their opinion, supported by reasoned explanations, as
to whether this solution could be effected in their districts. In so doing, they were to consider all the papers
which had been placed on the prepared lists of confessionally oriented journals. For those which could not be
brought into such a structure they were to indicate whether
the establishment should be closed or continued.[8]

[8] LV Rundschreiben, No. 81, Dec. 3, 1935; File 1, BDC. A
December 15 deadline was set for submission of the reports. In
an additional subject paragraph, Rienhardt again urged Landesverband authorities to give serious consideration to the social and
political results of the application of the Amann ordinances. "Even
though their application—especially the closing ordinance—serves
the purpose of eliminating unhealthy conditions and thereby re-

By November, application of the Amann ordinances was sufficiently advanced for Rienhardt to comment on this aspect of the Reichsverband's operations at the autumn meeting of the regional directors in Berlin. He admitted that the recent months had been trying. The ordinances had been difficult to formulate and to apply. It was not easy to make decisions concerning established publishing firms which had been built up through years, even decades, of professional and business endeavor. They had to make many exclusions from the RPK and many enterprises had been closed. It was admittedly hard but he believed it was in the interest of the publishing business as a whole. The exclusions were based upon checks and observations made over a period of two years. One publisher had appealed to the Führer, but the evidence which the Reichsverband possessed was conclusive and Paragraph 10 had to be applied. The closing actions, where overcrowding and unhealthy competitive conditions existed, had been equally difficult, Rienhardt said, but the investigations of the Cura staff had shown that in more than 200 cases action could not be postponed. "For if we had not effected these closings in the present year, then double the number that was closed (from 200 to 300) would have gone under, so far as we could judge. The remaining publishers, whom you represent, would have suffered still more during such a prolonged weeding-out process." With regard to interpretations that were being placed upon the actions taken, it was not true, he said, that the party and the Führer regarded

---

moving the danger of even greater unemployment in the industry, still great social and political hardships will ensue in those cases where action must be taken immediately. It is our task, employing all our powers, to reduce these effects to the minimum possible. I therefore request that you do everything in your power to find employment in other publishing firms, or in other suitable positions, for those who will be affected. You will not only help these individuals but also render a distinct service to the whole program."

the privately owned papers as "just a necessary evil." The Führer had decided that there should be both a party-owned and a privately owned press. He must also emphatically deny the rumor circulating that the party intended to acquire fifty-one per cent of the stock of all privately owned papers. "The party becomes a shareholder in those publishing companies where on special political grounds there appears to be a necessity for such action, but it has no intention of assuming such economic obligations as would make private ownership in the publishing industry illusory." [9]

In referring to party participation in private publishing companies, Rienhardt was touching upon one of the main features of the political and economic cleansing to which the publishing business was being ruthlessly subjected. This aspect of the final solution will be dealt with later in detail. To what extent the Landesverband directors were informed of this part of the operation we do not know. In the beginning they probably knew very little as this side of the operation was directed from Berlin. The curtain was lifted slightly in April 1936 when Rienhardt sent a communication, marked "strictly confidential," to all leaders and executive secretaries of the regional associations: "The Vera Verlagsanstalt GmbH, and the Phoenix Zeitungsverlag GmbH, stand in a special relationship to the party. We request that you take note of this fact in your operations." [10]

## The Catholic Press and the Phoenix Publishing Company

The Phoenix Publishing Company was established by Rienhardt in 1935 as a holding and management concern for former Center party papers which could not be left in

[9] Conference protocol, Nov. 13, 1935; LV Rundschreiben, File 1, BDC.

[10] LV Rundschreiben, No. 73, April 30, 1936.

the hands of their current publishers but which the Nazi authorities wished to continue under camouflaged party control. Its stock was held jointly by two Eher subsidiaries, the Standarte and Herold organizations, and the company worked closely with the staffs of the Reichsverband and the Cura. Most of the papers acquired by the Phoenix company were in the Catholic regions of Rhineland-Westphalia and South Germany. It is not possible, nor is it necessary, to list all the small and medium sized papers acquired by the Phoenix company. Among the principal acquisitions were papers in Cologne, Münster, Karlsruhe, Mainz, Paderborn, Würzburg, and Worms.[11]

Two of the more important acquisitions were the Verbo and Zeno combinations, whose dissolution was a specified objective of the Amann ordinances. The Zeno cooperative group comprised fourteen small local papers in Westphalia using joint advertising, purchasing, and stereotyping services with central headquarters in Münster. Since they served a Catholic clientele and since such combinations were prohibited under the Amann ordinances, the shareholders had no choice but to turn the enterprise over to the Phoenix company. The same fate befell the Verbo group in southern Württemberg. Here a group of thirty-two small-town publishers had formed a cooperative and established a modern printing plant in Friedrichshafen, with centralized stereotyping service, advertising agency, and general business office. Each paper retained its identity but printed only the local part of the paper in the town of origin. The group operated efficiently, produced superior local papers, and appeared to have found a solution to the problem of survival for the small-town publisher. Operating in a Catholic community, the papers were strongly confessional in tone. Since they formed a combination, the organization could not continue under the Amann ordinances. When

[11] Fritz Schmidt's listing of Phoenix papers is both incomplete and incorrect. *Presse in Fesseln*, p. 81.

this was made plain to the shareholders by Phoenix representatives, they surrendered their stock in the central establishment, which operated thereafter as the Oberschwä-
bische Verlagsanstalt GmbH. The acquisition of control
over these small Catholic papers was the solution which
Rienhardt had been seeking as an alternative to closing
them "by the dozen." A similar solution was reached in
the Munich area where a group of thirty-two small town
newspapers were brought together to form the N-S Zeitungsblock Oberbayern. This, however, was not a Phoenix
undertaking, but owed its existence to the enterprise and
initiative of Adolf Müller and his business associate, Max
Amann, who together with Müller held the majority
shares.[12]

One documented case concerning a large and important
Verlag throws much light on how the confessional political
papers were dealt with. The *Bayerische Volkszeitung*, published by the Sebaldus Verlag in Nürnberg, was the leading
organ of the Bavarian People's Party in Franconia. The
Sebaldus Verlag also produced a large line of books and
periodicals suitable for a Catholic clientele. The SA had
stormed the building and destroyed the book stocks on
the same night in 1933 that had witnessed the looting of
the SPD *Frankische Tagespost*. The Nazis then began the
usual campaign to intimidate subscribers and advertisers.
Circulation and advertising revenue declined and the
Verlag operated with a deficit. As a joint stock company,
the Verlag fell under the Amann ordinances and the director, Balthasar Moeckel, was excluded from the RPK as
politically untrustworthy under Paragraph 10. With the
notice of expulsion was coupled the demand that the publishing rights and titles of the Verlag be surrendered to

[12] Schmidt erroneously attributes ownership to the Phoenix concern (*Presse in Fesseln*, p. 81). Amann gave a full account of his
partnership with Müller in his appeal to the district court in Munich. (Amann, Spruchkammer file, appeal dated Nov. 2, 1951.)

the Phoenix company. A contract was then negotiated and signed (September 27, 1935) by Julius Mundhenke, staff director of Cura, for the Phoenix company, and Moeckel for the Sebaldus Verlag. For the publishing rights and titles Phoenix paid 50,000 RM calculated on the basis of 3 RM per subscriber. Half the purchase price was paid in twelve monthly installments, beginning January 1, 1936, and the balance in quarterly payments with interest at four and one-half per cent. The technical plant remained in the hands of the original owner who accepted a printing contract for the paper from the new proprietors. Moeckel agreed to support the new company, to hand over all books, accounts, and files, and not to purchase materials from Jewish suppliers. The Phoenix corporation agreed to retention of the editorial and clerical force, reserving the right to discharge those who were "unsuitable." This kind of contract, where only the publishing rights and titles were acquired, while the original publisher became a printer of what was now a Nazi paper, was used in hundreds of acquisitions by the Eher Verlag subsidiaries. The cost of acquiring control was minimal and, under existing circumstances, large profits could not be anticipated from operating the printing plant.[13] In many of the larger enterprises, Eher's participation included the plant as well as the publishing rights and titles.

For the papers gathered into the Phoenix group, centralized direction and control was provided from the Berlin headquarters. The objectives of this operation were more political than financial. While the records are not available,

[13] In 1949 Moeckel filed a restitution and indemnity claim with Allied authorities for 620,000 RM. His claim was rejected because under the restitution law those publishers who received printing contracts from the Eher subsidiaries and continued in association with the Nazi tenants could not qualify as political persecutees or opponents of National Socialism. The complete file on the Sebaldus Verlag, including a copy of the contract, is in the Bavarian Restitution Office, File 3820/III, Pressesachen.

it is safe to assume that large profits were not derived from the operatıons of this holding company, since most of the papers were small or at best middle-sized; many were later transferred to the local Gau publishing companies or merged with other Eher undertakings.[14] For the Nazi "simplifiers," the Phoenix apparatus served its purpose well. The history of these papers was such that they could not be taken over immediately by the Gau publishing companies and issued as party-owned papers stamped with the swastika emblem. That would have meant sudden death in predominantly Catholic communities. But by bringing them into a camouflaged combination under party control, the editors could be changed, all former financial and political ties severed, and all those characteristics of a confessional press to which the Nazi leaders took vigorous exception, could be gradually eliminated without alienating the local subscribers and advertisers.

A special target of the Nazi publishing policy was the Pötz newspaper chain in the Ruhr-Rhineland region. Catholic owned and oriented, and an especially tough competitor of the local Gau papers, the Pötz enterprises received special attention from the Nazis from 1933 to 1936.[15]

The Volksverlag, parent unit in the chain, was founded in 1918 by a group of Catholic business men. Pötz became the principal shareholder and head of the enterprise, and, adding by purchase to the original paper in Oberhausen, developed a chain of local Catholic papers. A position of importance was acquired for his journals in Düsseldorf, Cologne, Krefeld, and Oberhausen. His organizational and business methods were modern and aggressive and he operated on a sound financial basis. The Pötz papers were

[14] W. R. Beyer, "Die gesellschaftsrechtliche Geschichte des Eher-Verlages," pp. 9-10, File 3820-b, Gutachten im Pressesachen, BWB.

[15] This account is based on the richly documented dissertation by A. O. Limburg, *Der Pötz-Konzern* (Bonn, 1946).

not notably political in tone and content, but were designed for middle class Catholic families who formed the
solid core of his circle of readers. Neither before nor after
1933 did the Nazi papers make any great inroads upon his
circulation and advertising. When Hitler came to power,
the Pötz press generally took evasive action, avoiding prov-
ocation, recognizing Hitler as a constitutional chancellor,
but without altering at all the confessional tone and character of the papers. When collisions occurred with the
local Nazis, the publisher protested sharply and vigorously
by letter and telegram to the Nazi agencies, the police presidents, mayors, Gauleiters, provincial authorities, and the
publishers' association. In 1933, the main offices in Düsseldorf were not stormed, but the printing establishment in
Oberhausen was twice occupied by the SA. Gauleiter Terboven was present at one of these illegal entries.[16]

This was only the beginning of a campaign of harassment and chicanery that was pursued relentlessly toward
the publisher. During the next two years the Pötz papers
were cited sixteen times for alleged breaches of laws and
regulations. In twelve instances papers were suspended for
short periods or the offending issue confiscated by the
police. Public agencies and officials regularly withheld
news releases and announcements from the Pötz reporters.[17] In the circulation war which raged in 1933, Pötz
fought the Nazi papers—especially the *Volksparole* and
the *National-Zeitung*—for every subscriber, and indeed
not without success. In Düsseldorf the *Tageblatt* gained
8,000 subscribers between January and June 1933. The
Nazi competitors employed their customary tactics—uni-
formed solicitors, threats and pressures directed at subscribers, ruinous rumors, and charges of philo-Semitism.
More damaging to Pötz was the order by the Nazi president of the government employee's association that all

[16] Limburg, pp. 55-60.
[17] Limburg, pp. 60-75, gives details of these actions.

members must cancel their subscriptions to the Catholic papers and subscribe to the *Volksparole* or the *National-Zeitung*. Officials who could not show a subscription receipt would be reported to the Gauleitung. The cost of meeting the Nazi challenge was high. In 1934 the Pötz paper in Oberhausen spent 43,000 RM on special circulation advertising without gaining a compensating number of new subscribers.[18] The Catholic press in the Rhineland, and especially the Pötz papers, made a sustained effort to win the subscribers and readers of the former SPD press. Boldly these papers in large display advertisements made their appeal: "We Have Also Been Suppressed. In Our Circle of Readers You Will Find Yourself in Good Company!" In the Catholic clerics the Pötz papers also found helpers. From the pulpits, congregations were urged to subscribe to Catholic papers and many pastors undertook to distribute free advertising copies to their communicants. This direct support for the Catholic press led Gauleiter Florian to issue a public proclamation denouncing the alliance: "Whoever makes the public appeal—'Catholics read Catholic papers'—demoralizes the nation and is a traitor to German unity. There can be no Catholic press, only a German press!"[19] Despite the pressure and competition from the Nazis, the confessional newspapers in Rhineland-Westphalia gained circulation during 1934 while the other papers lost or barely held their own.[20]

In the spring of 1934 the bitter competition between the *Neue Tag* of the Pötz group and Terboven's *National-Zeitung* brought the issue of the Catholic press to the point of decisive action. In the Duisburg-Hamborn area the *Neue Tag*, in a determined counterattack, recovered from the Nazi paper some thousand subscribers. Representatives

[18] Limburg, pp. 80-83.
[19] Limburg, p. 98.
[20] Report of the executive director of the Landesverband (Krefeld), cited by Limburg, p. 87.

of the *National-Zeitung* in SA uniform visited these canceled subscribers and threatened reprisals and boycott if
they did not renew with the *National-Zeitung*. Pötz' representatives brought charges in the state court (Landgericht),
seeking an injunction against "unfair competition" by the
Nazi competitor. When the injunction was denied, Pötz'
attorneys took the case to the superior court (Oberlan-
desgericht) where the injunction was granted. This created
a sensation and precipitated action by the Reichsverband
and the Propaganda Ministry against the Catholic press.
The drive, which ended with the elimination of confessional papers from the publishing scene, opened with a
blast from Goebbels: "With all possible emphasis," he
declared in a public statement, "I must reject the standpoint that there is in Germany a Catholic and a Protestant
press, or a worker's press, or a farmer's press, or a city press,
or a proletariat press. There exists only a *German* press.
The government has assumed the protection of the confessions, and we do not propose to leave this responsibility to
those newspapers which in the past had an opportunity to
defend the churches but instead protected Marxism." [21]
Concurrently, the Reichsverband issued a confidential order to the publishing industry strictly prohibiting the use of
confessional appeals in soliciting subscribers, or indeed
even mentioning confessional orientation in subscription
advertising and canvassing. However, in the continued competition the *Neue Tag* sailed as close to the line as possible,
incurring two reprimands from the Reichsverband and an
order to drop even the saint's day calendar from the masthead of the paper. Finally, the Gestapo arrested and interrogated five of Pötz' solicitors whose statements were used
as a basis of a list of charges brought by the Reichsverband
against the publisher. It was alleged that the canvassers
emphasized their paper was Catholic oriented; that it was
less Nazi than other journals; that it played down the

[21] Limburg, p. 100.

Catholic foreign exchange scandals; and that members of the organization had been sentenced to jail for their convictions.[22] These charges were added to the dossier on the Pötz papers that was building up in the central office of the Reichsverband.

Pötz and his associates, through unauthorized channels, acquired copies of the draft ordinances and Rienhardt's "Commentaries," so they knew well in advance that they were marked for liquidation. A dozen of the prohibitions in the Amann ordinances applied to the Pötz organization, but two especially made its liquidation certain—it was a newspaper chain and its papers were unreconstructed confessional journals. On July 9, 1935, the Reichsverband office in Berlin notified the publishers that their papers had been carefully examined with regard to the application of the ordinances. They were given barely two weeks in which to comply with the terms—that is to reorganize financially and to cleanse the papers of all evidences of confessional orientation. On appeal the deadline was extended to September 23, but the extension was accompanied by a sharp reminder that compliance must be prompt. A month later an inquiry as to reorganization plans was dispatched by the Reichsverband; this was followed in a few weeks by a reminder that since the conversations in Berlin between the Reichsverband officials and the Pötz representatives nothing further had been heard from them. The publisher was given ten days to submit concrete proposals. Again Pötz and his associates played for time but on December 12 the Reichsverband wrote categorically: "Negotiations on the practical possibilities of a solution can only be conducted with the Vera Verlagsanstalt GmbH, Berlin NW 87, Brückenalle 3, with whom we advise you to make contact immediately." [23] Further delay being impossible, Pötz and his associates made their pilgrimage to the Vera offices

[22] Limburg, 101-102.
[23] Limburg, p. 108.

and negotiations with Winkler began in early February. On April 7, 1936, an agreement was concluded transferring all publishing rights and titles to the Vera trust for 550,000 RM. A long term contract was concluded with the old firm for the production of the Vera controlled papers in the Pötz printing plants, which were left in the possession of the original owners. In the direction and editing of the Pötz papers, the Vera management was moderate and cautious, but under the party trust the special character of the papers disappeared—and so did the subscribers. Using a favorable opportunity, in June 1941, the principal Pötz newspapers were discontinued and the remaining subscribers supplied with a substitute Nazi paper.[24]

## Winkler and the Generalanzeiger Press

While the Phoenix company was used to hold and manage the confessional papers which Amann wished to acquire and publish, the Vera Verlagsanstalt, an Eher subsidiary under the direction of Max Winkler, operated on a larger scale with higher capital stakes. The Vera company was employed to manage the mass circulation Generalanzeiger papers and the provincial political dailies which were brought into the Eher combination. This company was not a new creation. Organized in 1917 by Alfred Hugenberg and associates, it provided management, auditing, and technical advisory service for provincial newspapers. It was closely associated with a finance company specializing in loans to newspaper publishers and during the unsettled post-war years played a significant role in the Hugenberg trust. By 1935, when the Vera company was acquired by the Eher interests, together with Hugenberg's holdings in fourteen provincial newspapers, its operations had been greatly curtailed and it was scarcely more than a corporate

[24] Limburg, p. 109. On the Catholic daily press see also K. A. Altmeyer, *Katolische Presse unter NS-Diktatur*, Chap. III.

shell.[25] The Vera company was reorganized in November 1935 with a capital of two million marks. The stated object of the company was participation in newspaper enterprises and the management of newspapers and periodicals. The principal shareholder was the Herold Verlagsanstalt—a completely owned Eher subsidiary—and the minority stockholders were the Phoenix company (100,000 RM), Winkler's personal Cautio company (29,200 RM), and an unliquidated minority holding of 1,500 RM assigned to the "heirs of Pastor Paulsen." In 1937 the capital stock was reduced to one million RM and in 1938 the shares held by Phoenix were transferred to the Standarte company. In 1939, when relations with Amann became strained, Winkler surrendered his shares, the Vera company was merged with the Herold combination, and the name Vera canceled from the corporation register.[26]

Since the Vera company functioned as a trustee and management firm, the amount of the capital stock did not reflect the importance of its operations. Nonetheless, substantial amounts of capital were required for the Vera purchases even though many acquisitions were forced sales at distress prices. As previously stated, the operating capital was derived from a thirty million RM loan from the former German trade union bank, now under party control. The loan was repaid in 1939-1940 from the profits derived from the Vera holdings in the numerous publishing enterprises under its control. The participation of Vera in a publishing house usually worked to the firm's advantage because Vera was obligated to insure that the unfair competition of the party papers ceased. This ended the ruinous competition

[25] Ludwig Bernhard, *Der Hugenberg-Konzern*, pp. 80-81; Schmidt, *Presse in Fesseln*, p. 59. This transfer reduced Hugenberg's newspaper and periodical holdings to the Scherl Verlag in Berlin.

[26] "Auszüge aus den Handelsregisterakten des Amtgerichts Berlin-Charlottenburg," BWB.

for subscribers and frequently enabled the papers to make substantial profits which flowed into the Vera accounts.[27]

Occupying a position similar to the Vera firm in the Eher corporate structure was the Herold Verlagsanstalt GmbH. In the general drive against the middle class press it was planned originally that the acquisitions and participations would be grouped under one of the holding companies according to the character and origin of the acquisition— Phoenix for the confessional papers, Vera for the Generalanzeiger press, and Herold for the non-confessional political press. The separation, however, was far from rigid. Vera acquired the Pötz papers because presumably they were of the Generalanzeiger type, and the separation of the Vera and Herold controlled firms was far from consistent or logical. In both Vera and Herold, Max Winkler functioned as trustee shareholder and executive director, a straw man for Amann and the Nazi party. The Herold company traced its history from the founding in 1904, by Louis Hirsch, of the Herold Depeschenbureau GmbH, an early news agency rival of the Wolff service. In 1922 it was acquired by Hugenberg and the business merged with his Telegraph Union. Until 1935, when it came into the hands of Max Winkler, Herold was scarcely more than a title in the official corporation register. It was then reorganized and the name changed to Herold Verlagsanstalt GmbH and its purpose declared to be the acquisition and management of printing and publishing enterprises. While the capital shares amounted to only 20,000 RM, as a trustee the company administered capital assets booked at over 27 million RM. When Winkler and Amann fell out in 1939, Rienhardt became the managing director and the Eher Verlag acquired all the shares. Among the three companies there was continuous shifting of properties and capital stock. The Phoenix corporation was liquidated in 1940 and Vera in 1944. Even

[27] Statement by Willy Imhof for the Bavarian Restitution Office, File 3820-b, BWB.

before this date Herold had become the major holding and management concern under the Eher Verlag.[28]

For the greater part of three years, from 1935 to 1938, Max Winkler, under Amann's direction, devoted his talents as a business negotiator and organizer to the purchase of many of the most important German newspapers. Circumstances determined whether an enterprise was wholly acquired or whether Winkler purchased the controlling interest in the publishing house. The acquisitions of the Phoenix company in the confessional newspaper field were minor compared to Winkler's operations, which were concerned with the Huck and Girardet combinations, the provincial Generalanzeiger papers, and the old established political dailies whose owners and publishers the Nazis regarded as unsuitable or unreliable. His successes must be attributed mainly to the pressure under which the publishers now found themselves. With multiple newspaper holdings banned under the Amann ordinances, with the two customary corporate forms of organization prohibited except with Amann's express approval, with the threat of closing on competitive grounds hanging over the individual publisher, and with the Paragraph 10 test as a final hurdle, it is not surprising that Winkler found most of the publishers approached willing to sell or to admit one of Winkler's companies as a majority stockholder in their publishing enterprise.

The state of mind of the independent publisher under these pressures has been described by Dr. Walther Jänecke, former publisher of the *Hannoverscher Kurier*: "It was difficult for the provincial publisher to hold out against the pressure of the Gau and central authorities for he stood alone with no organization to support him. He was always

[28] "Auszüge aus den Handelsregisterakten . . . Berlin-Charlottenburg," BWB. The dates of the Herold entries are: Dec. 12, 1935; Feb. 12 and 21, April 19, Dec. 31, 1939. Also Beyer, "Die gesellschaftsrechtliche Geschichte des Eher-Verlages," pp. 8-10.

under pressure from the party officials and the strain and worry were terrific. After applying pressure a representative of the Gauleiter, perhaps even Winkler, would appear and an offer would be made accompanied by a warm recommendation that he sell. 'This offer may not be repeated', he would be warned. And the publisher would think: 'In another year they can kill me off financially with dirty competition. Their resources are unlimited, mine are not'. He would usually sell or surrender fifty-one per cent of his shares if it were an incorporated company. Frequently he retained his printing plant and continued as a contract printer for his former paper." [29] In less graphic terms the former executive director of the Reichspressekammer, Dr. Ildephons Richter, expressed the same view of the plight of the publisher: "The circumstances were such that the greater part of the publishers had to submit for they saw little possibility of circumventing the logic of events." [30]

A less sympathetic view of the plight of the private publisher is expressed by Wilhelm R. Beyer, a legal authority on the restitution and indemnity laws: "Almost all the 'old publishers' (Altverleger) were actually members, and some were old members, of the NSDAP. They all made considerable money during the Third Reich. To be sure, they could no longer *publish* their papers but they could *print* their papers. . . . The fact is that during the Third Reich the printing establishments earned considerable revenue. That the publishers would have earned more if they could have continued as publishers of their newspapers is correct. But a newspaper is always a political business. . . . Only one case is known where for this reason alone—refusal to give up his publishing rights—one of the old publishers was taken into custody. Erich Köllreutter of Metzingen (Württemberg) and his lawyer, Dr. Klett, were held in custody

[29] Interview notes, Aug. 18, 1958.
[30] Unsworn affidavit on behalf of Max Amann, 1947; Spruchkammer Munich i, Amann, main file.

for approximately fourteen days. In the other cases, connections were made with the Eher concern because this brought an abundance of contracts to the printing plant. It is not correct today to represent all these arrangements as having been made under compulsion." [31] With regard to some, perhaps many, of the publishing cases this caveat is doubtless valid, but it takes no account of the human desire to save something of the family patrimony by enduring an unpleasant association; and it appears to require that a publisher be a proven martyr in order someday to vindicate his rights and secure indemnity.

The procedure in applying the Amann ordinances to force the large publishers to surrender their holdings was fairly uniform. All the means of pressure and intimidation were in the hands of officials of the Reich Press Chamber and the Reichsverband; and the Eher trust was the only purchaser in the field. The compliance features of the Amann ordinances required the publishers, or their representatives, to contact the officials of the Reichsverband. Here the official attitude would be explained, including a statement as to what the publisher must accomplish or surrender, in order to conform to the requirements of the ordinances. Heavy pressure would be applied by referring to the Paragraph 10 investigation and the possibility that the publisher might be found wanting. He would be urged not to take the risk but rather to agree to a reasonable compromise which would leave him in possession of anywhere from thirty to forty-nine per cent of his capitalized company.

When the publisher was properly conditioned by Rienhardt or his right-hand man, Anders, he would be referred to Winkler. The latter would express sympathy for the victim's plight, and would then propose one of his famous "compromises" which would earn the thanks of the de-

[31] Beyer, "Die gesellschaftsrechtliche Geschichte des Eher-Verlages," pp. 31-33.

spoiled person but would represent what Amann, Rhien-
hardt, Mundhenke, and Winkler had previously agreed
upon as a goal. After the group's objective had been
achieved no difficulty was made with regard to Paragraph
10 unless the person had made himself utterly intolerable
to the regime. A variant procedure was one in which Winkler made a direct approach after the publisher was thoroughly entangled in the net. Winkler would then appear
with a commission from Amann. In executing his mandate, he was always considerate, conciliatory, and as unctu-
ous as a small-town undertaker. Using the soft approach,
he sympathized with his victims as he despoiled them. "The
Führer has decided," he would say, "that you must withdraw from the publishing business or dispose of fifty-one
per cent of your shares in the XYZ publishing company. I
have a commission to negotiate a reasonable and advantageous settlement through the sale of your interests. If my
proposals are rejected, I can only return my mandate and
let matters take their course. There is no predicting what
the result will be." And he would add with a sly wink:
"One never knows how these gentlemen have slept the
night before." When he closed a deal, the seller did not
know whether he had disposed of his property to Hitler personally, the Nazi party, or indirectly to the Eher company.
The relations of Eher to the Vera, Phoenix, and Herold
concerns were not matters of public knowledge; and it was
not politic to try to penetrate these mysteries of the Third
Reich.[32]

Throughout the latter part of 1935 and the greater part
of 1936 Winkler was engaged in negotiations with two
principal newspaper combinations belonging to the families
of Huck and Girardet. Both published papers that were
popular, politically colorless, and directed toward maximum

[32] The procedures have been described by participants in numerous publishers' restitution cases since 1945—Huck, Girardet, Madsack, Bosch, Schünemann, Broschek, Pielenz, and others.

circulation and advertising revenue—in other words "a business press," which in the eyes of Rienhardt and the doctrinaires was a sin against the National Socialist spirit. The break-up of these combinations and the transfer of the properties to party hands was a principal objective of the Amann ordinances. The Huck concern owned completely or held the controlling interest in seven publishing companies in Mannheim, Dresden, Kassel, Stettin, Halle, Breslau, and Munich. In addition, Huck held eight per cent of the stock of the Stuttgarter Zeitungsverlag, which published three papers in the Stuttgart area. Huck and his father, while not politically active, had been identified with the Democratic party, and both had been financial backers of Max Reinhardt in his theater ventures. The Wolff brothers, of Jewish descent, were shareholders and managers of Huck's Dresden publications, and another Jewish family held substantial stock in the Munich paper. While the Huck press did not oppose National Socialism before 1933, it did not favor or promote the movement, and after 1933 maintained a politically neutral line—that is, the Huck papers did not become vehicles of Nazi propaganda or endeavor to turn their readers into convinced National Socialists. Personally, Huck was unsympathetic toward the Hitler regime and he lightened considerably the burdens of business associates and employees affected by the racial laws. On the other hand, his character and principles being those of a prudent business man, he accommodated his interests to the political circumstances created by National Socialism. Huck was not of the clay from which political martyrs are made. In the crisis produced in his affairs by the Amann ordinances, he made the best settlement he could; he was subsequently certified in the RPK as "reliable and qualified" from the Nazi standpoint, and in 1940 joined the party, seemingly as a further measure of protection for his dwindling interests as a newspaper publisher. He confessed to associates that this was the most difficult decision of his life and that the party emblem in his lapel "burnt like a coal of fire."

Huck was one of the first to initiate legal action after issuance of the Amann decrees. Because of his contacts and reputation, the lawyer Von der Goltz was retained to represent the interests of Huck and others. His unavailing efforts to move the ministry of justice to intervene have already been noted. There then began against Huck the usual procedure of leaks and pressures. Anders, who was the staff specialist in the Reichsverband for the General-anzeiger papers, was reported to have said that Huck would have to divest himself of all his holdings; hostile and omi-nous comments allegedly made by Rienhardt and Amann reached Von der Goltz and Huck's representatives in Ber-lin; and there was the pointed reminder that the Paragraph 10 decision was still pending. Since all avenues of influ-ence and counteraction appeared to be closed, Huck made the first concession in December 1935, when he signed a contract transferring his shares in the Stuttgarter Zeitungs-verlag to the Vera company. This divestment was arranged by Winkler and appears to have appeased Amann and Rienhardt to the point where they were willing to accept a "compromise" with regard to the main Huck holdings.[33] Under this arrangement the Huck papers in Stettin, Bres-lau, and Kassel were sold to the Vera company, permitting Huck to retain the papers in Munich, Dresden, and Halle. (The Mannheim property had been sold in 1933.) Huck became the responsible publisher of the *Dresdner Neueste Nachrichten* and two of his nephews became—*pro forma,*

[33] Winkler testified later that both Rienhardt and Amann had repeatedly referred to the Huck papers as "unbearable for National Socialism." He testified further that his first commission from Amann had been to negotiate the transfer of all Huck papers and that he later proposed the compromise accepted by both parties. (Case of Wolfgang Huck vs. Land Baden-Württemberg, Aug. 16, 1956, pp. 38-39.)

since they were minors—responsible publishers of the papers in Halle and Munich. One nephew was also permitted to acquire the Jewish-owned shares of the *Münchener Zeitung*. After the combine was broken up and this concentration of power in the publishing industry reduced, Huck and his nephews were admitted unconditionally to the RPK and received clearance certificates under Paragraph 10.[34]

In his confidential memorandum on the Amann decrees, Rienhardt had predicted that the Rhenish publishing family of Girardet would be less vulnerable than the Huck concern under the provisions of the ordinance prohibiting multiple ownership of papers. The Girardet company published the *Hamburger Anzeiger,* with the largest circulation in the city, the *Düsseldorfer Nachrichten,* the *Niederrheinische Nachrichten* in Duisburg, and the *Essener Allgemeine Zeitung.* The Girardet press had been cited by Rienhardt as standing in the way of further development of the party papers in these cities. But he also pointed out that, because of the Girardet family relationships, the chain

---

[34] A 48-page decision and rationale of the Restitution Chamber, Landgericht Stuttgart, in an action brought by Huck to secure indemnity for his shares in the Stuttgart publishing company, gives all the details of the Huck negotiations and the court's evaluation of the facts. Huck won his suit in the state court, but the judgment was reversed by the Supreme Restitution Court under Allied Control Council Law 59. Under this law a claimant had to prove that he belonged to a racially or politically persecuted group, or that the confiscation was effected because the person was a known opponent of National Socialism. The appellate court held that, for a claimant to recover, "opposition to National Socialism must be proven as a reason for the confiscation by the preponderance of the evidence." The opinion stated further: "The fact that one secretly does not endorse the ideology of National Socialism and is in disagreement with its principles does not make him an opponent. The Huck combine and its members did everything possible to appease the Party and to appear in accord with its ideology." (Supreme Restitution Court, Case No. 1771, April 25, 1958.)

could be reorganized and operated as single newspapers. No details are available on the negotiations with the Girardet brothers, but the principal properties were brought under the control of the Vera company through the acquisition of fifty-seven per cent of the stock of the *Hamburger Anzeiger* and fifty per cent of the stock of the central publishing house in Essen.[35]

A third newspaper chain, less important than the Huck and Girardet enterprises, was owned and directed by the Saxon industrialist, G. P. Leonhardt. A principal manufacturer of newsprint and paper products, Leonhardt had acquired several newspapers which he combined with his main business as a newsprint and paper supplier. The principal Leonhardt papers, all of the Generalanzeiger type, were located in Chemnitz, Brunswick, and Kiel. According to Fritz Schmidt, by dissolving the central management company and transferring ownership to members of the family, Leonhardt was able to meet the requirements of the Amann ordinances. However, in the suspensions and mergers effected in 1941 and 1943 as war emergency measures, the Leonhardt papers were brought under Nazi party control.[36]

During the two years of Winkler's greatest activity, he acquired through the Vera company majority shares in many of the most important provincial papers of the Generalanzeiger class. In this category, the principal acquisitions by Winkler and his agents were: the *Leipziger Neueste Nachrichten*, published by the Verlag Herfurth; *Rostocker Anzeiger*, Verlag Boldt; *Lübecker Generalanzeiger*, Verlag Colemann; *Magdeburger Generalanzeiger*, Verlag Faber; *Hannoverscher Anzeiger*, Verlag Madsack; *Würzburger*

[35] Organization and participation chart of the Eher publishing company, 1943. The widow Girardet, two daughters, and a son-in-law were certified and admitted to the LV Nordmark after the reorganization of the firm. (*Zeitungs-Verlag*, No. 6, Feb. 6, 1937.)
[36] *Presse in Fesseln*, p. 57.

*Generalanzeiger,* Verlag Richter.[37] The proprietors of these papers represented some of the most highly respected publishing families in Germany. To be sure, their efforts were directed toward maximum circulation and advertising but they fulfilled essential social and economic tasks even though they propagated no clear political line. This was what the Nazi party leaders could not overlook—the prosperity of these papers and their neutral political tone. The Nazi view was well expressed by Ildephons Richter, executive director of the RPK. "The elimination of the General-anzeiger press was a program for which the need had appeared even before the National Socialists came to power. These papers were directed solely toward advertising and had gigantic revenues without following any clear political line. In this respect they had a great advantage over the political press. It was quite obvious that the time had come to place limitations upon these papers. In the course of time most of them offered to sell out." [38] How they "offered to sell out," under extreme pressure from the party and its agents, has been recorded in numerous indemnity cases adjudicated in the German courts since 1945.

## The Provincial Political Press

As previously stated, the Amann ordinances were devised to expropriate or gain control of three important segments of the newspaper publishing industry—the confessional papers, the Generalanzeiger press, and the provincial political papers. The provincial press posed problems of a special kind. Deeply rooted, and in many instances economically sound, these journals represented political tradi-

---

[37] Organization and participation chart of the Eher publishing company, 1943; Schmidt, *Presse in Fesseln,* pp. 58-59. A number of acquisitions attributed by Schmidt to Vera were actually made by the Phoenix company.

[38] Deposition by Richter, 1947, Spruchkammer Munich I, Amann, main file.

tions that often antedated the Bismarckian empire; they were frequently in the hands of prominent publishing families which had directed their fortunes through two or three generations; and they were strongly representative of the provincial middle classes and their local interests and loyalties. Usually liberal or moderately conservative in their views, they represented the best in German journalism—the *Kölnische Zeitung, Bremer Nachrichten, Hamburger Fremdenblatt, Hannoverscher Kurier, Frankfurter Zeitung, Leipziger Neueste Nachrichten, Stuttgarter Neues Tagblatt, Münchner Neueste Nachrichten,* and *Magdeburgische Zeitung.* These papers and their publishers were noted for a sense of responsibility, patriotism, and participation in the political life of the region and nation. A totalitarian political power claiming a monopoly of the citizens' loyalty had two alternatives with regard to the political symbols and institutions of the preceding system—to suppress or eliminate them, or to capture and exploit them in the interest of the Nazi political community. To this problem Amann, Rienhardt, Richter, and Winkler, together with their corps of assistants, devoted themselves with zeal and determination. The view prevailing in the Reich Press Chamber with regard to these papers was well expressed by Ildephons Richter: "I must . . . admit that on our part the tendency existed to let the obviously provincial political press go under. After the Gleichschaltung through the National Socialist party and the continuation of only one party, there was no longer a need for these papers." [39]

In fact, the elimination of this segment of the press began before the promulgation of the Amann ordinances. In these cases the initiative was often taken locally by the Gauleiter, or the party Verlag director, with a view to improving the position of the Nazi paper in the locality by eliminating a serious rival. Political and financial support would be sought from the party directorate, and the local owners

[39] *Ibid.,* deposition by Richter.

put under severe pressure until a purchase or merger was effected. A typical case was that of the liberal *Westfälische Neueste Nachrichten* of Bielefeld. Those concerned in this affair were Rudolf Hess, Edgar Brinkmann, leader of the RVDZV, Gauleiter Meyer (Westphalia-North), and Director Osthoff of the Bielefeld branch of the Dresdner Bank, who represented the owners of the paper. The key document is a communication from Brinkmann on the letterhead of the Reichsleitung, dated May 20, 1935, addressed to Director Osthoff. Sharp and peremptory in tone, Brinkmann referred to their previous negotiations concerning the "accommodating offer of Minister Hess" to purchase a controlling interest in the paper. He would like to know whether the offer was accepted or rejected. He had no interest in new proposals or further discussions and he could not hold the offer open as it would be in contravention of the recently published ordinances of Reich Leader Amann. The failure to close the deal had embarrassed him with Hess and he must have an acceptance or declination by noon, May 25. Otherwise the case would find its solution under the recently published ordinances. Gauleiter Meyer, he said, fully concurred in the views expressed. What course the negotiations took immediately thereafter we do not know, but the merger of the *Westfälische Neueste Nachrichten* with the insignificant *N-S Volksblatt für Westfalen* was announced the following August.[40]

The affair that gave the Nazi dictators the greatest difficulty, involving the party leadership from Hitler down to the Gau officials, and which gave rise to massive litigation after the war, was the case of the Stuttgarter Zeitungsverlag, publisher of the *Stuttgarter Neues Tagblatt*, the *Württemberger Zeitung*, and a local paper in suburban Cannstatt. The former paper was recognized as the leading spokesman for the Democratic party in South Germany. It had wide

[40] *Zeitungs-Verlag*, No. 34, Aug. 24, 1935. Brinkmann's letter to Osthoff is in Amann's Spruchkammer file.

circulation and despite the economic depression, a strong financial position. The founders and original shareholders had participated in the enterprise from political conviction or sympathy, and the character and standing of the paper had not altered when Robert Bosch, the Stuttgart industrialist, became the majority shareholder. Carl Esser, managing director of the firm, had distinguished himself as an opponent of National Socialism before 1933, and thereby earned the bitter enmity of Gauleiter Murr and Dr. Otto Weiss, Gau press warden and head of the N-S Zeitungsverlag. In their complaints to Hitler and the press authorities in Berlin, Esser was described as a "red swine," the publishing company as a "nest of democrats" and a "pig sty," and the *Stuttgarter Neues Tagblatt* as a "Scheissdemokratenblatt." In the process of Gleichschaltung in 1933 Esser was forced to resign, but this in no way abated the party leaders' animus toward the papers and their stockholders.[41]

Publication of the Amann ordinances placed the Stuttgarter Zeitungsverlag in greatest jeopardy. As a corporation the Zeitungsverlag had been admitted originally to the RPK, but under the new ordinances a corporate personality could not hold membership. The Verlag also possessed the GmbH form which was likewise prohibited except by special permission of Max Amann. That this concession would

[41] The case of the Stuttgarter Zeitungsverlag is presented in detail in the restitution case of Ilse Pielenz vs. Finance Ministry of Baden-Württemberg, Sept. 28, 1953. Pielenz was the heir of Alfred Amann, a minority stockholder not related to Max Amann. The decision and rationale, setting forth the documented facts as well as the argument, runs to eighty-eight legal-size pages. Among the witnesses and deponents were: Max Amann, Rolf Rienhardt, Max Winkler, Ildephons Richter, Otto Dietrich, Werner Stephan, Graf von der Goltz, Friedrich Michahelles, former director of the Stuttgart Landesverband, and Fritz Schmidt, author of *Presse in Fesseln* and former director of the newsprint allocation office of the RPK.

be made to Bosch and his associates was unthinkable. Finally, the principal shareholders, including Bosch, were not professionally or occupationally identified with the publishing business. Only the granting of an exception could permit them to continue their participation.[42] When Esser's successor, Verlag director Dr. Wolf, proposed to Rienhardt that the company be reorganized under a dispensation from Amann, Rienhardt replied that this was not possible because of special plans which the RPK had for the Stuttgarter Zeitungsverlag.[43] These plans, as subsequent events showed, envisaged taking over the Verlag to strengthen the NSDAP in Württemberg in the field of the press.

When action on the important provincial papers began in the central office of the Reichsverband and the RPK, all derogatory material available on the owners and publishers of the Stuttgart enterprise was assembled by the Gauleiter, Kreisleiter, and the Gau press warden. The evaluations that accompanied this material to Berlin were, of course, adverse and unflattering. Weiss, who expressed the view that the stockholders were a "democratic clique" who ought to be taken out and shot, returned from one of his visits to Berlin and jubilantly told an associate that he had "fixed the Stuttgarter Zeitungsverlag." [44] In addition to his fanatical hatred of the "democratic clique," Weiss wanted to bring the privately owned company into his N-S Gau Verlag. This would have been a major step toward the party monopoly which he was striving to establish in Württemberg.

---

[42] Pielenz vs. B-W, pp. 38-39. Bosch was an industrialist, Alfred Amann a manufacturer, and other stockholders were business men in Stuttgart and Heilbronn. Altogether there were approximately twenty stockholders.

[43] Madsack heirs vs. B-W, Aug. 16, 1956, p. 13.

[44] Pielenz vs. B-W, pp. 36-38.

The first attempt to purchase Bosch's interest in the Stuttgarter Zeitungsverlag was made without success in the summer of 1935. Winkler sent a representative to Stuttgart after arranging an appointment with one of Bosch's directors and associates. Winkler's representative, a Herr Debach from the Deutscher Verlag, stated to Bosch's associate that it was "the Führer's will" that industrialists withdraw from newspaper publishing and that Bosch would have to divest himself of his shares. As a leading industrialist, Bosch thought he could resist the pressure and the Winkler-Debach overture was rejected. This was reported to Amann and Hitler, and the latter authorized Göring to bring pressure upon the Stuttgart industrialist. Göring telephoned Bosch and asked him to come to Karinhall, where he was presented with Hitler's firm demand that he get out of the publishing business. With the delivery of this ultimatum Bosch had no recourse but to sell his holdings to Winkler's company. All the witnesses in the postwar restitution cases arising out of the expropriation of the Stuttgart publishing firm were in substantial agreement that the major cause for action was the political reputation and the suspected unreliability of the "democratic clique of stockholders."

While Göring and Winkler dealt with the prominent figures among the Stuttgart shareholders, Rienhardt negotiated with the minority participants, none of whose holdings was large. They were pointedly informed by letter from the central office, on January 4, 1936, that under the provisions of the Amann ordinances they must surrender their shares to the Vera company in Berlin. No exceptions were allowed even though some of the minority shareholders were engaged in the publishing business and some had more than made their peace with the Nazi party. When Bosch was expropriated the others saw no chance of protecting their interests. As one witness in the Pielenz case put it, "When the Duke falls, the cloak must also fall." [45]

One of the Stuttgart group proved recalcitrant and put up determined resistance. Alfred Amann visited the central office in Berlin and exchanged blunt letters with Max Amann. But this availed him not at all. The last of the minority stockholders to surrender, he did so when a threatening communication from the president of the RPK informed him that no further delay would be tolerated. It could only be inferred from the tone of Max Amann's letter that if he did not accept the Vera offer he would be expropriated without compensation. [46]

One of the original founders of the *Stuttgarter Neues Tagblatt*, and a stockholder in the company, was August Madsack, owner and publisher of popular middle class newspapers in Hanover and Königsberg. After his death in 1933 the family business was continued by his sons, Erich and Paul Madsack. With the promulgation of the Amann ordinances the Madsack family was subjected to extremely heavy pressure with regard to its papers in Hanover and Königsberg. As a part of one of Winkler's compromises, the Madsacks were allowed to retain their interests in Hanover, but the family was required to sell its Stuttgart shares to the Vera company. [47] With the acquisition of the Madsack and Amann shares the Stuttgarter Zeitungsverlag became a wholly owned subsidiary of Max Winkler's Vera company, thus establishing the Nazi party's domination of the press in Württemberg.

The case of the Stuttgarter Zeitungsverlag is instructive as well as illustrative of the methods employed by Amann and Winkler. Two of Germany's prominent publishers— Huck and Madsack—were forced to surrender their holdings; Robert Bosch, one of Germany's leading industrialists, was likewise forced out of the field of newspaper owner-

[45] *Ibid.*, pp. 76, 79, 81, 85.
[46] *Ibid.*, p. 87; Max Amann to Alfred Amann, April 8, 1936.
[47] Madsack heirs vs. B-W, Aug. 16, 1956, pp. 8-10.

ship, and the smaller stockholders were expropriated with little difficulty.[48]

How a closely held family concern was dealt with is illustrated by the case of the Madsack family of Hanover. August Madsack had founded the *Hannoverscher Anzeiger,* a middle class popular paper, which he developed into a substantial property. He was one of the co-founders of the *Stuttgarter Neues Tagblatt,* and acquired the controlling interest in the *Königsberger Allgemeine Zeitung.* His papers were not primarily opinion making journals, although Madsack was a member of the Democratic party and his papers followed a liberal line. Although the Madsack family conformed to the new situation created by Hitler's advent to power, this did not prevent party attacks and the usual unfair competition from the local Nazi press. In 1933 the circulation of the paper in Hanover declined from 120,-000 to 67,000. To appease the new order, Erich Madsack joined the N-S Motor Corps (NSKK) and made other concessions and compromises in the interest of the family business. This did not erase the impression, or suspicion, in Rienhardt's office and in the RPK that the Madsack family was basically unreliable and unsuitable from the standpoint of Nazi party requirements. With the Paragraph 10 examinations running parallel to the application of the Amann ordinances, the Madsack brothers were in a precarious position when summoned to Berlin to a conference on the future of their publishing interests. Here it was

[48] Most of the stockholders, including Bosch's heirs, the Madsacks, and other minority participants, won a favorable judgment in the Restitution Chamber and were indemnified from confiscated Nazi assets. Each claimant however had to prove that he was entitled to be reckoned a member of "the democratic clique" and an opponent of National Socialism whose expropriation was a political objective of the Nazi party operating through the RPK. Some claimants were unable to establish this identity. The favorable decision in the Huck case was reversed by the Court of Restitution Appeals.

intimated to Erich Madsack that he would probably not receive clearance as a publisher. He then engaged a lawyer, Dr. von Brandenstein, to represent him in subsequent negotiations with the central authorities. Brandenstein conferred with Anders, a relative of Rienhardt's, who had conducted the examination of the middle class provincial press and assembled the derogatory material on the publishers and their papers. Anders pointed out that the *Hannoverscher Anzeiger* had carried a full page campaign advertisement for the SPD in the March 1933 election period, the paper had been attacked by local party officials as a "Jewish Generalanzeiger," and its reputation was so questionable that a party mob had endeavored to storm the building in May 1933. The impression conveyed to Brandenstein was that his client's case was weak and that the family would probably have to get out of the publishing business.

Conforming to the established pattern, Winkler entered the scene at this point with a compromise proposal that would save something for the Madsack family from their publishing enterprises. These negotiations, conducted by Winkler and his right-hand man, Dr. Erwin Reetz, resulted in the sale of the family's Königsberg and Stuttgart interests to the Vera company and the reorganization of the publishing firm in Hanover. With regard to the latter, the Madsacks were allowed to retain the land, building and plant under separate incorporation while the newspaper was organized as an independent company. In this company the Vera concern held fifty-one per cent of the stock, the Madsacks the remainder. Erich Madsack was given clearance under Paragraph 10 and allowed to remain as chief editor and publisher of the paper, an exception to the RPK regulation which required that these two positions be separated. He was ousted from his post as editor in 1943 but retained his position as publisher until the *Hannoverscher Anzeiger* was suspended some months later under the general wartime closing action. In the Madsack restitution case, the defendants were able to cast serious doubt on Erich Madsack's alleged difficulties with the party in his post as editor and publisher. They also noted that he joined the party in 1937 and that his personal income was larger in 1943 than in 1935. Nevertheless the court gave a verdict in favor of the Madsack heirs.[49]

An example of ruthless expropriation under severest pressure is afforded by the Vera acquisition of the controlling interest in the Schünemann Verlag, publisher of the *Bremer Nachrichten*. The Schünemann family had a long tradition of liberalism and through their paper had strongly combated National Socialism from 1930 to 1933. The brothers, Carl and Walther, who directed the enterprise, conformed to the Editor's Law and accepted the necessary changes in their editorial staff in 1933. However, they could not escape the suction pump of the Amann ordinances. To meet the new requirements they must reorganize the company, which required RPK approval. Moreover, the Paragraph 10 investigations were in progress. They were approached by Amann's representative in November 1935 with an offer to buy a controlling interest, but the brothers delayed and resisted to the point where they incurred expulsion from the RPK. In the official notification of expulsion (July 12, 1936), signed by Amann, it was stated in justification that: "The *Bremer Nachrichten* combated the NSDAP and the National Socialist movement in a most hateful manner up to the assumption of power. . . . The person of the Führer was ridiculed and treated with scorn. A further examination of the paper to 1935 has revealed that the *Bremer Nachrichten* has not met the requirements demanded of the press in the National Socialist state. . . . All the facts communicated to you lead to the conclusion

[49] Madsack heirs vs. B-W, Aug. 16, 1956, especially pp. 8-11, 14-15, 21-22, 23-30, 32-35. Dr. Paul Madsack and five members of the family and firm were also admitted to the RVDZV on Jan. 12, 1937. *Zeitungs-Verlag*, No. 3, Jan. 16, 1937.

that you do not fulfill the requirements and conditions established for publishers in the National Socialist state. It is therefore not possible to permit you to continue participation in the shaping of public opinion. Publication of the *Bremer Nachrichten* under your direction must therefore cease. The execution of this decision is postponed until July 31, 1936, to permit an appraisal of the printing and publishing plant. If my decision has not been executed within the period specified, I shall be forced to require its execution by the competent police authorities." In consequence of this order, Walther Schünemann withdrew from the business, turning his interests over to his brother, Carl. The latter, to save something for the family, effected a corporate reorganization and sold fifty-one per cent of the stock to the Vera company for 1,900,000 RM. The Schünemann affair was such a flagrant expropriation and so manifestly political that the family had no difficulty after the war in securing cancellation of the Vera contract and restitution of their property.[50]

Almost as brutal as the Schünemann case in Bremen was the expropriation of the *Hamburger Fremdenblatt* and the book publishing firm of Kurt Broschek and Company. The *Hamburger Fremdenblatt* was one of Germany's leading papers with outstanding financial, industrial, and maritime news services. Both politically and economically it reflected the broad outlook of the Hamburg business classes. It therefore had slight affinity for National Socialism. Following the customary cleansing of the editorial staff and coordination of the paper's political line in 1933, it continued publication under the direction of Kurt Broschek, son of the original founder. By his fellow publishers Kurt

[50] Circular No. 4, 1950, "Nur für die Mandanten," prepared by Dr. Bertold for clients in the publishing business. (Institut für Zeitungswissenschaft, Munich.) Also a detailed account published by the Schünemann brothers in the *Bremer Nachrichten*, March 2, 1950.

Broschek was rated well below his father in intelligence and ability. His father, too, apparently shared this view and prior to his death placed the direction of the paper in the hands of a commission. What motivated Kurt Broschek to commit the provocative act which resulted in his expulsion from the RPK and the loss of his business is still a matter of speculation. In violation of the Editor's Law, he forced the publication in his paper of a report of a chapter meeting of a Masonic lodge in Hamburg! In consequence of this rash act he was excluded from the publishing business and forced to sell seventy-six per cent of the stock of his company to the Vera concern. Thereafter, according to Fritz Schmidt, he operated a steam laundry in Berlin.[51] Acquisition of the *Hamburger Fremdenblatt* together with Girardet's mass circulation paper gave the Nazi party a near monopoly in newspaper publishing in Hamburg.

For prestige as well as political reasons the press in Munich had a special interest for Amann and the party leaders. Three newspapers enjoyed substantial circulations in the Bavarian capital—Huck's *Münchener Zeitung,* a popular paper of the Generalanzeiger type, the *Münchner Neueste Nachrichten,* published by the old firm of Knorr and Hirth, and the party's own *Völkischer Beobachter.* In dealing with the Huck syndicate, Amann desired to take over or close the *Münchener Zeitung,* but was dissuaded by Rienhardt from an act so crass and obvious. The *Münchner Neueste Nachrichten,* because of its ownership and political attitude, was a special case. Distinctly political, the paper had long followed a course hostile to National Socialism in Munich and Upper Bavaria. Its political line was best described as national-clerical-Bavarian. During the economic unsettlement after the First World War, the

---

[51] *Presse in Fesseln,* p. 58. Both Dr. Jänecke and Rolf Rienhardt commented on the Broschek case in interviews with the author. Winkler conducted the negotiations which were long and difficult but finally resulted in the transfer of Broschek's interests.

controlling interest in the publishing company had been acquired by Rhenish steel interests, the Gutehoffnungs-hüte, and the Vereinigte Stahlwerke. Franz Haniel, a Ruhr industrialist, represented the majority stockholders as chairman of the management board of Knorr and Hirth. Hitler thought he had the *Münchner Neueste Nachrichten* neutralized in the presidential campaign in 1932 through an agreement with Paul Reusch, general manager of the Gutehoffnungshütte. When the management board rec-ommended to the administrative and editorial staff that a more reserved position be taken, and sails trimmed to the new political winds, this pressure was successfully opposed. Although they resisted the management board, the policy makers on the paper were not politically united. Fritz Büchner, the chief editor, Dr. Anton Betz, the Verlag director, and Professor Paul Nikolaus Cossmann, the gen-eral manager, were clerically oriented, while Erwein von Aretin, the political editor, was a leading Bavarian mon-archist. Fritz Gerlich, former chief editor and a fanatical opponent of National Socialism, had withdrawn from the staff to publish his *Gerade Weg* which earned him persecu-tion and death at the hands of the Nazis. Despite extreme pressure from the principal owners, the anti-Nazi line was maintained until the seizure of the state government by the National Socialists in March 1933. Hess and Himmler inter-vened immediately causing the arrest of Betz, Von Aretin, Cossmann, and Büchner. Betz and Büchner were released, then rearrested; Von Aretin went eventually to Dachau, and Cossmann died in Theresienstadt in 1942.

In March 1933, clothed with authority by Hess and Himmler, Leo Hausleiter had been appointed trustee and Verlag director of the Knorr and Hirth firm. Prior to this appointment Hausleiter had held a minor position in the publishing house and rendered good service to the party leaders as an informant. Under his direction the staff and business office were purged of approximately fifty employees some of whom were arrested and held for interrogation by the Gestapo.[52] Amann, who had been forestalled in the action against the paper and its staff, developed a special animus toward Hausleiter, whom he charged with deceit, incompetence, and corruption. As long as Hausleiter enjoyed the support of Hess and Himmler, the director of the Eher Verlag could take no action. When Amann became president of the RPK and czar of the publishing industry he forced Hausleiter out of his post, which he alleged earned him the warm thanks of Franz Haniel. This was the only action for which Haniel might have thanked Max Amann, for in the end the party's objective—acquisition of the Knorr and Hirth company with its profitable publications—was achieved. According to Amann, Haniel was admitted to the RPK as the responsible publisher, but after some months offered to sell the concern because his interests and activities did not permit him to function as a publisher. In December 1935, the Eher Verlag made a direct purchase of the company's stock for three and a half million RM, which Amann boasted was paid in cash. He said nothing about the pressure that was put on Haniel by Göring to dispose of his publishing interests.[53]

Further recital of cases in which important provincial

[52] Among those arrested and dismissed was Werner Friedmann, the present editor of the *Süddeutsche Zeitung* in Munich.

[53] Petition filed by Amann with the appellate chamber of the denazification court in Munich, Nov. 2, 1951, pp. 7-8, Spruchkammer file, Max Amann. There is much documentation on the case of Knorr and Hirth and the *Münchner Neueste Nachrichten*. The action in 1933-1934 is described in detail in Erwein von Aretin, *Krone und Ketten*, pp. 49-50, 65-66, 70-72; and on the performance of Hausleiter, pp. 193-95, 258-59, 429-30. Also the events of 1933 were narrated in detail by the former Verlag director, Dr. Anton Betz, in a lecture sponsored by the Institut für Zeitungswissenschaft in Munich. (*Münchener Merkur*, Feb. 2, 1959.) Winkler testified in the Huck case to the pressure applied to Haniel by Göring. (Huck vs. B-W, p. 33.)

newspapers and publishing firms were despoiled would
serve no useful purpose. The pattern was well established
and many times repeated. Outwardly the ordinances were
applied uniformly but in fact they were used as an instrument to achieve objectives desired by the party authorities.
This comes to view not only in the positive actions but also
in the matter of exceptions, which were granted under the
special powers conferred upon the president of the RPK.
Such exemptions were granted where important economic
interests were involved or the publisher had a powerful
friend in the party hierarchy. Hugenberg was permitted
to retain his Scherl Verlag because Goebbels interceded for
him. The I. G. Farben concern was likewise granted an
exemption and for a time retained its control of the *Frankfurter Zeitung*. The Stinnes heirs continued to hold the
*Deutsche Allgemeine Zeitung* and, as has been noted,
Haniel was granted an exception and permitted for a time
to retain his newspaper interests.[54] In short, the ordinances
permitted all kinds of deviations and combinations, allow-
ing the press authorities to do with the publishers and their
properties whatever they decided would serve the interest
of the party and its program.

## Impact of the Amann Ordinances

How many publishers were excluded from the RPK, or
expropriated, under Paragraph 10 and the Amann ordinances? Unfortunately the loss of the records of the Cura
company and those of the central office of the RVDZV
makes it impossible to give a precise answer. Application
of the ordinances and issuance of the Paragraph 10 letters
were substantially accomplished by May 1936, although
some actions were still pending and some new cases were
developed. As noted previously, the lists of publishers who
finally received clearance certificates were removed from

[54] These exceptions are noted in Pielenz vs. B-W, p. 71.

the small surviving collection of Reichsverband records, possibly after they came into Allied custody. Rienhardt has stated that not more than a hundred publishers were denied political clearance and in his remarks at the Landesverband directors' conference, in November 1935, he referred to "two or three hundred papers" closed for economic reasons. If we take his highest figures we shall probably not be far from a reasonably accurate total. The standard *Sperling's Periodical and Newspaper Directory* for 1937 presents a significant statistical table showing the number of newspapers published in each German state and Prussian province in the years 1935 and 1937. These of course were the two years during which the German press was subjected to the Nazi "cleansing process." In 1935, excluding Memel and Danzig, but including the Saar, there were 2,629 newspapers published in Germany, not including sub-editions. In 1937, there were 2,208 papers published in the same area, making a loss of 421 papers over the two years. The figures are not complicated by new starts and failures as there had been a flat prohibition on founding newspapers since the autumn of 1933, except with Amann's permission, which we may assume was only granted where new party papers were launched. Some of the 421 papers that disappeared were probably voluntary closures or liquidations, but the overwhelming majority ceased publication as a result of the Amann ordinances. The geographical incidence of closings is significant. The losses were heaviest as would be expected, in the Catholic areas—Bavaria (79), Baden (55), Silesia (25), Rhineland (32), Westphalia (28), and Saar (10). Areas that had been notably liberal-democratic also suffered substantial losses. Württemberg, already subjected to the plundering operations of Otto Weiss, lost an additional twenty-five papers. The North German states and provinces were least affected, although about half the total loss of newspapers was registered in these more populous areas.

Another impression of the scope of the suspensions, mergers, and transfer of rights and titles, can be secured from the notices in the weekly organ of the publishers' association, *Zeitungs-Verlag*. With the publication of the ordinances many of the small publishers doubtful of their future were prepared to sell to a party competitor. There resulted a great flurry of acquisitions and mergers at the Gau level, recorded in *Zeitungs-Verlag* under the rubric "Among the Publishers." The Gauverlag Bayerische Ostmark acquired eight small dailies in the Upper Palatinate. Four more dailies were acquired by Gerhard Kuhn for his Gauverlag in the Saar-Palatinate; and there were further party acquisitions in Pomerania, Silesia, and Baden. By July 1937, the Gau Verlag in Pomerania had acquired and consolidated twenty local papers.[55]

Beginning in January 1936, as the compliance requirements specified in the ordinances took effect, the number of notices greatly increased. From January through June, two hundred closures, mergers, and transfers of titles were recorded. The largest number noted in one week was twenty-three. After June 1, the notices taper off to three or four per weekly issue. Many of these notices recorded mergers of two or more papers "by voluntary agreement," a substantial number reported suspension of publication, and a very large number reported acquisitions and mergers effected by the Gau publishing companies. The latter reveal much as to the concentration of the local press under party ownership or control. But what is missing in these notices is of even greater significance—the acquisition of large newspaper properties by the Eher subsidiaries, the Vera, and Phoenix companies. These were not recorded in the trade journal of the German publishing industry.[56]

[55] *Zeitungs-Verlag*, No. 28, July 10, 1937.
[56] Acquisitions by the Gau publishing companies continued in many districts until a clean sweep of the local press was achieved. The Gauverlag Bayreuth, between 1935 and 1941, acquired the

As the operation drew to a close, Amann and his associates were confident that their objectives had been achieved. In his party congress address in September 1936, Amann concluded his report as Reich Leader of the Press with the assertion that "The 2,300 newspapers that exist today are of more value to us than the former 3,250 newspapers which worshipped at other altars than those of the fatherland and in consequence had to be sacrificed to the fatherland." And in 1938, in the same vein, he declared: "We have freed the newspapers from all ties and personalities that hindered or might hinder the accomplishment of their National Socialist tasks." [57]

In conclusion it should be emphasized again that in the application of Paragraph 10 and the Amann ordinances there was no judicial determination of a publisher's reliability and suitability, only an administrative investigation through the regional office of the RVDZV, the Gestapo, and party agencies. Depending upon the result desired, the attitude of a paper in the past could be charged against the publisher or it could be disregarded. That applied also to the publisher's own political past. If a newspaper after the Nazi assumption of power conformed and placed itself upon "a basis of fact," then the publisher could be charged with lack of character. But if the political conversion was not accomplished with acrobatic speed, and the paper as-

---

publishing rights and titles of fifty-eight local papers in the Upper Palatinate and Lower Bavaria. The price ranged from 70,000 RM for the *Bamberger Tageblatt* to 100 RM for a small-town weekly. ("Verlagstitel des Gauverlags Bayreuth," File 3820/III, Pressesachen, BWB.) In Regensburg, the former minister president, Heinrich Held, who had permitted Hitler to reestablish the NSDAP in Bavaria in 1925, received the usual Nazi reward when he was excluded from the RPK and his paper suspended. (Facsimiles of suspension notices in H. Walter, *Zeitung als Aufgabe*, p. 157.)

[57] *Zeitungs-Verlag*, No. 38, Sept. 19, 1936; and No. 1, Jan. 8, 1938.

sumed a reserved attitude in order to distinguish itself in tone and content from the Nazi press, this could be cited as highly suspicious and sufficient ground for depriving the owner of his publishing rights. To support a charge of unreliability under Paragraph 10 it was sufficient to show that a publisher had not reported a charity concert sponsored by the SA, or a children's party arranged by the Kreis leaders. To exclude a publisher from the RPK on grounds of unreliability it was also sufficient to show that his newspaper on February 10, 1933, had stated that "Hitler's *Mein Kampf* was undoubtedly the worst book that had ever been published in the German language." [58]

Once the dossier of derogatory information against a publisher was completed, he was usually given an opportunity to respond to the charges either in person, or in writing, or through a legal representative. However, there was no judicial consideration of the facts or their significance. The power to close publishing companies on economic grounds was exercised in an equally arbitrary manner by the directors of the Cura and the Reichsverband. Here, too, the publisher was blocked from access to the courts for a judicial determination of his rights, just as he was denied compensation for his losses. The only suitable comment on the entire procedure would be that it was a disgrace anywhere the words "law and justice" are understood and respected.

## The Nazi Verlagspolitik—Motives and Objectives

The Nazi party raid upon the publishing industry in 1935-1936 was probably the largest confiscation of private property that occurred under the Third Reich. After 1945, the interpretation of the restitution and indemnity laws raised the issue of motives and objectives in numerous cases brought by publishers to recover property or to secure com-

[58] These cases are cited in Pielenz vs. B-W, pp. 52-53.

pensation. A deeper probing of the motivations of the Amann ordinances is therefore justified.

Amann's address at the party conference at Nürnberg, in September 1935, was devoted to an explanation and defense of the decrees, which he presented as a needed work of "cleansing and reform" in fulfillment of Point 23 of the party program. The specific goals he described as: 1) the exclusion from the publishing business of all non-Aryans and all selfish interest groups, whether they were economic, class, or confessional, and all servants and functionaries of such interests; 2) to eliminate the influence of anonymous capital exercised through trusteeships and juridical personalities, as well as the corruption of the press through subventions; 3) to promote the cultural-educational tasks of the press and to guard it against injury through trustification and exploitation by profit-hungry business interests; and 4) to enforce the principle of personal responsibility of the publisher for his newspaper. Amann recognized that German industrialists had sometimes invested capital in newspaper properties to keep them from falling into Marxist hands but this need no longer existed, he said, since the combating of Marxism had been made the highest obligation of state and party. While he paid special tribute to the party press he reaffirmed the policy of fostering a mixed press, in which private ownership and initiative had a legitimate and prominent place.[59] Such was the surface explanation and justification of the ordinances as presented to the public by the party leadership.

Another level of interpretation is presented in the publisher's restitution cases which have been before the German courts since 1945. Legal counsel for claimant publishers have striven to establish for their clients a position analogous to that of a persecuted group in the sense that

[59] *Zeitungs-Verlag*, No. 38, Sept. 12, 1935.

members of the Jewish community, Social Democrats, and Communists were so regarded and treated. The forced sale of properties and publishing rights to the Eher concern, they maintain, was equivalent to expropriation. They have also emphasized the political motives of the Nazi publishing policy and insist that their clients constitute a persecuted group.

Counsel for the defendant German states, who hold the confiscated property of the defunct Nazi party, counter with the argument that the decrees expressed a general policy of the dictatorial regime and were applied to private publishers without regard to political views. They emphasize that even prominent Nazis—Goebbels for example— were required to surrender their holdings in publishing companies. The publishers have not been able to establish in the courts their position as a persecuted group automatically entitled to recovery or indemnity. To recover, each claimant has been required to prove that the sale was equivalent to confiscation and that it was an act of persecution because he was a known opponent of, or suspected of being in opposition to, National Socialism. If a publisher under pressure sold his publishing rights to a party concern and received a contract to continue as printer of his paper, he cannot recover. This has created a large aggrieved group among the "old publishers." [60] However, the restitution chambers and the Court of Restitution Appeals have consistently held that "the Third Reich's coordination and consolidation of the bourgeois press into the Nazi sphere

[60] On this point a decision of the Court of Restitution Appeals, interpreting Military Government Law 59, has been followed by the subordinate state chambers: "The claimant in proving his claim for restitution must show that one or more of the confiscatory acts took place and such confiscation was caused by or constituted a measure of persecution for reasons of race, religion, nationality, ideology or political opposition to National Socialism." Case No. 70, Rolf Boes vs. legal successor of the NSDAP, Feb. 6, 1951.

was an exercise of political power by the dominant political party" and was not *per se* an act of persecution.

The economic motive underlying the Amann decrees is the major theme of the book by Dr. Fritz Schmidt, *Presse in Fesseln*, a work cited frequently in publishers' restitution cases. The theme of this book is the intention of the Nazi leaders to eliminate the private publishers as competitors of the Nazi press, and to build a giant party trust enjoying a monopoly of newspaper publishing in the Reich. In developing this thesis Schmidt highlights the larcenous instincts of Max Amann, the massive vanity of Max Winkler, and the ideological fanaticism of Rolf Rienhardt. While objective consideration of the evidence supports the view that financial-economic considerations played a role, it would be incorrect to emphasize these motives to the exclusion of all others. Amann's greed and ambition were important factors, but Hitler would never have permitted Amann to disturb so deeply the property relations of the publishing industry solely to enrich himself or the party. In the middle ages the church confiscated the property of a convicted heretic, but it would be incorrect to assume that the church convicted the person just to enrich itself with his property.

Another approach to the problem of motives and objectives of the Amann decrees is that of Dr. Martin Löffler, a leading legal authority on the press, who has probably heard more testimony and delved deeper into the facts and implications of the publishing policy of the Third Reich than any other expert.[61] In his opinion, Hitler was the author of the Nazi publishing policy and the motives were neither basically ideological nor financial, but essentially

[61] Löffler has served as chief or associate counsel in numerous publishers' restitution cases and is the author of the standard work on the law of copyright and publishing, *Presserecht—Kommentar* (Munich, 1955). The views set forth were expressed in an interview with the author in August 1958.

the acquisition of power. "How do I achieve my principal objective, which is the consolidation of my regime?" Hitler may have asked. The solution required the acquisition of absolute control over the media of mass communications —press, film, and radio. The radio was already in the hands of the state and the film industry was so organized in large units that it was easy for Goebbels and Winkler to nationalize it. With the newspaper press it was more difficult. There were approximately three thousand newspaper publishers in Germany, of whom not more than five or ten per cent were Nazis. Nothing prevented the suppression and confiscation of the SPD and KPD publishing enterprises in 1933, but it was not possible to proceed in the same manner against the middle class press. Economically and politically this solution was too radical. Goebbels presented his solution to Hitler and it was the first one adopted —the Editor's Law. They could control the content and opinion of the papers by controlling the editors and journalists who created the product. In this way the publishers, who were unreliable or at best neutral, would be short-circuited and deprived of policy control over their papers. Amann and Rienhardt objected to this emasculation of the publisher and the monotonous uniformity which Goebbels' ministry imposed upon the press. Both insisted that a reliable corps of publishers, positive in their attitude toward National Socialism, could be created. Amann's position was: Work with the publishers rather than the journalists and editors, who after all were only hired hands. By purging and transferring ownership a responsible body of publishers in the National Socialist sense could be created. Then the Editor's Law could be repealed and the authority of the publisher over his enterprise restored.

There is evidence to support this interpretation. Amann and Rienhardt fully shared the publishers' hostility toward the Editor's Law and repeal or modification of this meas-

ure became an *idée fixe* with Rienhardt, especially as he
saw the press in its editorial and news services becoming a
barrel organ grinding out propaganda ministry tunes. In
1937 he attempted to secure a basic change in the system
but without success. Hitler found the barrel organ press
a useful instrument.

The evidence on the ordinances as a means of consolidating Nazi power by purging unreliable or suspected publishers is extensive and incontrovertible. On this point no
one has testified more frankly and convincingly than
Werner Stephan, former chief of the press division in the
propaganda ministry. Stephan was general secretary of the
German Democratic party from 1922 to 1929, when he was
appointed to the press division of the Reich government
by Stresemann. When this office was transferred to Goebbels' domain, Stephan remained in his post without abdi-
cating his own political views. He used his influence whenever possible to mitigate the injustices of the Nazi press
policy. In a sworn statement, as an expert witness, he has
testified that in committee meetings and conferences Max
Amann always emphasized that "the press is an affair of
the NSDAP." "He liked to refer to the party program and
emphasized that every newspaper acquired by the NSDAP
strengthened the political and propaganda position of the
party. In this matter he was in complete agreement with
the Reich propaganda minister, Dr. Goebbels." Stephan
further relates that when he intervened on behalf of the
publisher Broschek, in the case of the *Hamburger Fremdenblatt*, Rienhardt said: "What do you want? Amann
will not allow these old liberal publishers to remain any
longer in possession of the big newspapers. If we were to
have a real serious crisis what would these old democrats
and clericals do? The Führer demands that these unreliable
recruits (unsicheren Kantonisten) be gradually eliminated
from the press. They can keep their printing plants. It is

not a question of business but a question of political power!"

Stephan further relates how he interceded for the publisher of the *Hartungsche Zeitung* in Königsberg, whose merger with its Nazi competitor had been ordered on the 200th anniversary of the founding of the paper. To the officials of the RPK Stephan explained that this would result in a loss of German prestige in the Baltic area. "Don't be so sentimental," he was told, "Reich Leader Amann is of the opinion that a paper with such a progressive (freisinnigen) tradition simply cannot be continued. Whether it is merged with the party paper just before or just after its anniversary makes no difference at all." When he intervened with the RPK in the case of the Schünemann family and the *Bremer Nachrichten*, on whose staff he received his journalistic training, he evoked an answer from Anders in the same vein: "This concerns a typical liberal publishing family which inspires no confidence. On political grounds a change of ownership is imperative." When Stephan emphasized the economic loss that would inevitably result, Anders replied in Amann's name: "Financially we can be entirely accommodating. This is not a question of money but a question of power." And from Goebbels and Amann, he received a similar reply in the cases of Huck and Girardet.

The same political motives prevailed, according to Stephan, in the sweeping drive against the Catholic press. These papers were expropriated because of their political significance, not for their modest profits. "Both Amann and Goebbels emphasized this repeatedly when the crass injustice of these arbitrary interventions was alluded to. Financially, the Amann concern was at that time already so powerful that such manipulations were quite unnecessary. The drive for continued expansion came from the determination, supported by Hitler, not to tolerate any longer politically neutral publishers, or publishers who stood in a position of estrangement from the NSDAP."

Stephan testified further that in justifying the elimination of middle class publishers both Amann and Goebbels cited the experience of the party before it came to power: "The advancement of the NSDAP in the time of struggle prior to 1933 was achieved in opposition to the press. Almost all middle class newspaper publishers placed every possible obstacle in the way of the party and remained completely indifferent and uncomprehending toward the ideas of the Führer. One cannot leave in the hands of such men an important propaganda instrument like a newspaper." [62]

The tenor and substance of Stephan's expert opinion points to ideology, power, and the totalitarian demands of the NSDAP as the forces at play in the drive against the independent publishers and their press. The corollary of this view is that economic and financial considerations played a minor role. Insofar as Hitler and the party high command were concerned, Stephan's judgment is unassailable. This does not hold entirely, however, with regard to the motives of Amann, the Gauleiters, and the Nazi Verlag directors who, because of their responsibilities for the party press, viewed the removal of competition as a desirable if not an imperative development. With regard to Amann especially it was quite evident that he joyfully pocketed the direct profits resulting from further trustification of the industry and the throttling of competition. In his case desire for gain merged completely with his National Socialist principles.

Rienhardt's motives were rooted in National Socialist

[62] "Beglaubigte Gutachten," March 28, 1949, Institut für Zeitungswissenschaft, Munich. In the Pielenz case Stephan testified that in the press division of the propaganda ministry, the Amann ordinances were regarded as a device to eliminate Catholic and liberal publishers from the industry. (Pielenz vs. B-W, p. 46.)

convictions, a strong reforming bent, and distrust of the middle class publishers. This stands out clearly in a statement made at a closed meeting of the officials and staff of the publishers' organization on July 16, 1936: "There can exist no doubt that by application of National Socialist standards to the German publishing firms a large part of the owners must be excluded from the press and their property transferred to other hands. This transfer of ownership results from the unreliability of the individual publisher, not from some imaginary but non-existent principle which would require the progressive transfer of the press to party or state ownership, a principle which would be in complete opposition to National Socialist views on private property. These assumptions lead to the question, *who* should be the new owners? As claimants, the party's own press has priority insofar as suitable properties are concerned. Where no party Verlag is involved and local competitive conditions favor a merger, then the strongest enterprise, if it is politically reliable, should have priority. And finally, holding companies must be available for the acquisition of those publishing firms which are not suitable party property, or which cannot be merged with another reliable publishing company. These holding companies are the Vera Verlagsanstalt and the Phoenix Zeitungsverlag. It is their task to educate the readers of these newspapers, insofar as they do not transfer their subscriptions to party papers, in the principles of National Socialism." [63] Always in justifying the drastic assault upon the private publishers, Rienhardt placed the main emphasis on the necessity for a politically reliable body of publishers. At the same time he defended private ownership and repudiated the demand for a party monopoly.

[63] Quoted in Ludwig Winter, *Neue wirtschaftliche Grundlagen des deutschen Zeitungswesens,* pp. 39-40. Winter had access to Rienhardt's prepared statements and addresses before the RVDZV and the regional associations.

Dr. Walther Jänecke, former publisher of the *Hannoverscher Kurier* and a leader in the pre-1933 publishers' association, judges the motives of the Nazi leaders to have been almost solely ideological and political. In his opinion, Amann made no distinction between financial gain and party objectives. Goebbels, on the contrary, regretted the loss of many middle class papers as a weakening and worsening of his propaganda machine. Disdainful of the party press, including the V-B, he did not conceal his views from his collaborators and praised the middle class press as superior in journalistic quality. But he was under party pressure and the prisoner of the ideology which he espoused. Jänecke thinks the same applied to Rienhardt, who was completely aware of the enormous damage which his sweeping action produced. But the realization of the ideological plans of the NSDAP and the achievement of the expressed aims of Adolf Hitler outweighed his objective doubts and scruples. Hitler, in Jänecke's opinion, was the originator and driving force behind the Verlagspolitik which eliminated the private publishers. When he stated publicly that he desired both a strong party press and a privately owned middle class press he was simply following the pattern of his other actions—alleging the contrary of what he in fact planned and desired. "The systematic assault against the press showed all the signs of a political campaign of destruction planned and directed at the highest level." [64]

In concluding this presentation of the views of participants and expert witnesses on the objectives of the Amann ordinances and the Paragraph 10 actions, certain conclusions appear justifiable or inescapable. First, the publishing policy which the ordinances expressed had Hitler's full endorsement even if he was not its immediate author.

[64] Walther Jänecke, Gutachten, May 13, 1949, Institut für Zeitungswissenschaft, Munich.

Second, the principal motive was to strengthen the power position of the party and to consolidate the hold of the dictatorship on the country. It was not sufficient that the editors and journalists be subject to the authority of the propaganda ministry, the publishers and owners also must be convinced National Socialists. Hence the drive to eliminate the "unreliable recruits" from the newspaper publishing field. A third consideration with the Nazi leaders was to make the press a completely reliable and subservient instrument in indoctrinating the German people with the principles—what they always called the Gedankengut—of National Socialism. Finally, the ordinances were designed to secure for the party-owned press that position of preeminence in their localities which the party rank and file, as well as the leadership, insisted was its due. Political considerations, the consolidation of party power, the elimination of uncertain elements from the publishing business, and the competitive position of the party press were interwoven strands in the Nazi publishing policy.

# VII. The Captive Publishing Industry, 1936-1939

## Newspaper Production and Circulation

After the major work of "cleansing" had been accomplished, Rienhardt and his staff associates visited the Landesverband conferences to assure the surviving members that the worst was over, that they were now in possession of their Paragraph 10 clearance, and on political grounds had nothing more to fear. During April and May 1936 Rienhardt visited most of the regional organizations and made the same speech at each stop. It was a long address, full of National Socialist "idealism" and clichés, justifying the Amann ordinances and their mode of application. He urged the publishers to renew their efforts in developing their papers as cooperating agencies in the national tasks which lay ahead under National Socialist leadership. He acknowledged that the past year, when new foundations for the publishing industry were being constructed, was a time of anxiety and uncertainty for all publishers and that positive developments and advances were not to be expected. Among the immediate tasks emphasized by Rienhardt were the regaining of public confidence in the press, the publication of papers that people would buy and read, and the restoration of economic health to an industry that had suffered from the depression, overcrowding, and political developments. Kurt Mix, business manager of the Reichsverband, addressing a district conference in Hanover, said: "If for the year 1935-1936 we use the headline 'Cleansing of the German Press', then for the year 1936-1937 we should use the headline 'Strengthening the Economic Position of the German Publishers'—those who now have the honor, in consequence of the Paragraph 10 action, of belonging to the German Press Chamber." He warned his hearers not to use their Paragraph 10 clearance in circulation advertising or to publish it in their newspapers! He denied two rumors that appeared to be circulating widely in publishing circles: One, that new ordinances of a more drastic nature were being prepared, and two, that all papers of less than 1,000 circulation were to be closed. These rumors he described as "foolish" and "mendacious." Turning to the business situation, he said they could look forward to improved conditions. Higher rates had been established for the advertising agencies and the anticipated limitation upon direct mail advertising, resulting from the increase in postage rates, should benefit the newspapers.[1]

Rienhardt in his remarks to the provincial trade conferences announced a massive national advertising campaign on behalf of the newspaper industry with a view to increasing sales and circulation. This would be a joint undertaking of the Reich propaganda ministry and the RPK for the benefit of all newspapers. While the launching of this campaign was not a measure of desperation, it expressed the concern of the Nazi press lords over the persistent decline in newspaper circulation. In each of the three years—1933, 1934, 1935—sales and circulation had declined by nearly one million annually. Among the positive beneficial actions of the regime had been the requirement of periodic reporting of exact circulation statistics. What these figures revealed was disturbing. The loss of over a million subscribers resulting from the suppression of the SPD and KPD press had never been recovered. Also unemployment and general economic depression had adverse effects upon newspaper sales and distribution. Moreover, forced consolidations and the closing of weak enterprises resulted in some permanent loss of newspaper readers. The usual experience with mergers showed there was always a substantial loss of subscribers when two papers were consoli-

[1] Conf. Rept., Lattmann file 2, May 18, 1936; BDC.

dated. Many people, when they could not get the paper they preferred, subscribed to no paper at all. While the weeding out of weak enterprises and the closing of many Catholic and liberal papers strengthened the financial position of the remaining publishers, it did not increase the volume of business or total newspaper distribution.

Highly relevant to this problem is an article by Gustav Kammann, "The Circulation of the German Press," in the trade organ, *Zeitungs-Verlag*.[2] He began with the assertion that the term "newspaper circulation" was nearly meaningless before January 1, 1934, when for the first time certified statistics were required of all publishers by the Reich Press Chamber. He challenged the estimated total daily figure— 26 million copies—given in the *Handbuch der deutschen Tagespresse* for 1932. The certified 1934 figures showed the total average daily circulation for the Reich to be 16.6 million, a startling difference. Some of the author's explanations of this disparity are plausible: the 1932 statistic was an estimate based on voluntary reports of only one fourth of the newspapers; there was a wasteful overprinting of free advertising copies; many journals classified as newspapers in 1932 were now classified correctly as periodicals; the "scandal press" had been eliminated; and the application of the Amann decrees adversely affected some segments of the press. However, the author could not deny that during 1934, and the first six months of 1935, "paid up subscriptions" had declined by 1.4 million. The statistics further showed that the average "total copies printed" during the first quarter of 1934, which amounted to 20,-253,374, had declined by the second quarter of 1935 to 18,692,880.[3]

[2] No. 1, Jan. 4, 1936.

[3] The author's tables give the quarterly averages over an eighteen month period for each Prussian province and German state. There was scarcely a province or Land that did not show a decline between January 1934 and July 1935.

For a regime dependent upon effective propaganda the decline in newspaper reading was disquieting since the party authorities understandably wanted an unfailing pipeline into every German household. The national campaign, launched in the autumn and winter of 1936, was designed to win old and new subscribers with a view to bringing the entire adult population under the influence of the controlled press. Before this could be done some elements in the party, which were still carrying on an active campaign against the non-party press, had to be called to order. This was done by Goebbels in a memorandum issued to all party agencies through the propaganda office of the party directorate. Because it has not been hitherto published this communication is quoted in full:

> "I am informed that recently in public meetings serious attacks have been made against the press and individual newspapers. These attacks are without factual foundation, for the speakers did not take the pains to investigate before making these serious charges.
>
> "After our seizure of power, the German press suffered a considerable loss of readers in consequence of necessary radical changes which were effected in this field. These people are not now reached by any newspaper and have therefore been quite inadequately influenced by the state and the party. Together with Reich Leader Amann, president of the RPK, I have initiated a great advertising campaign for the German press as a whole, which, while serving a political necessity, will also enlist from the circle of non-newspaper readers a large new mass of subscribers for the press. The success of this advertising campaign will be made null and void if at the same time party speakers through public attacks upon the press undermine people's confidence in this medium. The National Socialist

state will thus be renouncing a means of influencing people which it cannot afford to forego in this age of modern technology.

"When on the one hand I have banned all criticism *in the press,* then I must on the other hand expect that all criticism *of the press* be stopped. If legitimate complaints are made anywhere against one or more newspapers or periodicals, then those party members who have been entrusted with the direction of the press give every assurance that such justified complaints will result in energetic action and every ground for criticism removed. From this time henceforth, however, public criticism of the press is under no circumstances permissible." [4]

Goebbels' appeal pointed to a serious condition which the National Socialist revolution had produced in the country with regard to the press—a severe crisis in confidence and a general environment of criticism. The Nazi rank and file repudiated the bourgeois press; and those circles indifferent or hostile to National Socialism would not accept the Nazi papers.

All advertising media were employed throughout the Reich for the campaign that began in September and ran through the fall. Stereotyped material was provided without cost by the sponsoring agencies. The weekly illustrated press, which was doing well, was widely used for circulation advertisements, as were billboards, streetcar placards, and newspaper space. One amusing cartoon sequence was widely published—the Hase series. Under the caption, "Mein Name ist Hase und Ich weiss von nichts," the series was designed to shame uninformed people into reading newspapers. More direct were placards and slogans pro-

[4] Signed by Goebbels, Nov. 12, 1936, the directive was issued by Hess as Party AO, No. 143/36; Bezirksamt Neu-Ulm, File 17, "Presse, Rundfunk, Film," BDC.

claiming, "Who Reads Newspapers gets Ahead Faster!" and "Without Newspapers one Lives in the Moon." Toward the conclusion of the campaign, publishers were urged to support the national effort by aggressive local action to attract more subscribers and readers. To highlight the campaign, Goebbels and Amann proclaimed "German Press Day" to be held in Berlin on December 8-10. Here the trade and occupational groups represented in the Reich Press Chamber organized suitable exhibitions and conference programs, culminating in a mammoth rally in the Deutschlandhalle. Amann's proclamation announced: "For the first time in the history of the German press, all the German Volksgenossen who are occupationally engaged in the work of newspaper publishing will meet in one great conference, in order to demonstrate to the whole world that the unity of the German press has been achieved and is a reality." [5]

This intensive effort to restore the standing of the press resulted in some increase in newspaper production and circulation, but it made up only part of the losses of the preceding years. This conclusion is fully supported by publication of the production statistics for 1936, which was the occasion of an extensive analysis of production and circulation for the preceding three years.[6] Again the compiler and analyst insisted that comparison with 1932-1933 would be misleading and that they had reliable figures only since 1934. The detailed quarterly figures by province and

[5] *Zeitungs-Verlag*, No. 43, Oct. 24, 1936. The campaign was a central feature of this journal from Nos. 36 through 52, Sept. 5 to Dec. 29, 1936. Another highlight of the campaign was the production and release of a newspaper feature film ("Togger") from a script chosen by a panel of judges from among 2,500 submissions. Shown in fifty-two major cities, this piece of Nazi propaganda, which cast the publisher as the villain, could not have inspired much confidence in the German press.

[6] "Die Gesamtauflage der deutsche Zeitungen—Entwicklung der Jahre 1934, 1935, 1936." *Zeitungs-Verlag*, No. 25, June 19, 1937.

Gau, published in *Zeitungs-Verlag,* showed a considerable decline in production and circulation in 1935 as compared to 1934. There was a slight over-all recovery trend in 1936, but in many provinces production and circulation continued to decline. While the second half of 1936 showed a modest recovery, the paid-up subscriber column revealed continued weakness. This was in part balanced by the increase in single-copy street and newsstand sales. (The 1936 Olympic games in Berlin gave a big boost to street sales.) The daily average of newspapers produced in the fourth quarter of 1936 amounted to 18,775,000, barely 100,000 more than for the first quarter of 1934. Paid-up subscriptions, which totaled 13,748,554 in the first quarter of 1934, stood at 14,059,036 in the last quarter of 1936. Street and newsstand sales which amounted to 1,368,321 in 1934 had increased to 2,060,500 in the fourth quarter of 1936.

A year later, on February 20, 1938, Hitler made a boastful accounting to the Reichstag of the achievements of his regime. Comparing the years 1932 and 1937, he recited details of gains made in every branch of economic, social, and cultural endeavor from the building of bridges to the birth of babies. The only significant cultural activity unmentioned was newspaper production and circulation. The explanation is obvious—there was no increase to boast of between 1932 and 1937. Hitler cited only the statistics for increased production of illustrated weeklies, which suggests that people wanted to be entertained if they could not be informed.[7] Had Hitler given the comparative statistics on the newspaper press he would have revealed an embarrassing fact—that millions of Germans had given up reading newspapers because they were too dull, politically offen-

[7] Norman H. Baynes, *The Speeches of Adolf Hitler,* I, 950-70. Fritz Schmidt, using the *Ala-Zeitungskatalog* statistics, estimated the daily circulation decline at ten per cent between 1933 and 1939 in the area of the Reich, excluding the Saar, Austria, and Sudetenland. (*Presse in Fesseln,* p. 179.)

sive, or boringly uniform in content and opinion. This is the more significant when one recalls that by 1938 workers had jobs and could again afford to subscribe to a newspaper. Only with the outbreak of war did eagerness for news produce substantial increases in press sales and circulation.

## Problems of the Reorganized Press

By 1937 the revolution in the German press had reached a point of stabilization. At the expense of private publishers the economic position of the official party papers had been made secure; the remnants of Catholic and liberal papers had been liquidated or brought into one of the Eher holding companies; and the Generalanzeiger press—the "business press" so obnoxious to the Nazis—had been brought in large part under the control of Winkler's Vera concern. The Gau publishing companies and the Eher subsidiaries continued to make acquisitions after 1936, but the salient features of ownership remained fairly stable until the war produced further suspensions and consolidations. We may assume that the relative position of privately owned and party-owned journals was about what the leaders desired, or considered necessary for support of the regime.

To examine and describe in detail the structure of newspaper publishing in every Gau or Land of the Reich would extend the limits of this study beyond reason, and in many instances would not be possible of accomplishment on the basis of surviving sources. We do have a sharp picture of conditions in the state of Württemberg, whose press, owing to the aggressive activity of Dr. Otto Weiss, was more completely under Nazi dominance than the press in other sections of the country. Yet even here the features were typical rather than unique. In 1937 there were 92 publishing firms in Württemberg, which published 120 newspapers, excluding local editions. The N-S Kurier Verlag in Stuttgart published the *N-S Kurier* and the *Württem-*

*bergische Landeszeitung.* The Gau press concern—N-S Presse Württemberg—was sole owner of twenty papers in principal towns such as Ulm, Tübingen, Heilbronn, and Gmund. The Gau publishing company was also the majority stockholder in twenty-three additional papers in towns of the rank of Esslingen, Crailsheim, Göppingen, and Vaihingen. The Eher subsidiary, Phoenix, held the majority stock in seventeen papers, mainly in the Catholic section of southern Württemberg—Friedrichshafen, Ravensburg, Biberach, etc. The three leading newspapers in Stuttgart, previously owned by Robert Bosch and associates, were now wholly owned by the Vera company. Altogether fifty-five papers remained in the hands of private publishers but they were relatively small and unimportant. Their combined average circulation was 167,680, compared to the party press which had a circulation of 528,280. The relative position of the two segments of the press in Württemberg was 76 per cent party and 24 per cent independent. What is especially worthy of note is that the party press occupied a commanding position in all the principal cities and towns.[8]

While the Württemberg press was not wholly uniform with the rest of the country, an approximate pattern had been achieved throughout the Reich. This was revealed by Amann in his party congress speech in September 1937. Entitled, "The Result of the New Order" ("Das Ergebnis der Neuordnung"), and doubtless prepared by Rienhardt and his staff, it was a glowing account of the achievements of the party in the publishing field, a statistical statement of these achievements, and a spirited defense of the Nazi press system against foreign critics. With regard to the party posi-

---

[8] These statistics, provided by the former director of the Landesverband Württemberg, are cited by Biesenberger, *Der Schwarzwälder Bote,* pp. 39-42. Other areas where comparable party dominance was achieved by 1937 were: East Prussia, Pomerania, Rhineland-Palatinate, Silesia, and Bayreuth-Upper Palatinate.

tion in newspaper ownership, he stated there were 1,890 publishing companies in Germany producing 2,241 daily papers with 391 local and sub-editions. The National Socialist press comprised 122 publishing companies producing 231 daily papers with 378 local editions. This included the official party press and papers "administratively connected with the party." Of those with daily editions of 20,000 or more, the Nazi press held 70 per cent of circulation. Of the total Reich daily circulation, the party press and party-controlled press accounted for 54 per cent. The publishing industry gave employment to 72,000 workers and professional people, and of this number 34,000 were employed in party or party-related enterprises. In wages and salaries 99 million RM were paid out annually. Amann estimated that the circulation and effective impact of the party press had increased twentyfold since 1932.

Nothing concrete was revealed in Amann's address as to the methods employed to achieve this commanding position in the press, beyond citing Nationalist Socialist virtues and principles. He acclaimed the party publishers for their achievement in converting an opposition political press into a leading newspaper press. This, he said, was accomplished by avoiding the mistakes of previous party organizations in Germany. The Nazis had made individual performance the standard and touchstone in the development of every party publishing house. Leadership, individual responsibility, and performance had been required of everyone working in the party press. He could assert that not a single mark from state or party had been channeled to their publishing companies, and that today not a single party Verlag was operating at a loss. "The reconstruction of the German press was not a question of ownership, but decisively one of conviction and character. Neither in the Kampfzeit, or after, did the Führer propose to eliminate private property in the press—a principle which National Socialism views as an inherent element of civilization—

but always emphasized as a basic principle the service of the entire press to the nation."

Amann's address then spun out the standard theme that freedom of the press as normally understood was not true freedom of the press. True freedom existed in Germany where the press had the mission to support the leadership of Hitler and the Nazi party. "To be bound by the common good was not to be unfree." Amann then turned to the foreign critics of the Nazi publishing policy, citing and refuting many of the criticisms: that under National Socialism Germany had only one newspaper in a thousand editions and only one reader; that the Reich had been made a graveyard of newspapers; that he had eliminated private property, performed the hangman's act upon the press, and ruined the German publishing industry. In refuting these charges Amann alleged the flourishing condition of the newspaper industry, and cited statistics to show that newspaper production and circulation had increased by 1,750,000 between the summer of 1934 and the spring of 1937.[9]

While Amann's address revealed the main features of the reconstituted press in Germany, it ignored the serious current problems that concerned thinking people in the publishing industry. These deserve brief attention.

As the German economy was directed to the requirements of the rearmament program, measures to spare raw materials were instituted in various sectors of the productive economy. The party and private publishers were affected by an RPK order in March 1936 which prohibited overprinting of copies in excess of twelve per cent of paid up subscriptions, regular recipients, and single issue sales. If in any month a publisher exceeded the twelve per cent

[9] To show this increase Amann took the figures for the 1934 summer quarter, when sales and subscriptions are lowest for the year in Germany, and compared these with the spring quarter of 1937, when sales and circulation are seasonally higher. The address is given in full in *Zeitungs-Verlag*, No. 37, Sept. 11, 1937.

limit he was required to report the circumstances and the justification to the central office of the RVDZV in Berlin.[10] Institution of the Four Year Plan imposed further restrictions upon the consumption of newsprint, machinery, and printing supplies. In December 1936, a questionnaire was sent to all publishers requiring detailed accounting of past and present newsprint consumption. This was followed by stringent rationing instituted by Göring's order in July 1937. The Göring ordinance assigned to Amann, as head of the Reich Press Chamber, sole authority and responsibility for the rationing of newsprint and paper. This responsibility Amann delegated to Rolf Rienhardt, who established a Newsprint Allocation Office (Papierwirtschaftstelle) in the Reich Press Chamber to administer the program.[11] Later during the war, a rationing committee of the Reichsverband was added to the structure. Quite aside from the considerable economic significance of the rationing ordinances, these measures placed another powerful weapon in the hands of Amann and Rienhardt. In reduced advertising space, special supplements, and entertainment sections, the German press soon showed the effects of these measures.

Recruitment of journalistic and publishing personnel was another problem that concerned both private and party publishers. Scarely a month passed that some aspect of this question was not treated or referred to in the trade journal of the RVDZV. From these discussions it is evident that the flow of able young people into journalism was drying up, and that the profession was not attracting the

[10] *Zeitungs-Verlag*, No. 10, March 7, 1936. Over-printing usually signified an excessive number of free copies for circulation advertising.

[11] *Zeitungs-Verlag*, Nos. 3, 27, 29; Jan. 16, July 3 and 17, 1937. Fritz Schmidt, author of *Presse in Fesseln*, was placed in charge of this new office by Rienhardt. (*Ibid.*, No. 1, Jan. 1, 1939.)

considerable number of trained persons from other fields which had formerly supplied the press with writers, editors, and reporters. The average annual class of university students which completed journalistic training was about 300. This number had not changed appreciably since 1932 and was quite insufficient to meet the replacement needs of the profession. The business side of publishing and advertising was also less attractive and rewarding to young people. In discussing the problems of professional recruitment, those in authority never came to grips with the basic cause —the Nazi system of restraints which made the profession unattractive to talented, original, and sincere young people. There was no place in the system for critical and creative minds.[12] Even in the non-political sections of the newspapers severe restrictions had been imposed. For example, at Hitler's instigation art editors were forbidden to write "art criticism," but had to write "art appreciation." The pressures upon editors, writers, and publishers were intolerable.

Another notable feature of the Nazi press was dullness and uniformity. Hitler's vaunted "orchestra of the press" produced a very low order of music. After the "cleansing" and reconstitution of the publishing industry, the directing authorities in the Reich Press Chamber and the RVDZV sought to stimulate publishers and editors to produce more original and interesting newspapers. A study of 650 papers over a week's period was made in the central office to determine the extent of uniformity in handling the news of the week's principal events. That conditions were found to be highly unsatisfactory can be assumed from the recurrent appeal to the editors and publishers to show more original-

[12] Two frank articles on the subject are by Dr. Wendelin Hecht: "Heranbildung eines tüchtigen Nachwuchs"; and "Wie steht es mit den Nachwuchs?" *Zeitungs-Verlag*, No. 27, July 4, 1936, and No. 42, Oct. 15, 1938.

ity, creativeness, and brightness in presenting their material to the readers.[13]

"Goodbye to Uniformity" became a major theme in Rienhardt's addresses to the Landesverband members as he toured the Reich. Uniformity in will and direction in the political life of the country did not impose upon the press an obligation to uniformity in make-up, content, and commentary, and he quoted Goebbels and Amann in favor of more originality, initiative, and creative imagination in presenting and clarifying the news of the day. The authority of Hitler was likewise invoked: "It is not at all my desire that the press simply print what is handed out to it; it is no great pleasure to read fifteen newspapers all having nearly the same textual content." [14] At Cologne a year later, Rienhardt developed the same theme with variations—"Nicht Moniteurpresse, sondern Volkspresse," he urged, as he paraded all the stock phrases of the new order—"comradely cooperation," "creative freedom," "confidence in the state, the party and the circle of readers." [15]

But it was a cave of the winds. The system did not permit of originality, creativeness, or brightness. That the publishers and editors were cautious, uncertain, and anxious is understandable; and this was reflected in their product. Better a bulletin board for the local Gauleiter and the propaganda ministry than to get into trouble. One alternative was to deal in irrelevancies, and this many of them did, bringing harmless but tasteless articles on "A Wedding Night in the Snow," or "Twenty Times Divorced," or a boring article on Bolivia gotten up from an encyclopedia.

[13] *Zeitungs-Verlag*, No. 16, April 18, 1936.

[14] Cited by Rienhardt, "Vertrauen, Eigenarbeit, Entfaltungs-freiheit," *Zeitungs-Verlag*, No. 41, Oct. 9, 1937. The same issue, however, carried a notice of expulsion of two publishers from the RVDZV for infraction of regulations.

[15] *Zeitungs-Verlag*, No. 13, Jan. 15, 1938.

The German press had become a barren desert of conformity.

Another problem of the reconstructed German press, one that affected both party and private papers, was the enormous expansion of press bureaus and public relations offices sponsored by the state and party. Being official, or officially sponsored, they brought tremendous pressure at all times upon the editorial and publishing staffs of the daily press. This pressure and interference extended from the local level, where Kreisleiter, Gauleiter, and party organizations demanded maximum coverage for their meetings and pronouncements, to the highest level in the propaganda ministry where the authorities dictated the content and commentary of the main news releases of the day.

A brief description of the parallel and overlapping publicity agencies suggests that the complaints of editors and publishers were wholly justified. After the old Reich press office of the central government was transferred to the propaganda ministry, it was greatly expanded in its new location. The ministry itself established a subordinate office in each Gau headquarters. The Reich press office of the Nazi party—Otto Dietrich's apparatus—maintained a parallel organization with a press officer in each Gau and Kreis. Every Reich Leader also had a press office or at least a press officer—Göring, Hess, Ley, Himmler, Hierl, etc. And for the financial and organizational management of the party press Amann had established his administrative office in Berlin with Rienhardt in charge. Most of the Reich ministries, if they did not have a press bureau with regional apparatus, hastened to establish one or greatly expanded the organization they already possessed. It was doubtless inevitable in a system that emphasized propaganda that these press bureaus and agencies should have shot up like mushrooms after a rain. The result was the flooding of editorial offices with announcements, articles, and handouts accompanied by demands that they be published in the most prominent portions of the paper. Had all this been printed there would have been no room for independent work by writers and editors. Demands for publication by party and state public relations officers infringed upon the basic right of the editor to determine what was to be included and what excluded from his paper. Also strongly evident was the tendency on the part of these press officers to interfere directly with the functions, personnel, and management of the papers. Recalling that the daily editorial conference in the propaganda ministry fixed the main content and policy line for the entire press, and that observance of directives was mandatory under the Editor's Law, the terrific pressure upon editor and publisher is clearly apparent. These demands upon the press by state and party were frequently discussed in Landesverband and Reichsverband conferences and protests were aired in *Zeitungs-Verlag*. Even the pliant Wilhelm Weiss, chief of the *Völkischer Beobachter* and head of the Reich journalists' association, publicly criticized the demands and pressures from the multitude of press offices in a speech at a journalists' conference in Dessau, in 1937.[16]

Neither complaints from the industry nor mild objections from persons in positions of leadership produced any notable change or relaxation. Under the Nazi press system—indeed under any totalitarian regime—the press was restricted to a reportorial function and the editors and publishers were excluded from any part in shaping independently and creatively the public opinion of the country on important questions. Even at the local level this field was largely preempted by the party and its representatives. The

[16] Weiss, Spruchkammer file 2, "Stellung zur N-S Pressepolitik." In the same address Weiss denounced Julius Streicher for his brutal threats against journalists in Nürnberg. Otto Dietrich demanded Weiss' dismissal but Amann, who viewed this as a prestige issue, supported Weiss.

system required the journalists to write what the Nazi leaders wanted them to, and this was called "freedom of the press."

## Inside the *Völkischer Beobachter*

What were the conditions of work and employment in one of the Eher trust papers? How did editors react to the strict regimentation imposed upon the professional personnel? Partial answers are afforded by a descriptive statement submitted by one of the editors of the *Völkischer Beobachter* in the denazification case of Wilhelm Weiss. While the deposition was designed to place Weiss in a favorable light as regards his professional activity, it also opens a window on conditions in the party papers, Amann's principles of management and direction, and the degradation of the editorial functions under Nazi press policies. As managing editor of the Berlin edition of the V-B, Joachim Schieferdecker found his superior, Wilhelm Weiss, to be mild, reasonable, and professional in dealing with the staff, which he insisted was not a group of party fanatics but a corps of competent journalists, trustworthy National Socialists who were chafing constantly under the restrictions of the system and the management principles of the Eher Verlag. Far from being a cooperating force in the Nazi system, the V-B was even more rigorously observant of the official regulations and directives than the non-party press. Nor did it have the relations to party and government leaders that some of its competitors enjoyed. It had the name but scarcely the function of "Central Organ of the NSDAP." In Berlin, on the contrary, the *Nachtausgabe* was close to the Berlin Gauleitung, the *Deutsche Allgemeine Zeitung* was favored by the foreign office, the *Börsen-Zeitung* by the Wehrmacht, and in the propaganda ministry Dr. Kriegk of the Scherl Verlag was treated as Berlin's leading journalist. The staff of the V-B enjoyed none of these special and rewarding relations.

As the official organ of the party, the staff was required to observe the multitude of regulations and directives with the greatest care. The sorry lot of the editor is described by Schieferdecker:

"Twice daily the so-called press conference was held in the propaganda ministry at which the "Tagesparole" of the Reich Press Chief was released with endless commentaries. Taken down stenographically and placed on our desks for guidance, the material amounted daily to ten or twelve closely typed pages, containing many prohibitions and few permissions. It prescribed the treatment of the specified themes with regard to space, tone, headlines and placement down to the last detail. If it were a recurring theme the directive might be valid for a month during which time it had to be carefully observed. The initiative of the editorial staff was mainly exercised, at least occasionally, in attempting to evade the prescriptions. During the war, when the V-B described Roosevelt as a 'gangster', 'criminal', or 'madman', and Churchill as a 'drunkard' or 'idiot', these expressions did not come from the vocabularies of the editors but were officially prescribed; and if repelled by these rude characterizations we dared to use other expressions, we were reprimanded or warned. From 1933 onward editors became more and more simply rubber stamps for officially stated views, placing their mark on the daily copy to indicate that they had worked the material, and nothing more. The DNB reports, almost fifty per cent of which the press was required to publish in their exact wording, served as directives to be strictly followed by the editors. As independent journalism the work of professional editors from 1933 to 1945 did not deserve even the name, because the essentials of access to unbiased information, the open door to sources, and the necessary respect of official and private persons for the profession of journalism simply did not exist.

"During the war these conditions steadily worsened. The military censorship kept the press on even shorter leading strings, and one had to be constantly on guard lest one touch on some fancied military secret or violate some similar regulation. It is no joke, for example, that the word 'Russian' was prohibited and had to be replaced by 'Bolshevik', so that the censor made out of a 'Russian winter' a 'Bolshevik winter'. To the editor was left hardly more freedom of action than to lend his good name to this anonymous official nonsense, and by every unguarded word he might use he ran the risk of being called sharply to account." [17]

Of working conditions in the Eher Verlag papers, the witness had nothing favorable to report. Amann's publishing principles prevailed one hundred per cent. Rosenberg held the title of publisher after 1933 but devoted little time to the affairs of the paper, although he continued to receive reports from Weiss on internal organization, personnel matters, and general policy. The chronic friction and antipathy between Rosenberg and Amann seems to have abated somewhat as Weiss assumed the duties of chief editor and supervisor of the editorial staff. The latter's authority in this sphere included the *Beobachter* staffs in Munich and Vienna as well as in Berlin. The business affairs of Germany's "leading paper" were, as they had always been, under Amann's firm control exercised through his Verlag director, Wilhelm Baur. The news and editorial staff was still regarded as an unproductive nuisance, while economic and financial objectives overrode all other considerations. Although the party line denounced the "busi-

---

[17] Sworn statement by Joachim Schieferdecker, managing editor of the Berlin V-B, July 28, 1948; Wilhelm Weiss, Spruchkammer file.

ness press" no publisher ever pursued financial ends so assiduously in his own enterprises as Max Amann.

Schieferdecker's testimony on working conditions in the Berlin office of the V-B is also worth quoting at length:

> "The general contempt for the journalist gang (*Journaille*) was especially noticeable in the offices of the Zentralverlag of the NSDAP. The manager-publishers were at best simply business men, strangers in the intellectual world of the editorial staff, which they basically mistrusted. When I joined the V-B, the manager remarked to me that editors brought in no money, drank heavily, chased women, and accumulated debts! After a trial period of employment, my salary was set at 100 RM below what had been promised. This was characteristic of the Verlag. No newspaper of the size and prominence of the V-B was ever produced with such meager expenditure; of the reported wealth of the Zentralverlag we never saw any evidence. Of all the newspapers in Berlin we occupied the meanest quarters, where the central stairway was so dark and narrow that two people could barely meet and pass, and the offices so poorly and sparsely furnished that visitors could scarcely get used to it. Only the central reception room of the chief editor could be called an exception. The technical printing plant available to us was inferior and inadequate, which made our work more exhausting and affected even the appearance of the paper. Sixteen linotype machines, pounding away 24 hours a day without a break, had to produce not only two editions of the V-B but also *Der Angriff, Das Schwarze Korps, Der Arbeitsmann,* and the *NSKK-Mann.* We only had a decent printing plant in Berlin for a short time, when, after a heavy bombing raid, we were temporarily housed in the Ullstein build-

ing, where we also occupied adequate offices and work-rooms.

"Likewise in the matter of personnel we worked with inadequate resources and heard with astonishment and envy about the large editorial staffs of other news-papers. Also the number of reporters and correspond-ents outside the central office, and especially abroad, was kept scandalously small. Service trips at the ex-pense of the Verlag, which were generously granted by other papers with a view to informing and developing the staff, we experienced only occasionally and then on the tightest of schedules with meager expense allow-ances. The entire editorial staff of the V-B in Berlin never had but one automobile available for its service trips. These examples of penury under which we had to work by no means exhaust the list." [18]

Conditions of work and salary on the V-B, the leading party organ, were undoubtedly common to other papers under Eher control. As director of the Verlag and boss of all party papers, Amann issued directives to the Verlag directors on matters of business, administration, and finance. Typical was his circular order (Rundschreiben No. 42) of March 4, 1935, which forbade editors and staff members to attend meetings or to travel without the permission of the Verlag director. Although Hitler and Amann boasted that the V-B was the first German paper to reach a million circulation, this was not achieved through its qualities and service as a leading newspaper. Weiss and Dr. Walter Schmitt, the foreign editor, sought to develop the staff of foreign correspondents but their efforts and proposals were of no avail with Amann. The issue reached the proportions of a civil war between the editorial staff and the Eher Verlag. The system of part-time

[18] Schieferdecker, sworn statement.

correspondents abroad, who received a small monthly stipend with additional pay for work submitted and published, was maintained. The monthly stipends were unbelievably meager—Sofia 350 RM, Tientsin 300 RM, Madrid 250 RM, Brussels 150 RM. The total budget for foreign representation in 1934-1935 amounted to only 12,650 RM. In Stockholm the German Auslandsgruppe made the V-B correspondent a present of a telephone connection! And the embassy protested to the foreign office, calling it "shameful" that the V-B did not pay a decent wage and provide its representative with an adequate office and services.[19]

Amann boasted at the party congress in 1937 that not a single party Verlag was operating in the red. This was probably correct. But the low quality of newspapers produced was owing, in no small degree, to the cheese-paring and restrictive budgetary policies enforced by the head of the Eher Verlag.

## Rienhardt's Campaign Against the Editor's Law

Many of the difficulties and shortcomings of the reconstructed press were attributed by Rienhardt to the Editor's Law—the abandonment of the profession by qualified journalists, the difficulties of recruiting talented people, the monotony and uniformity of the papers, and the public indifference and distrust of the press in the Third Reich. The replacement or revision of the Editor's Law became for Rienhardt almost an obsession. In his conception of newspaper publishing, the intellectual, technical, and economic functions formed an inseparable whole. The dichotomy of editor and publisher, established by the Editor's Law, produced all the difficulties and weaknesses from which the system suffered. He therefore sought to release

[19] National Archives, Micro-copy T-454, R-55. This microfilm roll contains many letters and reports from Rosenberg's papers dealing with the internal affairs of the V-B.

the pressure of the Editor's Law upon the journalists, relax the centralized direction, and restore to the publisher the authority he formerly enjoyed over the content and policy of his paper and over the editorial employees who produced it. After 1936, with a substantial part of the press owned by the party and the private publishers purged of lukewarm and anti-party elements, he thought the road was clear for a major move against the Editor's Law. While he defended the centralized press policy in public, in his professional view it was a hangman's noose for the German press. Rienhardt was not without support in his drive for revision of the Editor's Law. Wilhelm Weiss, head of the journalists' association, shared his views, as did Walther Funk, state secretary in the propaganda ministry, and himself an experienced journalist and editor. Winkler, who managed the mass circulation papers under the control of the Vera company, likewise shared Rienhardt's concern over the long-range effects of the law. Amann was influenced by Rienhardt's powerful mind and still smarted over the defeat suffered when the Editor's Law was promulgated by the cabinet over his objection. He would understandably approve any measure to restore the authority of his Verlag directors over the editorial and reportorial staffs. In the Zentralverlag he paid precious little attention to the paragraphs of the Editor's Law. He was firmly committed to the leadership principle in the publishing business, which in his primitive view meant that the paymaster should be the boss.

Goebbels' position was somewhat dichotomic. As the sponsor of the original law and master of the propaganda machine he could scarcely repudiate his handiwork. But he was intelligent enough to appreciate the consequences for the profession and was aware of the poor quality of the work produced by the regimented press. On one occasion he confided to his aide, Rudolf Semmler, that he "would find it intolerable, and for any person with intellectual

powers undignified, to attend daily at the official press conference to have ten commandments, all beginning with
'Thou shalt not', handed out by Hans Fritzsche." Goebbels
went on to say "that the work of the daily journalist had
become quite unsatisfying. He had to find his way through
a mass of instructions, bans, and political considerations,
and the results were boring, flat phrases. Real journalistic
talent could not be stimulated by the daily round." [20] However, Goebbels never gave his support to revision of the
Editor's Law.

Rienhardt was most active in his efforts to modify the
system in 1936 and 1937. Also opposed to revision were the
legal division of the propaganda ministry and the Reich
press chief, Otto Dietrich. Whether Rienhardt bombarded
the propaganda ministry with memoranda, as Fritz Schmidt
alleges, cannot be confirmed, but of his activity in this
direction there is much evidence.[21] The issue appeared to
be moving toward a stage of decision after the party congress of 1937. On December 2, Rienhardt wrote to Amann:
"I am enclosing for you the draft of a letter to Dr. Goebbels, together with a draft memorandum. In December
1936, the Führer remarked to State Secretary Funk that
he had the impression the press was being too tightly controlled. Moreover, as a result of frequent discussions among
State Secretary Funk, Dr. Winkler, and myself of the
problems set forth in the attached memorandum the State
Secretary has expressed the view that these matters, which
are the most acute and basic for the future development of
the press, should be clearly set forth in detail and made the
subject, on an appropriate occasion, of a thorough discussion with the Führer. Unfortunately it was not possible for
me to prepare the statement at an earlier time. . . . Both
Captain Weiss and Dr. Winkler have read the draft and

[20] Rudolf Semmler, *Goebbels—The Man Next to Hitler*, p. 22.
[21] *Presse in Fesseln*, p. 35. Schmidt presents the issue as a power
struggle between Amann and Dietrich.

are in agreement with its substance. Weiss especially emphasizes that the clarification of these questions is absolutely vital for our publishers and editors since the very best men—even in the Eher Verlag—are doubtful about being able to fulfill their professional tasks and, in consequence, are strongly inclined to leave the profession. I would have gladly presented the draft memorandum to you in person but I am not yet permitted to travel. In view of the impending change in assignments in the propaganda ministry I dare not hold the memorandum until my next conference with you; for it is important to act in this matter while State Secretary Funk, who has the greatest understanding of these questions, is still in his old position and will concern himself with the problem."

The draft letter opened with reference to Goebbels' discussion of the problems of the press at a recent informal meeting of N-S publishers and editors in Nürnberg, and went on to propose that he and Amann initiate a discussion of the problems that affected both their spheres of responsibility. These problems were set forth in the enclosed memorandum but he would emphasize as the most critical the drying up of the sources of qualified personnel to staff the newspapers. The profession appeared to have lost its attractive force; and this was his foremost concern as a publisher. "Therefore I regard as the most urgent matter the reawakening of confidence in the professional value of journalism, the satisfaction that results from professional performance, and respect for the profession. I am sure you will appreciate why this and other problems set forth in the memorandum are of the deepest concern to all publishers and why I hope you will let me have your reactions to the questions raised and your suggestions for further procedure."

Whether the basic discussion of press controls with Hitler was ever held, or whether the memorandum became lost in the labyrinth of bureaucracy, cannot be determined. Rienhardt states that concrete proposals were placed before Hitler and rejected. At the Goebbels-Amann level the only concrete action was a proposal that the three persons most directly concerned—Goebbels, Amann, and Dietrich, together with their staff advisers—meet periodically to coordinate their overlapping responsibilities toward the press. Goebbels signified his willingness but Dietrich sabotaged the plan by simply ignoring the invitation and not appearing.[22] At the end of the year Funk moved from the propaganda ministry to the post of minister of economics, and Dietrich acquired his titles of Press Chief of the Reich Government and State Secretary in the Propaganda Ministry. With the beginning of the Austrian crisis in March 1938, the attention of Hitler and his associates shifted from internal to external affairs. In fact, the only change made in the Editor's Law had the effect of tightening rather than relaxing political control of editors and journalists. In an ordinance issued on Goebbels' authority, paragraph 21 of the Editor's Law was altered in a manner that gave the Gauleiter a specific right of concurrence in certifying the political reliability of applicants for admission to the professional journalists' list in his district.[23] The Editor's Law and centralized control of press and propaganda remained intact until the end of the regime.

[22] The draft letters, but unfortunately not the memorandum, are in the Spruchkammer file of Wilhelm Weiss; Rienhardt's statement was made to the author, and Fritz Schmidt gives a highly colored account in *Presse in Fesseln*, pp. 28-39. Rienhardt proposed to scrap the Editor's Law and return to the old press law of 1874, which was in force during the Reich and Weimar periods. In the statutes of the Reich, the Editor's Law repealed and replaced paragraphs 7 and 8 of the "Reichsgesetz über die Presse" of May 7, 1874.

[23] Previously the law required only a police investigation and clearance certificate. The amendment is published in *Zeitungs-Verlag*, No. 24, June 1, 1938.

## Expansion and Further Acquisitions

Between 1936 and the outbreak of war the Nazi press system and the empire of the Eher Verlag were further expanded. This resulted from two lines of action: the territorial expansion of Hitler's Reich and the purchase by Amann of additional privately owned newspapers.

A witty Viennese journalist asserted that when Hitler's tanks arrived in Vienna in March 1938, amidst a shower of flowers, they were closely followed by a detachment of Amann's press people—well in advance of the infantry—who had come to recast the Austrian press in the image of the Nazi Reich. While this is doubtless apocryphal, Amann and Adolf Müller did fly to Vienna forthwith to establish the Vienna edition of the *Völkischer Beobachter,* and Amann played a key role in the purging and coordination of the Viennese publishing industry. His first concern was to extend the influence of the V-B to Austria. For this he was fully prepared, having acquired with the Ullstein properties, in 1934, the Waldheim-Eberle publishing firm. In less than a week the Vienna edition V-B, printed by Müller in the Waldheim-Eberle plant, was on the newsstands. Subsequently the Vienna company was sold to the Adolf Müller firm.[24] This was scarcely more than a transfer of titles since Amann and the Eher Verlag held two-thirds of the shares of the Müller publishing company.

The coordination of the Austrian press and the extension of the press laws and ordinances of the Reich to Land Austria were accomplished swiftly and efficiently. Anti-Nazi papers in Vienna were seized by local SA and SS squads and forcibly coordinated. The *Telegraph am Mittag,* for example, appeared immediately as the *N-S Telegraph;* state commissioners were placed in charge of a number of

[24] Amann, Spruchkammer file, Berufungs-Register, No. 166/49.

papers; and many editors and publishers voluntarily coordinated themselves with the new regime. Papers that
stood for an independent Austria on March 10-11 enthusiastically endorsed Hitler's solution on March 13-14! [25]
Within a month the official Austrian news agency was
merged with DNB and the entire apparatus of the Reich
Chamber of Culture, the Reich Press Chamber, and the
Amann ordinances were established by decree in Austria.
Soon the Austrian publishers' association was merged with
the RVDZV.[26] The Editor's Law and the professional
journalists' list were not applied immediately, owing no
doubt to the high percentage of Jewish persons engaged
in journalism whose immediate replacement was not feasi-
ble. With the establishment of the party organization in
Austria, each of the seven Gaue was provided with a Gau
Verlag which published one or more official party papers
for its district.[27] Max Winkler, too, it appears, became
active in Vienna with the application of the Amann ordinances and acquired for the Vera company some of the
leading Vienna papers. These were controlled through two

[25] "Ausbruch der Presse im deutschen Österreich—Freiheit zum
Bekenntnis"; an eye-witness account in *Zeitungs-Verlag*, No. 13,
March 26, 1938. Helmut Sündermann, Otto Dietrich's deputy, was
also active in the coordination of the Austrian press and has given
an account of his experiences in *Die Grenzen fallen* (Munich,
1939).

[26] The implementing decrees were published in *Zeitungs-Verlag*,
Nos. 19, 26, 27, 51; May 7, June 25, July 2, Dec. 17, 1938. At the
party congress in September, Amann devoted a part of his report
to the take-over in Austria. His main point was that they had
purged the journalists' corps of all Jewish elements and the party
had taken over Jewish owned newspapers. Austria now had a National Socialist press and people were happy! (*Ibid.*, No. 37, Sept.
10, 1938.)

[27] The Gaue were: 1) Vienna; 2) Nieder-Donau; 3) Ober-
Donau; 4) Steiermark; 5) Kärnten; 6) Salzburg; 7) Tirol-Voral-
berg.

publishing firms whose majority stock was held by the party trust.[28]

With the annexation of the Sudetenland in October 1938 and the creation of the protectorate over Bohemia-Moravia in March 1939, the Nazi publishing system was extended to these areas. On October 1, 1938, Amann issued an RPK order prohibiting for the time being the exportation of Reich newspapers to the Sudetenland beyond the number normally sold in that area before October 1. Likewise, sales, subscription canvassing, and advertising solicitation by Reich publishers were prohibited. By the end of October an official party newspaper, financed and controlled by the Standarte company, was established in Reichenberg and the Reich Press Chamber statutes and ordinances were extended to the area of the Sudetenland.[29] The same pattern of action developed in the autumn of 1939 with the annexation of Polish Upper Silesia, West Prussia, and Posen.

Besides the territorial expansion of the Nazi party's newspaper empire through Hitler's conquests, further acquisitions by purchase were made in the area of the Reich. The ownership structure of the German press might have stabilized at the 1936-1937 point—two thirds party, one third private—had it not been for two factors that produced further consolidation and trustification. One was the greed of Max Amann; the other was the impact of war. For Amann, what remained of the private publishing business was like a pot of gold into which he constantly dipped for another handful. With the enormous competitive power and resources of the Eher Verlag at his disposal, Amann con-

[28] The Druck und Verlagsanstalt "Vorwärts" KG, and the Österreichischer Druck und Verlag GmbH. (Eher participation chart, July 1, 1944.) Fritz Schmidt lists eleven papers in Vienna acquired by the party but I have been unable to verify the listing. *Presse in Fesseln*, pp. 72-73.

[29] *Zeitungs-Verlag*, Nos. 41, 43, 44, 45; Oct. 8, 22, 29, and Nov. 5, 1938.

tinued to buy up publishing enterprises at bargain prices. A number of these acquisitions were well-established, highly regarded papers which had strong support in industry and finance but had not been sucked into the trust under the Amann ordinances. Among the prominent papers in this group, which now passed to Eher control, may be mentioned the *Deutsche Allgemeine Zeitung*, the *Frankfurter Zeitung*, the *Schwäbischer Merkur*, and the *Berliner Börsen-Zeitung*. These acquisitions were made through the Herold holding and management company of which Rienhardt was now the managing director. It was perhaps indicative of future developments that Winkler and his Vera concern were not used in these deals. The *Deutsche Allgemeine Zeitung*, a respected daily of national scope with an extensive foreign news service and a distinguished editorial staff, was the only newspaper of the once large Stinnes trust still in the hands of the family. Reportedly, Winkler's Vera company had acquired a minority interest before the paper was purchased by the Eher interests in 1938. DAZ, as it was familiarly known, was then transferred to the Deutscher Verlag and published as a substitute for the *Vossische Zeitung*, which had been allowed to go under. Of the Berlin newspapers during the war years it was by far the best, retaining its identity, written and published in a good style, and sometimes bringing news and views not to be found in the Nazi mass circulation papers.

The *Börsen-Zeitung* was another Berlin paper that came into Amann's hands during this period. A family enterprise since the mid-nineteenth century, the principal owners were the retired General Joachim von Stülpnagel and his brothers-in-law of the family Killisch von Horn. It was a class paper, with an aristocratic tone, finding its readers and subscribers among the civil service, military, and financial circles of Berlin. It was especially noted for its economic coverage and was one of the few papers that printed the complete daily stock market reports. Walther Funk had been the economic and financial editor. Through this position he became one of the principal liaison men between German industry and the leaders of the Nazi party. The depression brought the paper into financial difficulties and a merger with the *Berliner Börsen-Courier* gave it only temporary financial respite; bank credits also failed to restore financial health. At this point, according to Fritz Schmidt, Walther Funk, and Otto Dietrich, with Goebbels' endorsement, developed with the publishers an ambitious plan to reorganize the paper, broaden its appeal, and publish a high class journal as a substitute for the now defunct *Vossische Zeitung*, the languishing *Berliner Tageblatt*, and other papers of their level which had disappeared from the Berlin newspaper scene. The plans, which were far advanced were blocked by Amann and Rienhardt through the Reich Press Chamber, and Stülpnagel was forced to sell the *Börsen-Zeitung* to the Amann trust. Later, in 1945, Amann insisted that he deeply sympathized with Stülpnagel in his difficulties and paid him twice what the property was worth, although this is scarcely credible. During the negotiations with the owners of the *Börsen-Zeitung*, Amann and Rienhardt learned that the firm also owned the flourishing Wehrmacht Verlag which published for the Propaganda Office of the Armed Forces High Command the popular illustrated journal, *Die Wehrmacht*. By the outbreak of the war the circulation and sales had reached three-quarters of a million; it had a high advertising rate, and financially it was a bonanza. It became an immediate target of Amann and his staff director. The principal records of this deal have been preserved in the files of the OKW and are worth exploring in some detail as they present an illuminating case history of what can happen to publishers under a totalitarian regime.

In 1936 the Propaganda Office of the War Ministry launched *Die Wehrmacht* as a means of popularizing the armed forces with the German people. It was not a service journal of limited interest but was patterned on the popular illustrated weeklies, its format and content being designed for the general public. Hitler took an interest in the enterprise from its inception and gave it his blessing. Stülpnagel organized the Wehrmacht Verlag and received a contract for printing and publication of the journal. The War Ministry specified maximum security regulations, controlled appointments and editorial policy, and prepared many of the articles. Indeed, after 1938 the OKW appeared on the masthead as the publisher. Who inspired the drive to bring the publication into party hands cannot be determined, but immediately after Amann acquired the *Börsen-Zeitung* he began to put pressure on the OKW to cancel the contract with the Wehrmacht Verlag and put the journal in the Eher trust. The opportunity to intervene decisively was presented by the publisher's request for approval to merge the Schroter news photo agency with the Wehrmacht Verlag in order to round out the latter's technical services. The OKW Propaganda Office supported the publisher's request and this gave Amann and Rienhardt an opportunity to intervene. Amann's letter to General Keitel, May 5, 1939, read in part as follows: "On the basis of your letter of March 4, I took occasion to discuss with the Führer's Deputy, Party Member Rudolf Hess, my basic principle that the journalistic representation of the tasks of the Army in the periodical press (excluding technical publications) could best be achieved organically through the party publishing house. The continued promotion of the merging of army ideals with the basic principles of National Socialism would, in my opinion, be especially promoted and practically realized through the application of this principle. My views on this subject coincide generally with those of the Führer, namely, that the basic ideological indoctrination of the German people should be effected through publishing companies owned by the party. I therefore represent the position that these periodicals in principle should be published only by party Verlage, from which it follows that existing contracts with non-party publishing companies should, in a fair and proper manner, be terminated. The Deputy of the Führer informed me that in this matter he personally shares my view. Because of these basic considerations I must for the time being withhold a decision on the merger of the Schroter firm with the Wehrmacht Verlag, at least until I can first discuss with you and obtain your views on the basic question of transferring to party ownership those armed forces journals which are issued for the public." In closing, Amann expressed to Keitel the hope that they could discuss the matter on his next visit to Berlin and in the meantime referred him to Rienhardt and the staff director's office in Berlin. On the margin of the communication Keitel wrote: "Aha!"

In reply, Keitel strongly defended the position of the OKW and the contract with the Wehrmacht Verlag, reminding Amann that the agreement made in 1936 had been approved by Hitler and the war ministry, and that he, Amann, had been informed. Considerations which supported the arrangement at that time prevailed even to a greater degree in 1939. They still needed to contract with a small firm which could be directed by army authorities, which was qualified to do this specialized job, and which could meet maximum security requirements. During the past three years the Wehrmacht Verlag had fully met these conditions and he saw no reason to propose to the Führer a change in the publishing arrangements. He hoped that Amann would accept this position and reminded him that the Verlag had met the requirements of the 1936 ordinances by converting from a corporate form to a simple partnership.[30]

[30] The OKW was in error here. In 1936, ordinances similar to those for the newspaper publishing sector were issued for the periodical field. The Wehrmacht Verlag had applied for permission to reorganize, but this too was held up in the RPK.

Amann's reply to Keitel of July 6 reiterated his earlier arguments against a private contract and sought to convince him that a party publishing house could meet the OKW requirements, including that of security. When he had approved the original contract he had done so with the expectation that this would bring financial support to the *Börsen-Zeitung;* however, it had not had this result, and at the beginning of the year he had taken over the paper in order "to insure the development and the future of this worthy organ." Again he sounded the note of Hitler's approval for the policy which he upheld.

During the spring and summer heavy pressure was kept on the OKW Propaganda Office and the Wehrmacht Verlag. Approval of the merger with the photo news service was withheld; an allocation of newsprint for a special edition on the Condor Legion in Spain was refused by the RPK; and Amann blocked approval of the conversion of the Verlag from a corporation to a limited partnership. This finally produced a personal letter from Stülpnagel to Keitel reviewing the circumstances of the original contract, underscoring the success of the Verlag and the periodical, and summarizing Amann's opposition to the private contract relationship. He urged Keitel to take the matter up with Hitler and get a decision; they could not continue to operate in the present condition of uncertainty and stalemate.

The Polish crisis and outbreak of war postponed a final settlement of the disagreement between Amann and the OKW. By this time the dispute had developed into a power struggle between the party and the army. As seen by the OKW, it was a question of whether it could communicate directly with the German public through a periodical like *Die Wehrmacht,* or whether the armed forces were to be dependent in publicity matters upon the party. An OKW briefing note of July 21 stated baldly the army's objective: To support the publishers of *Die Wehrmacht* and keep the Verlag and its publications out of party hands and under the immediate control of the Armed Forces High Command.

Meanwhile, Amann had an opportunity to press his views directly with Hitler, and apparently with success. A briefing note, of September 3, stated that further support by OKW of the claims of the Wehrmacht Verlag had little hope of success. Inquiries made by Colonel Schmundt (Hitler's adjutant) revealed that Amann had made strong representations to Hitler concerning objectionable maneuvers by the Verlag at the time of the transfer of the *Börsen-Zeitung*. Colonel von Wedel, chief of the propaganda department, suggested that it might be wiser to make the first move toward negotiations with Amann rather than wait for an abrupt order to transfer the contract. Von Wedel's pessimism was justified for under the National Socialist system the matter could have but one solution—Amann would acquire the Wehrmacht Verlag. When the issue was presented to Hitler for decision in early February, he supported Amann and the party position. This was conveyed in a personal letter from Keitel to General Stülpnagel:

"In response to your repeated requests for clarification of all questions relating to the periodical *Die Wehrmacht*, I have presented the matter to the Führer. In doing so I made the points that spoke strongly in favor of continuing *Die Wehrmacht* in its present relationship. The Führer in response to my presentation said that the periodical *Die Wehrmacht* in content and form had his complete approval. He had decided, however, that it would be more appropriate to transfer the Verlag to a party or state publishing company.

"Now that this decision has been reached by the Führer, I would recommend that in your own interest as business manager of the Wehrmacht Verlag you get in touch with Reich Leader Amann and his staff leader

Rienhardt, with a view to negotiating the transfer of the Verlag to a party or state publishing house. I believe that you personally, as well as the Verlag, will gain more by acting in this way.

"I should like to say in this connection that I fully appreciate how difficult will be the decision to give up tasks that have become dear to you. But in view of the Führer's decision I see no other possible course of action and regretfully I cannot give you any other advice."

All the details of closing out Stülpnagel's interests in the Wehrmacht Verlag were in Rienhardt's hands. Stülpnagel and his associates received two million marks for the shares; the OKW received a letter from Amann, drafted by Rienhardt, pledging continued OKW control over policies, personnel and content of the periodical; and the Eher concern acquired a publication whose circulation on November 8, 1939, reached one million copies.[31]

The newly acquired property was placed in the Herold holding company but production of the periodical was shifted to the former Mosse concern, whose facilities for printing graphic material in large volume were unexcelled in Germany. Other popular military journals were likewise transferred, and the Mosse presses that formerly rolled out millions of colorful advertising supplements, now produced millions of copies of *Die Wehrmacht, Unser Heer,* and *Ostfront Illustrierte.*

[31] The letters and memoranda relating to Verlag Die Wehrmacht are found in OKW—Wehrmacht Prop. Abtl., File OKW/ 613, Nos. 454/39 ff.; and on microfilm, NA Micro-copy T-77, R-1010, frs. 2475568-2476104. Fritz Schmidt states incorrectly (*Presse in Fesseln,* pp. 67-70) that Amann paid eight million marks for the rights and titles of Die Wehrmacht Verlag. In 1945 Amann told the author that he paid two million and recovered his money from the first year's profits. Amann also feigned concern about the moral propriety of a retired general holding large publishing contracts with the armed forces!

## On the Eve of War

By 1939, six years after the seizure of power, the Ver-lagspolitik of the Nazi party was established in all essential elements. The publishing industry had been completely re-structured, uneconomic enterprises eliminated by suspensions and consolidations, the advertising business reorganized and rationalized, and the most important sectors of the press brought under the immediate control of the party. As a major creation of the Third Reich, the main features of this edifice as it existed on the eve of the war merit brief description.

First, if one considers only the number of newspapers and publishers, a substantial sector of the press remained in private hands. With few exceptions, however, these were small and medium sized papers—the Heimatpresse—in the smaller towns and cities. Average circulation for these journals was 10,000 or less. Since their content and opinion-forming functions were controlled by the propaganda ministry, their continuation in the hands of private owners presented no political danger to the regime. The second conspicuous feature of the press edifice was the official party papers, now organized uniformly in each Gau under a Gauverlag, all grouped in the Standarte holding and management company and subject in their financial, personnel, and publishing policies to the direction of Amann and Rienhardt. By pressure, purchase, consolidations, and sharp competitive practices these papers had been developed to the point where they were either self-supporting or showed a good profit. Circulation averaged about 60,000 copies each, including their numerous local editions. To this extent, in circulation and advertising, the privately owned press had been thrust aside to make room for the official party newspapers. The third major feature of the Nazi publishing structure was the large sector of the press directly owned or controlled through the Eher sub-

sidiaries—the Vera, Phoenix, and Herold companies. These
papers were not identified as party organs, they did not
carry the Nazi emblem, they retained the firm name of the
old publisher, and it was not generally known that they
were owned by the party trust. Probably not more than 100
persons in all Germany could have traced the lines of ownership of these old established papers to the residential
building in the fashionable Tiergarten district of Berlin
on whose door appeared the modest brass plates bearing
the names of the Vera and Phoenix corporations. By 1939,
as an economic and financial enterprise, the Eher Verlag
together with its subsidiaries was Germany's largest trust.

If we seek the *raison d'être* of this giant organization,
erected on the ruins of the private publishing industry,
we find it succinctly stated without ideological wrappings
in the explanation given by Rienhardt to Colonel von
Wedel of the OKW, justifying the transfer of the Wehrmacht Verlag to party ownership. "The basis for the decision which has been rendered," Rienhardt wrote, "con-
forms to the general directive of the Führer, that the authoritative political leadership of the German people be
achieved preferably through publishing companies that belong to the party. Political leadership, as the fundamental
responsibility of the party, must therefore be exercised
directly in the publishing sectors; and this is so important
for the party and the state as to necessitate the maintenance of their own facilities and organizations. Reich
Leader Amann, who is charged by the Führer with this
responsibility, aims to concentrate in the publishing organizations of the party the totality of the intellectual, personnel, and material resources of the authoritative press. In
this way the guarantee is given that the financial gains from
this work will serve exclusively the improvement and development of all publications, and not be diverted from the
publishing field and used for other purposes." [32] This is

[32] Rienhardt to Wedel, March 6, 1940; NA Micro-copy T-77,
R-1010, frs. 2476063-4.

the frankest exposure of the motives and objectives of the Hitler-Amann press policy that can be found in available contemporary records. It identifies Hitler as the sponsor, a monopoly for the party's publishing organization as the objective, and the party trust as the financial beneficiary of the massive pillage of the publishing industry. Compared to this revealing statement, all the public explanations by exponents of the party's press policy are scarcely more than deceitful fabrications.[33]

All indications suggest that the party leaders concerned with the press considered the position achieved by 1939 to be politically and competitively satisfactory. The party-owned and party-controlled press held about two-thirds of the total circulation, the 2,000 privately owned papers the remaining third. This point of stabilization might have been maintained had it not been for the war which led to further closures and consolidations. Before examining this phase of Nazi press history the important developments of the last year of peace deserve brief treatment. Besides the expansion of the Eher trust into Austria and Bohemia, three events worthy of note occurred: the remnants of the

[33] I have not thought it worthwhile to collate and present the justifications of the Nazi publishing policy advanced for public consumption. The fullest presentation was made by Rienhardt at a meeting of editors, publishers, officials, and leading business men at Cologne University in June 1938: "Das Kern Problem: Muss Presse Sein," *Zeitungs-Verlag*, No. 25, June 18; also, "Führer—Idee—Wille—Tat," No. 12, March 21, 1936; and "Rede des Herrn Rechtsanwalt Rienhardt vor den Bezirksversammlungen im April, Mai 1936," printed but not for public distribution. Amann's party congress addresses and occasional pronouncements published in *Zeitungs-Verlag* are merely variations and restatements of Rienhardt's ideas: "Die Grundlagen des deutschen Zeitungswesen im N-S Staat," No. 50, Dec. 16, 1933; "Es gibt nur eine deutsche Presse," No. 17, April 27, 1935; "Die Grundgesetz der Standesgemeinschaft der Zeitungsverleger," No. 30, July 27, 1935; "Nationalsozialistische Pressepolitik," No. 38, Sept. 21, 1935; "Die N-S deutsche Volkspresse," No. 38, Sept. 19, 1936; "Unser Wort sei Tat," No. 37, Sept. 10, 1938.

private publishing business were organized within the RVDZV; Max Winkler withdrew from the field of the press; and the corporate structure of the Eher concern was recast and simplified.

In the summer of 1938 a rumor circulated among publishers that the Gau Verlag directors, with the support of Goebbels and Dietrich, were developing a plan to liquidate the remaining provincial papers and concentrate all local publishing in the Gau press. This was strongly opposed by Rienhardt, who persuaded Amann, as a blocking measure, to approve the request of a number of independent publishers that they be allowed to organize within the RVDZV a working group of privately owned newspapers (Arbeitsgemeinschaft der privateigenen Zeitungen). The stated aims were to consolidate and represent their interests, to provide cooperative services, and to exchange information beneficial to the members. About seventy publishers participated in the formal organization of the association on June 29, 1939. Officers were elected, dues assessed, and a business office established in Berlin, with Dr. Fritz Schmidt, whose services were made available by Rienhardt, installed as business manager.

The leading publisher in the Arbeitsgemeinschaft, and chairman of the executive committee, was J. K. von Zweck, a prominent figure in the pre-Hitler newspaper publishers' association. One of the principal purposes of the organization was to assist the members in revitalizing their papers and bringing them technically and economically up to the level of their party trust competitors. To this end a cooperative news and editorial service was established in Berlin, a uniform accounting system for middle-sized newspapers developed, and other assistance in business and technical organization rendered to members. The Arbeitsgemeinschaft brought the independent publishers out of their helpless position of isolation, gave them contact with one another, and provided representation of their interests to the publishing authorities in Berlin. Within the working group seventy of the more active and affluent members organized the cooperative news service—Dienst mittlerer Tageszeitung (Dimitag)—which became a strongpoint of defense against further encroachments by the Gau publishing companies. It was owing in no small part to this organization that some 600 middle-sized newspapers survived until 1944 when Amann dissolved the Arbeitsgemeinschaft.

Fritz Schmidt, who served as business manager, attributes to the organization the character and activity of a Nazi resistance group. Beyond their trade and economic objectives was the determination to maintain the independence of their papers for the day when the Hitler regime would fall and a free press would flourish again. He also alleges contacts between the group and the July 20 conspirators. The validity of his statements must be challenged. Certainly among the independent publishers of the Dimitag group were many who rejected the regime and all that it represented, but it must also be remembered that every private publisher had passed the Paragraph 10 examination and had been certified by the Reich Press Chamber as politically trustworthy from the National Socialist viewpoint. It would be more accurate to describe these hard pressed publishers as a group of men bound together for mutual assistance and the defense of their newspaper and publishing rights, which many of them had inherited from their fathers and grandfathers. But even in conserving and defending their property rights were they not also defending freedom? [34]

Within the party, the founding of the Arbeitsgemeinschaft produced immediate repercussions and persistent dissatisfaction. The Gau Verlag directors, the editors of the

[34] The fullest account of the Arbeitsgemeinschaft is in Fritz Schmidt, *Presse in Fesseln*, pp. 159-66. Significantly, the organization of the Arbeitsgemeinschaft was not reported in *Zeitungs-Verlag* or the daily press.

principal party organs, and the Gauleiters vigorously protested this "new course" initiated by staff director Rienhardt. Strong protests reached Goebbels, Dietrich, Amann, Hess, and Bormann. Rienhardt was subjected to sharp attacks and found himself fighting hard to maintain Amann's power over the publishing field. On occasion he was forced to conciliate his critics and opponents by concurring in Gau Verlag plans for further acquisitions and consolidations.

Another consequence of this party dissatisfaction was the withdrawal of Max Winkler from the publishing field. The Gau authorities had been unhappy over the assignment of the principal newspaper properties, acquired in 1935-1937, to the Vera and Phoenix companies instead of allocating them to the Gau publishing firms. They saw the profits and benefits flowing to Amann's Eher Verlag and their Gau papers still in competition with their old established rivals. Competitive tactics employed against these papers when they were privately owned were not permissible when they came under Eher control. Winkler and the whole Vera complex were much misliked and resented by the Gau authorities. Winkler's withdrawal was certainly not uninfluenced by the animosity felt toward him by many party leaders. All concerned—Winkler, Amann, and Rienhardt—have been reticent about the circumstances of Winkler's withdrawal from the Eher companies. After the war both Amann and Winkler denied that serious difficulties had developed between them, and Winkler submitted an affidavit on Amann's behalf in his denazification proceedings. In 1945 Amann spoke appreciatively of his former agent and collaborator. Personal relations between Winkler and Rienhardt certainly cooled as the staff director took over Winkler's managerial and board positions in the Eher controlled companies and then proceeded to recast the entire corporate structure of the party publishing empire.

Obviously by 1939 Rienhardt had learned his trade from the "old master" and was no longer dependent upon his advice, experience, and talents. Winkler also had other important irons in the fire. As Reich trustee for the film industry, he had become more and more involved in Goebbels' plans—the nationalizing of the film companies under the ministry of propaganda. By 1939, Winkler was the financial czar of the motion picture industry and was appearing with Goebbels at the gala premiere showings of its major productions. With the conquest of Poland, in September 1939, the "Reich Trustee for Everything" acquired a new responsibility—head of the Central Trustee Office East (Haupttreuhandstelle Ost) for the administration of confiscated Jewish and Polish property in the occupied and annexed districts of Poland. Only once during the war did Winkler return to the newspaper field, when he negotiated for Amann the purchase of Hugenberg's Scherl Verlag. We may assume that a combination of party pressure on Amann and Rienhardt and involvement in his new assignments removed the former mayor of Graudenz from the publishing scene.

Winkler's departure marked the beginning of a major reorganization in the corporate structure of the party's publishing system. Winkler's trustee shares in the Vera company were transferred to Eher, and Rienhardt assumed the post of managing director, a position he already held in the Herold concern. Soon he began to shift Vera properties to the Herold register. This continued during the early years of the war until Vera became an empty shell and was finally liquidated in 1944. The Phoenix company, which had been established to hold the titles and properties of the confessional papers, had now served its purpose. It too was liquidated in 1940. Most of its holdings were small or middle sized properties which were now transferred, some to the Standarte party trust, some to the Herold com-

pany. Those that went to the Standarte group were in most
instances merged with a Gau paper or suspended during
the war. During the following years there was also considerable shifting of properties from the two holding companies—Herold and Vera—to the Gau publishing companies. Many of these rearrangements are doubtless to be
regarded as concessions or sops to the Gauleiters.[35]

In the four years that elapsed between the promulgation
of the Amann ordinances and the outbreak of war, the
publishing industry experienced revolutionary changes. The
unsettlement caused by the Amann ordinances depressed
circulation and gravely affected the economic position of
the industry. By 1939 signs of adjustment and recovery
were clearly visible. The outstanding feature of the new
order was the position of predominance acquired by the
party press through expansion of the Gau publishing companies in the provinces and the acquisition by the Eher
Verlag of the most prosperous and widely circulated papers in the metropolitan centers. The press, like the film
industry and radio, was now the captive of the party and
the state. Weaknesses in the Goebbels-Amann press system
were obvious and gave concern to both party and private
publishers. In this respect should be noted the discontent
of editors and journalists with the stringent controls, the
uniformity and monotony of the publications which bored
or repelled readers and subscribers, the declining rate of
recruitment of gifted or qualified personnel, and the unsettlement resulting from the fear and uncertainty felt by
the remaining private publishers. Some of these problems
were intensified by wartime developments, some faded into

[35] It is not possible to specify the exact distribution of the news-
paper properties as the records of the Standarte and Phoenix com-
panies were destroyed in Berlin. Winkler's withdrawal from the
Eher companies was entered in the Berlin corporation register in
December 1939. Wilhelm R. Beyer, "Die gesellschaftsrechtliche
Geschichte des Eher Verlages," pp. 8-10; File 3820-b, BWB.

the background, some assumed new aspects. But more immediately, the beginning of the war presented new problems to every individual and firm, party or private, engaged in the work of the press.

# VIII. The German Press in Wartime

## The Conditions of Publishing

The invasion of Poland marked the opening of a new chapter in the history of the German press. While the Nazi publishing policy admitted of some private enterprise up to 1939, the war afforded the setting and justification for more radical measures in line with the party's demand for a monopoly of the press. War emergency measures that seriously affected the production of newspapers and periodicals were instituted, rigorous military censorship was added to the system of positive control that already prevailed, the drafting of manpower took a heavy toll in editorial and business offices and, beginning in 1943, Allied bombing attacks upon German cities destroyed printing plants and disrupted communications. War conditions and political radicalization brought further suspensions and consolidations of newspapers and publishing enterprises.

The basic raw material in the publishing industry is newsprint and periodical paper. In an attempt to reduce imports, Rienhardt endeavored in 1937 to secure through the RVDZV a voluntary reduction of consumption by ten per cent. Encountering passive resistance from users and suppliers, firm controls were then imposed through the Planning and Raw Materials Office of the Four Year Plan. This agency and its successors, the Ministry of Economy and the Speer Ministry of Armaments and War Production, made a specified quarterly allocation to the RPK for distribution to the publishers. In allocating this supply the newspaper press and the illustrated weeklies were favored over the periodical press. The monthly allocation to the newspaper press in mid-1939 amounted to 28,200 tons. This amount remained remarkably stable during the first four years of the war, but with the cutting off of Finnish sources of supply in 1944, it dropped to 8,500 tons monthly and by March 1945 to a mere 5,000 tons. Oftentimes this meager amount could not be delivered. The statistics for paper consumption of the weekly and illustrated journals parallel those for newsprint, while the allocation for general and specialized periodicals was sharply reduced until it amounted to only 1,237 tons monthly in 1944.[1]

With the outbreak of war the rationing system was reinforced by ordinances issued by the RPK regulating the size of newspapers and periodicals. Papers issued in the small format were limited to eight pages, including Sunday editions, those with the large format to six pages, weekly papers to sixteen, and the weekly illustrated papers to twenty-eight pages. As the raw materials position worsened during the war more drastic restrictions were imposed upon the industry. In 1944, a maximum size of four pages for all newspapers was ordered and publication was limited to six editions weekly; single issue sales were limited to an area within twenty-five kilometers of the place of origin and subscription delivery to within 100 kilometers. At the same time the delivery of newspapers and periodicals through the army postal system was prohibited. Likewise, in 1944, all weeklies with an entertainment character were suspended and the illustrated weeklies were limited to two —the *Berliner Illustrierte* and the *Illustrierte Beobachter*, both Eher publications. The suspended weeklies received these two publications in stereotype and issued them in their areas under a local title. This ended the German family custom of buying or subscribing to several illustrated weeklies. Finally, in March 1945, newspapers were reduced to a single page, issued irregularly as conditions permitted, and circulated only in the immediate locality.[2] As hostili-

[1] Schmidt, *Presse in Fesseln*, pp. 251-52, statistical tables. Schmidt sees in Rienhardt's paper rationing policy a sacrificing of the periodical sector to the newspapers of the party trust, but an objective judgment suggests that newspapers are more important to a war effort than periodicals.

[2] The ordinances and regulations of the RPK are summarized in Schmidt, *Presse in Fesseln*, pp. 252-53.

ties ended the publishing industry in Germany was dead.

Despite the newsprint and paper restrictions, decline in advertising revenue, and manpower and materials shortage, the war brought temporary prosperity to the publishing business. For those publishers who continued in business, and for the Eher Verlag, the years 1939-1943 were years of substantial prosperity. The reasons are obvious: Paper and newsprint costs remained stable; while advertising space was severely limited the rates were doubled; and subscription and sales price were maintained, although the purchaser received much less for his money. Also complete monopoly conditions prevailed. Considerable savings on wages and salaries were effected as men were called to military service and their work performed by the reduced staff that remained on the job. While comprehensive industry statistics are not available, we know that the Eher Verlag and its subsidiaries, now comprising seventy per cent of the industry, enjoyed their greatest prosperity from 1939 to 1943, when the bombing of German cities and the shortage of newsprint, machinery and power greatly reduced the volume of business and curtailed profits.

War makes news and creates an insatiable appetite for information. In Germany, as elsewhere in 1939, newspaper sales and circulation skyrocketed.[3] People not only bought papers and magazines but they read them. News photos and graphic materials used by the press doubled and tripled in volume. We have substantial statistical material which shows how the war stimulated the business of the Deutscher Verlag (formerly Ullstein), the largest enterprise in the Eher trust. In 1939 the principal publications of the Deutscher Verlag were: the *Deutsche Allgemeine Zeitung*, acquired by Amann as a quality replacement for the old *Vossische Zeitung*; the *Berliner Morgenpost*, with the larg-

---

[3] Amann stated that newspaper circulation rose during the war from 20.7 million to 26.7 million, and the weeklies and illustrated weeklies from 11.9 to 20.8 million. ("Die deutsche Presse im Kriege," *Handbuch der deutschen Tagespresse—1944*, p. xv.)

est circulation of the Berlin papers, the *B-Z am Mittag,* the *12 Uhr Blatt,* the *Berliner Volkszeitung,* the *Berliner Allgemeine Zeitung,* and the *Montagspost.* In the illustrated field the Deutscher Verlag published the *Berliner Illustrierte,* Germany's largest illustrated weekly, and *Koralle,* an educational and popular science weekly. For national distribution the Verlag published a considerable list of women's magazines, mode and fashion reviews, sports journals, and trade and industry publications. The Deutscher Verlag also executed a large number of printing contracts for other publishers. Using Ullstein methods and experience, the Verlag was a mass production enterprise for all kinds of printed materials.

In 1934, when the Verlag was acquired by Amann, the total circulation of Ullstein papers and magazines amounted to 3,671,000 copies; by 1939 circulation had more than doubled, to 7,421,700. The *Deutsche Allgemeine Zeitung,* in its Berlin and Reich editions, had a modest circulation of 60,000 when it was acquired by Amann. The circulation was up to 90,000 on the eve of the war, and by 1941 had risen to 251,000. The *Morgenpost* had suffered severely from the depression and Nazi boycotts. In 1934 its circulation was down to 337,000, but it made a good recovery and within five years it rose to 450,000 (Sunday 675,000). During the opening months of the war its circulation increased to 500,000 (Sunday 725,000). The popular midday street papers, *B-Z am Mittag* and *12 Uhr Blatt,* which had combined sales of about 150,000, in 1939, rose to 250,000 daily and at times of heavy front fighting to 600,000. The merged *Grüne Post* and *Braune Post,* a family magazine, acquired circulation of 750,000; and the *Berliner Illustrierte* shot up from two million in the early weeks of the war to three million at the end of 1940.

Two enormously successful publications were launched by the Deutscher Verlag in 1940. In April, the heavily illustrated *Signal* made its appearance. Designed to impress Europeans with Germany's military power, it was printed in fifteen languages and achieved a circulation of 1,600,000 copies (largest edition in French—444,000). Making its appearance in May 1940, the political-cultural weekly, *Das Reich,* had a phenomenal success. Except for Goebbels' weekly political contribution, the publication maintained high quality in its articles, reviews, and reporting. The customary tone and style of Nazi journalism was pointedly avoided and it demonstrated that there was still a large market for good taste and sound journalism. Goebbels took no interest in the publication beyond writing his weekly article, for which he was handsomely paid. *Das Reich* was mainly the creation of Rudolf Sparing, Rienhardt, and Amann. Within a year it had sales of over one million, attaining a circulation in excess of one and a half million copies in 1942-1943. As Germany dominated the continent militarily her publications gained ever wider circulation. The three weeklies—*Signal, Das Reich,* and *Berliner Illustrierte*—achieved foreign sales of 2,100,000 of each edition. In general the income from increased sales and circulation balanced the decline in advertising revenue. Total income from circulation in the Deutscher Verlag in 1938 was 44,300,000 RM; in 1940 it rose to 74,400,000 RM.[4] While the Deutscher Verlag was the largest and

---

[4] Revenue from circulation and advertising in the Deutscher Verlag from time of acquisition to 1940 was as follows:

|      | Advertising Income (In million RM) | Circulation Income |
|------|------------------|-------------|
| 1934 | 11.              | 29.6        |
| 1935 | 12.35            | 30.3        |
| 1936 | 14.              | 33.5        |
| 1937 | 15.              | 37.7        |
| 1938 | 17.15            | 44.3        |
| 1939 | 20.              | 56.4        |
| 1940 | —                | 74.4        |

The information on the publications of the Deutscher Verlag is derived from the presentation volume prepared by the staff for

most prosperous of the units in the Eher trust, available evidence indicates that with few exceptions the subsidiary companies produced substantial profits from 1939 to 1943. Private publishers, too, if they could get their paper contingent and stay in business, shared in this period of prosperity.

## The German Press in the Occupied Areas

As the German armies occupied the greater part of continental Europe, the Nazi party trust expanded its publishing activities into these areas. This work absorbed much of Rienhardt's time and much Eher capital and personnel. The papers established in the occupied areas were published in German, designed for civilian readers, identified themselves with the country or region in which they appeared, and were independent of the papers issued for the troops by the Wehrmacht propaganda staffs. They were German papers in style, format, and content, and served as communication channels between the occupation authorities and the indigenous population.

Rienhardt and his staff gained their first experience of operating in a conquered area, in close cooperation with the army, during the occupation of Poland. By mid-November 1939 four German newspapers were appearing in the annexed districts of Poland (the Warthegau) and in the General Government. These were the *Krakauer Zeitung* and its twin edition the *Warschauer Zeitung*, which were established at the request of Governor General Hans Frank. The first issue, appearing on November 12, brought greetings from Goebbels, Amann, and Dietrich. In Lodz, a former Volksdeutsche paper was converted to the new *Lodzer Zeitung*, and in Posen an official Gau paper was established by the Gauleiter—the *Ostdeutscher Beobachter*. The latter proudly proclaimed its mission to be "the

Amann on his fiftieth birthday. (*Deutscher Verlag, 1934-1941*, pp. 8-10, 14-16, 23-25, 26-29, 77-85.)

voice of Adolf Hitler in the Warthegau." In establishing these papers, the personnel and much equipment had to be brought from the Reich, connections with DNB established, the newsprint supply arranged, a distribution system established, and payments of all kinds assured.[5]

The opening of a new field of activity produced the customary grab for power among Hitler's lieutenants. After Amann's staff had installed editors and managers in these papers, Goebbels asserted his right "to inspect" and proceeded to fire them all. Thereupon Amann visited Goebbels in his office and for two hours "told him the truth"— what he really thought about his "miserable Ministry," how the Gauleiters unanimously disparaged it, and how "no one had any use for it." According to Amann, who told all this to Rosenberg after his session with Goebbels, the latter was conciliatory—"mein lieber Pg. Amann, etc."— and withdrew his claim to jurisdiction.[6] Thereafter Amann's power in the foreign publishing field was as undivided as it was in the domestic area.

The pattern of the German foreign press was finally established with the occupation of Norway, France, Belgium, and the Netherlands. The first paper was established in Norway on the initiative of Terboven, the Reich Commissar. Terboven approached Amann, requesting him to supply funds, an editorial staff, and the necessary business and technical personnel. The *Deutsche Zeitung in Norwegen* was so successful that similar papers were soon established in the other occupied territories.[7] To finance, direct, and

[5] The founding of these papers is described by Rudolf Sparing, "Herolde des Deutschtums im Osten," *Zeitungs-Verlag*, No. 48, Dec. 2, 1939. Until he became principal editor of the weekly *Das Reich*, Sparing was Rienhardt's principal assistant in establishing the occupation press.

[6] H. G. Seraphim, *Das Politische Tagebuch Alfred Rosenbergs*, p. 96, entry Jan. 19, 1940.

[7] Amann, Interview notes, Aug. 22, 1945. In Alsace-Lorraine and Luxemburg the nearest Gau publishing firm established the papers

administer these enterprises a holding and management company was set up in Berlin under Rienhardt's administrative office. The Europa Verlag, at the peak of Germany's expansion, administered about thirty publishing enterprises. The Berlin office drafted from the editorial and business staffs of the Eher papers essential editorial and publishing personnel, negotiated arrangements with the army authorities, provided telephone, telegraph, and radio communications, and requisitioned all necessary technical equipment from home stocks. Local circumstances usually dictated whether the printing facilities were requisitioned or whether a contract was given to a local firm. When an occupation paper was established it was customary for the military authorities to guarantee purchase of from thirty to forty thousand copies for the offices, staffs, and agencies of the occupation authority. The army also facilitated distribution through army canteens and clubs to the troops stationed in the area. These arrangements assured the financial foundation of the venture and confirmed Hitler's statement that "no business which was in the red . . . had the slightest interest for Amann." At the peak of circulation, in January 1943, the Europa Verlag papers were sold and distributed in over one million copies daily.[8]

---

in Strasbourg, Mulhouse, Kolmar, Metz, and Luxemburg in July and October 1940. These papers were managed by the Standarte company. (*Handbuch der deutschen Tagespresse—1944*, p. xvii.)

[8] "Die deutsche Presse im Kriege," in *Handbuch*, p. xxl. Also Amann's memorandum, "Zu dem Buch Presse in Fesseln," Oct. 30, 1947, pp. 15-16, Spruchkammer file. The Europa Verlag papers and their locations were as follows: Amsterdam: *D-Z in den Niederlanden*; Athens: *Deutsche Nachrichten in Griechenland*; Belgrade: *Donau-Zeitung*; Brussels: *Brüsseler Zeitung*; Bucharest: *Bukarester Tageblatt*; Hermannstadt: *Südostdeutsche Zeitung*; Istanbul: *Türkische Post*; Kovno: *Kauener Zeitung*; Cracow: *Krakauer Zeitung*; Kiev: *Deutsche Ukraine Zeitung*; Minsk: *Minsker Zeitung*; Oslo: *D-Z in Norwegen*; Paris: *Pariser Zeitung*; Prague: *Der Neue Tag*; Reval: *Revaler Zeitung*; Riga: *D-Z im Ostland*; Shanghai: *Ostasiatischer Lloyd*; Temesvar: *Südostdeutsche Zeitung*

Amann maintained in 1945 that, at his insistence, the occupation papers had greater freedom in news and editorial policies than the home press. His staff chose the best editors available, he said, and some of them got into serious trouble with Dietrich and Goebbels because they did not always follow press directives from the propaganda ministry. Field censorship, too, was likely to be less restrictive than that of the central authority. Dietrich threatened that if the editors did not conform, the papers would be barred from circulation in the Reich. Some papers, according to Amann, were so excluded, but as the responsible authority he supported the editors in their difficulties with Goebbels and Dietrich. "Since these papers were produced and read abroad, you had to have something more in them than National Socialist propaganda," he said. Anyone who read these papers consistently during the war found much of the familiar phrase threshing and tiresome stereotypes of Nazi journalism, but Amann's claim that in their regional functioning they were better news and information papers than their counterparts in the homeland is not without justification. Indeed, these papers, which were read in London and Washington by Allied intelligence authorities, frequently yielded more information of value than the German home press. They were a primary source for the actions and policies of the German occupation officials.

Something of a reversed image of the German papers published in the occupied capitals of Europe were the foreign language papers issued in the Reich for foreign workers and political emigrant groups. As larger and larger contingents of foreign workers were brought in to replace German workers called to the colors, weekly and bi-weekly papers in their native languages were provided for morale

(for the Banat); Trieste: *Deutsche Adria-Zeitung*; Zagreb: *D-Z in Kroatien*. Files of these unique papers are widely scattered, when they exist at all. One of the largest collections is held by the Library of Congress.

and informational purposes. This production was organized originally by the propaganda ministry and was managed by the Fremdsprachen-Verlag GmbH. In 1944 it published twenty papers in thirteen languages, of which the French, Russian, Polish, and Ukrainian papers had editions of over 100,000. The Europa Verlag also entered this field, financing and directing three publishing houses—Nowoje Slovo, Verlag Ranica, and Verlag Holos—which issued several papers in the Baltic, Russian, and Ukrainian languages. In 1944, the Allied occupation of France and Belgium sent a wave of political refugees, headed by Pétain and Laval, into the Lake Constance region. In the interest of these exiles, although what interest they represented is difficult to determine, the Verlag Interpress was organized to publish the French political daily, *La France*. To complete this account, the Metropress GmbH, Berlin, should be mentioned. A subsidiary of the Europa Verlag, it coordinated and controlled the sales and distribution of German newspapers, periodicals, and books in eleven European centers.[9]

## First and Second Press Closing Actions— 1941, 1943

The newspaper press was considerably affected by the outbreak of the war as the publishers encountered severe paper rationing, reduced staffs, war-time taxation and insurance, power and fuel rationing, and transportation difficulties. Some dwarf rural papers closed voluntarily for the duration, but such suspensions were of slight importance. In the periodical field, however, the cutting off of paper and newsprint effected the disappearance of hundreds of

[9] These distribution firms were located in Amsterdam, Athens, Belgrade, Brussels, Bucharest, Cologne, Istanbul, Kovno, Paris, and Riga. The firms in Cologne and Istanbul were probably active in the procurement of foreign publications for the German intelligence services.

non-essential publications. Germany produced the almost unbelievable number of 15,000 periodicals. Every local society, whatever its function, every trade and branch of trade, indeed every large firm and factory in Germany had its weekly, monthly, or quarterly publication. Most of this forest of club and business publications disappeared with the immediate interruption of the paper supply, which was reserved for war-essential publications. For the rest, the propaganda ministry recommended that by suspensions and consolidations the periodical list be reduced to three hundred. This radical proposal was submitted to the Propaganda Office of OKW with a request that the military authorities indicate which periodicals in their field were indispensable. Such a list was prepared but then the OKW stalled as it did not wish to be saddled with responsibility for putting all the other military journals out of business.[10] Apparently this drastic program was abandoned, for the German periodical list carried approximately 2,500 titles at the beginning of 1943, when a major program of suspensions and consolidations was effected.

The first extensive reduction in the number of newspapers occurred in May 1941, when the Reich Press Chamber issued suspension notices to approximately five hundred newspapers.[11] It was stated in the individual notices that the suspension was for the duration of the war; the order was justified as a measure to save paper, electricity, type metal, and other materials, and to free manpower for the armaments industry. Fritz Schmidt, in reviewing the list of suspended papers, concludes that Rienhardt's selections were directed toward political and monopolistic goals

[10] OKW—Wehrmacht Prop. Abtl., File OKW/613; National Archives, Micro-copy T-77, R-1010, frs. 2475166 ff.

[11] Amann gave the number as "540 kleinen und kleinsten Zeitungen neben rund 1,200 Zeitschriften." On January 1, 1942, there remained in the area of the "Greater German Reich" 1,246 daily newspapers. (Handbuch—1944, pp. xiv, xxviii.)

in the interest of the party and the Eher Verlag. Approximately twelve former Center party papers were suspended, including several that had been acquired by the Phoenix company for the Eher trust. A number of suspensions and mergers were also effected among papers belonging to the Eher group. These could be described as "tidying up" actions, reducing competition between party-owned papers, and closing out some unprofitable enterprises. Here Rienhardt was indeed pursuing a policy of consolidating the party's papers into larger, more economic, and effective units. The third aspect of the action was a considerable number of consolidations in towns where two privately owned papers competed for a limited number of subscribers and advertisers. Consolidation was mandatory where both papers were published by the same Verlag. Finally, between three and four hundred local papers with circulations under five thousand were suspended. As compensation for suspension of publishing rights, private owners were paid from 15 to 18 RM per subscriber by the area party Verlag, which usually took over the paid-up subscription list. As a result of this action, twenty-one papers belonging to the Arbeitsgemeinschaft of privately owned newspapers were suspended or consolidated. Viewed objectively the 1941 closing action appears to have been as much a program of economic rationalization as it was a war measure.

The radical curtailment of newspaper publishing in 1943, however, must be placed against the background of the unfavorable military situation that was developing for Germany. In the winter of 1942 Germany lost the initiative in the war. The Anglo-American invasion of North Africa, the British victory at El Alamein, the loss of the German Sixth Army at Stalingrad, and Allied mastery of the U-boat menace, all came within a period of five months and marked the decisive turning point in the struggle. Further, in March 1943, the first really damaging assaults from the air were made against Berlin, Munich, Nürnberg, and Essen. The terrifying attacks upon Hamburg came at the end of July, and the massive assaults on Berlin in November left a large part of the capital a smoking ruin. Henceforth it was not a question of who would prevail in the war, but how long it would last.

In this crisis, the measures taken by the German leaders to mobilize manpower and industrial resources approached for the first time the conditions of total war. Central to the program were two decrees published with much fanfare at the end of January 1943. The first ordered the closing of all retail specialty shops, handicraft shops, luxury restaurants, women's beauty salons, and workshops employing fewer than five persons, unless serving a war essential purpose. There was much resistance to this action and its execution had to be extended from ninety days to six months, but hundreds of thousands of small tradesmen, artisans, and retail clerks were forced out of their usual employment into the industrial labor pools. Concurrently with the business closing decree a compulsory registration order was issued requiring all men between the ages of 15 and 64 and all women between the ages of 16 and 44 to register at the employment office of their district for assignment to full-time essential war work. It was an obvious certainty that the publishing industry, which existed in a gray area between essential and non-essential enterprises, would be sharply curtailed.[12]

Drastic cuts were made in periodical publishing. The *Frankfurter Zeitung* (March 17 and 23) listed 28 film, fashion, and general periodicals with national circulation which would be suspended, and ten business, financial, and

[12] The decrees were published in *Völkischer Beobachter*, Jan. 29, and April 21, 1943. The effect in Munich is described in detail in the *Münchner N.N.*, Feb. 20, 26, 27, 1943. The decrees are also summarized in Max Seydewitz, *Civil Life in Wartime Germany*, pp. 232-36.

statistical periodicals. In regard to trade, industry, and technical magazines the number was reduced to one journal for each field and major branch. At the beginning of 1943 there were 2,500 registered serial publications appearing in Germany. Now approximately 1,000 titles disappeared through mergers and suspensions, leaving 1,500 periodicals on the publishing list at the end of the year. Further reductions in 1944 brought the number to around five hundred, the principal categories being science, technology, agriculture, medicine, industry, transportation, law, and administration. Significantly, while fifteen Nazi political and ideological journals continued publication, not one was left in philosophy, religion, theology, or religious art.[13]

In the newspaper press further suspensions and consolidations were effected by order of the RPK. In all, about 950 papers ceased publication. Hardest hit were the remaining private publishers in towns and cities with populations of 10,000 to 100,000, where two or more papers were still appearing. In almost every instance the party-owned or controlled paper benefited from the closing of its competitor. And it happened not infrequently that the mail delivery of the notice of suspension brought the publisher a summons to report for military duty. As compensation, the private publishers were offered three alternatives: First, they could sell their rights and titles to the nearest Gau Verlag at a price of 20-25 RM per subscriber; second, they could merge their paper with a local Gau organ in a partnership in which the party publishing firm would hold the controlling interest; third, they could lease the paper to a Gau Verlag for the duration of the war at a monthly rate of 50 to 80 pfennig per subscriber, which was about one third of the monthly subscription rate. Fritz Schmidt, who was still the managing director of the Arbeitsgemeinschaft, states that the majority of publishers chose the third alternative,

[13] Schmidt, *Presse in Fesseln*, pp. 212-13, gives the classified list and the number appearing in each group.

hoping to reestablish their papers after the war. Of the 243 members of the Arbeitsgemeinschaft, 73 were affected by the concentration order in 1943. Of these, 16 sold their rights and titles, 25 negotiated a merger, and 32 leased their rights. Whatever saving in manpower, raw materials, and machinery may have accrued to the war effort, it is obvious that the party's Gau papers benefited by acquiring the subscribers of their competitors. When the publisher sold or leased his rights he still retained his plant and equipment, but even these assets were placed in jeopardy by the ordinances issued by the Reich economics minister. Under these decrees the presses and all equipment were subject to requisitioning on Amann's authority and could be used to re-equip and maintain plants destroyed or damaged by bombing.[14]

One of Amann's personal and local objectives was achieved in 1943 when the *Münchener Zeitung*, principal competitor of the V-B and the *Münchner Neueste Nachrichten*, was suspended by order of the RPK. As one of the papers left in the hands of the Huck family, Amann had wanted to close the *Münchener Zeitung* in 1941, but Rienhardt had persuaded him that it would produce a bad impression. In March 1943, when Hermann Vitalowitz, the Verlag director, received the order to suspend, he went immediately to call on Herr Salat, manager of the *Münchner Neueste Nachrichten*. While he was in Salat's office, Amann called him on the telephone to inform him jubilantly that the "*Münchener Zeitung* was closing down." The subscribers were divided between the V-B and the *Neueste Nachrichten*, and compensation of 45,000 RM monthly was paid to keep the plant of the *Münchener Zeitung* in stand-by condition for the other two papers.

---

[14] Schmidt, pp. 173-75, for the terms and application of the closing regulations. Amann described this program as one to strengthen by merger the papers in the provincial centers. ("Die deutsche Presse im Kriege," in *Handbuch—1944*, pp. xvi-xvii.)

The compensation, Vitalowitz testified later, was paid promptly by the *Münchner Neueste Nachrichten,* but the V-B was always in arrears. Some of the additional terms of the agreement were also not fulfilled.[15]

With the press closing action of 1943 the Amann trust papers achieved a circulation position of such predominance that Amann could say at last: "The Party commands the press."

## End of the *Frankfurter Zeitung* and the Fall of Staff Director Rienhardt

The most notable casualty of the 1943 closing action was the *Frankfurter Zeitung,* one of Germany's best known and highly regarded papers, the journal most frequently quoted abroad, the paper which even in Nazi Germany attempted to maintain traditional standards of journalism. Closely related, but unreported in the press, was the break between Amann and Rienhardt and the banishment of the all-powerful staff director to one of SS-General Sepp Dietrich's heavy weapons companies.

The disappearance of the *Frankfurter Zeitung* was widely noted and commented on in the foreign press. Previously there had been much speculation as to how this leading liberal paper, founded and presumably owned by a Jewish publishing family, had been able to maintain itself during ten years of Nazi rule. Investigators at the end of the war, inquiring as to the circumstances of the paper's demise, were told by informants that it was closed on Hitler's order. As for the reasons and circumstances, there were many versions and most of them conflicting. The briefest explanation, offered by one witness, was Hitler's general aversion to the paper—"I don't like the name; it must be closed down." In fact, for ten years the *Frank-*

[15] Statement by Hermann Vitalowitz, Spruchkammer Munich I. Max Amann, Main file, No. 317.

*furter Zeitung* had lived from crisis to crisis, its existence threatened with each major change in the structure of the German press.[16]

Founded in 1856 by Leopold Sonnemann as a business and stock exchange paper, the *Frankfurter Zeitung* became one of Germany's leading journals, noted for the extent and authority of its news reports, the scope and reliability of its economic and financial news, and the variety and quality of its cultural material. Liberal-democratic in politics, the *Frankfurter Zeitung* distinguished itself in opposing National Socialism prior to 1933 and thereby incurred the burning enmity of the party leadership and the local fanatics. When the I. G. Farben company became a stockholder in the paper cannot be exactly determined, but as the enterprise encountered financial difficulties during the depression, the deficits were covered by the Farben board members. In 1933, when it became evident the family could not indefinitely retain its publishing properties, the majority shares were transferred to the Farben interests and the Sonnemann heirs withdrew from the direction of the paper.[17] The existence of the paper was again threatened in 1935, with the promulgation of the Amann ordinances. Hitler, according to Amann, wanted to suspend the paper. Finally an exception was granted to the Farben interests to retain ownership of the newspaper, but shortly before the war, by agreement between Goebbels and Amann, it was purchased by the Herold company, of which Rienhardt was the managing director.

The editorial staff, too, lived from one crisis to the next.

[16] Hitler's hatred of the *Frankfurter Zeitung* and the *Berliner Tageblatt*, as Germany's leading democratic papers, was of long standing. See *Mein Kampf*, I, 267-68.

[17] *Zeitungs-Verlag*, No. 23, June 9, 1934, carried a notice that the majority stockholders, Frau Therese Simon-Sonnemann and Drs. Heinrich and Kurt Simon, had transferred their interests to the minority stockholders.

In 1933, the staff, which numbered around seventy persons, was racially and politically unacceptable and had the Editor's Law been applied strictly the paper would have been forced to close. However, Dietrich and Weiss granted liberal exemptions and the core of the editorial staff, which included such figures as Benno Reifenberg, Dolf Sternberger, Erich Lasswitz, Paul Sethe, and Dr. Wilhelm Hausenstein, was maintained. Goebbels' position with regard to this paper and its continuation was that it served a useful purpose as an example, if perhaps only a single one, of a high quality paper in a sea of mediocrity. It made a good impression abroad and was a display item on the newsstands in Zurich, Paris, Milan, Brussels, and Amsterdam. It was also accorded a kind of 'fool's privilege' in comment, news reporting, and criticism. When the *Frankfurter Zeitung* became a property of the Eher concern, Amann placed an able publisher, Dr. Wendelin Hecht, in charge, made additions to the staff, and spent a considerable amount of money rehabilitating the paper. In 1945 Amann stated that "Eventually it was in good shape and the employment and pensions of many people were saved. But suddenly in August 1943, Hitler ordered the *Frankfurter Zeitung* closed. Goebbels told me personally that when he remonstrated with Hitler he only replied: 'I don't like its name.' At Goebbels' suggestion I wrote a memorandum for Hitler, but it did no good. We had to close it. We really needed such a paper because it was a credit to German journalism and was highly regarded abroad." [18]

Otto Dietrich gives this account of Hitler's action: "Sitting one day at table in the (Munich) Osteria Bavaria, he [Hitler] spontaneously ordered Bormann to stop publication of the *Frankfurter Zeitung*. He paid no attention to the remonstrances of the specialists on press matters who were present. The reason for this order was a complaint by

[18] Amann, Interview notes, Aug. 23, 1945.

the wife of Troost, the architect, who had taken offense at something in a column of that newspaper." [19]

Without repeating other versions of the incident, these are the ascertainable facts. Hitler loathed the *Frankfurter Zeitung*, describing it on one occasion as "the banner carrier for all the enemies of National Socialism." His animus toward the paper was not greatly abated when it was brought into the party trust. His suspicion and dislike was fed by the widow of the architect, Ludwig Troost, father of the Nazi style of architecture exemplified by the Haus der deutschen Kunst and the Nazi administration buildings in Munich. The *Frankfurter Zeitung* had published an article in which Troost's work was given rather critical treatment.[20] Thereafter, the widow, who held an important position in the Munich art museums in which Hitler was interested, regularly clipped from the *Frankfurter Zeitung* every item to which a dedicated Nazi might take exception. These she placed before Hitler on his visits to Munich. When the newspaper suspension list was made up in the spring of 1943, Hitler insisted upon closing the *Frankfurter Zeitung*. Everyone concerned—Goebbels, Amann, Rienhardt, Dietrich—regarded the decision as a mistake, each for different reasons, but Hitler remained adamant. Goebbels records in his diary, May 10, 1943, how in a conference with Hitler he sought to win a reprieve for the newspaper. "Unfortunately my view did not prevail in the question of continuing the *Frankfurter Zeitung*. The Führer gave a number of reasons why the *Frankfurter Zeitung* should be eliminated. . . . Personally I believe the reasons for retaining the *Frankfurter Zeitung* are stronger than the Führer realizes, but he is stubbornly of the opinion that it would be better to do away with it. I shall now carry out

[19] Dietrich, *12 Jahre mit Hitler*, p. 202.

[20] Because of its long row of ill-proportioned white columns, Munich wits referred to the Haus der deutschen Kunst as the "Athener Bahnhof" or the "Weisswurst Parade."

his wish and bring about the liquidation of the newspaper." [21]

Amann's appeal to Hitler was no more successful than
Goebbels'. The Führer's decision should have settled the
matter; however, the paper continued to appear. It continued to appear because Rienhardt took bureaucratic action to delay execution of the order. His first move was to
address a memorandum to the party chancellery and then
await a formal reply. When no reply was received a second
communication was dispatched while the suspension order
remained in Rienhardt's basket. After all, Hitler was directing a world war and might conceivably forget about
the *Frankfurter Zeitung*. But then came the final act. The
*Frankfurter Zeitung* published an article on "Poets of the
Movement" ("Dichter der Bewegung"), which dealt with
Dietrich Eckart as dramatist and poet. In the course of the
article the unlucky author referred to Eckart's addiction to
alcohol and narcotics. Who brought the article to Hitler's
attention is not known—whether Frau Troost, Bormann,
or Gauleiter Sprenger. Hitler was incensed and called
Amann sharply to account. Why was his order, which had
been issued twice, not obeyed? Clearly Rienhardt was at
fault and Amann was furious. Their relations, already
strained, moved toward the breaking point.

What then happened can best be described by one of the
principals in the drama, Prof. Erich Welter, at that time
deputy editor of the *Frankfurter Zeitung*, responsible for
editorial personnel. Welter and the offending author were
arrested by the Gestapo and after their release Welter was
charged before the professional journalists' court with
defamation of the Nazi party. Wilhelm Weiss, head of the
Reich journalists' association, let the case against Welter
drag until the storm had blown itself out. But not so

[21] *Goebbels' Diary*, pp. 366-67. As in many of his diary entries,
Goebbels exaggerates his position and authority. Only the director
of the Eher Verlag could liquidate an Eher trust paper.

Amann. He had Welter summoned to Berlin and in Rienhardt's presence addressed him as follows: "We must thank our Führer that in this case of the *Frankfurter Zeitung* he has taken decisive action to clean out the abscess. This cleansing of public life was long overdue. The question now is what should be done with the editors of the *Frankfurter Zeitung*. It has been proposed to make short work of it and put you all up against the wall. I have given it considerable thought and I think, perhaps, there is a way to make your staff associates useful in some degree to the state, despite the disloyal and disintegrating attitude they have displayed. Apparently the editors understand their work; one must simply prevent them from remaining together. My plan is to split them up and take several of the ablest into the staff of the V-B. There they can do no mischief. The editorial staff of the V-B is ideologically sound. I can imagine a kind of crossing taking place, and that the ideological reliability of my editors will fuse with the professional journalistic abilities of the editors of the *Frankfurter Zeitung*. Within a few days you will receive from me a list of those who will be offered transfers. . . . I certainly hope that those selected will appreciate fully the honor that goes with this offer of employment on the editorial staff of the party's leading paper. Should anyone have reservations about responding to this call, he will thereby confirm the suspicion that he has a hostile attitude toward National Socialism and will have to bear the consequences of this confirmation. You will hear more from me on this matter in the near future." There were about seventy persons on the editorial staff and it was agreed among them that those singled out for transfer to the V-B would sacrifice themselves as hostages for the security of the others.

When Welter and the Verlag director, Dr. Hecht, were summoned to Munich to receive the list, they dealt with Wilhelm Weiss, who took quite a different line from Amann. He explained that it was his desire to improve the V-B, and get it out of the rut of an official party paper by availing himself of some of the journalistic talent that had distinguished the *Frankfurter Zeitung*. While Welter and Hecht had no illusions about transforming the V-B, they appreciated Weiss's naïve sincerity and his moderation. The list of journalists to be transferred was considerably shorter than they had anticipated and by negotiation they reduced it still further. Welter learned that he had been selected for a new position, that of a general managing editor to supervise the three staffs in Munich, Vienna, and Berlin. He was able to convince Weiss in discussion that he was unsuited for this position and he was "let off the hook." "I shall thank Herr Weiss to the end of my days that he spared me this sacrifice and accepted my arguments that I was not the right man for the post." [22]

On August 18, the *Frankfurter Zeitung* published a front page announcement stating that as a result of "measures of war economy," it would cease publication on August 31. Subscribers who wished to receive a paper with national coverage were advised to place their applications with the *Völkischer Beobachter*, the *Berliner Börsen-Zeitung*, or the *Deutsche Allgemeine Zeitung*. After 87 years of distinguished service to the economic and cultural community of Western Europe the *Frankfurter Zeitung* was liquidated.

[22] Among those transferred was the distinguished journalist Paul Sethe, who henceforth wrote the military commentaries for the V-B. The source of this amazing account is the sworn affidavit of Prof. Erich Welter in the Spruchkammer case of Wilhelm Weiss. (File II, Beiakten, July 27, 1948.) Frau Troost's involvement was specified by two informants: Rolf Hoffman, successor to "Putzi" Hanfstaengl as chief of the foreign press department of the NSDAP (Interview notes, Aug. 21, 1945); and Eugen Maier, head of the Munich office of the Reich press chief (Interview notes, Aug. 20, 1945). The distinguished author and critic, Wilhelm Hausenstein, who wrote the article about Eckart, was purged from the RPK and barred from further literary and journalistic employment.

Rienhardt's dilatory handling of this case was not the immediate cause of his dismissal by Amann in November 1943, but it widened appreciably the breach between the two men. We can be sure that in making his explanations and excuses to Hitler, Amann placed the responsibility upon his staff director. For ten years, Rienhardt had done Amann's thinking, planning, and writing. His enormous but purposeful energy, which carried him through a four-teen-hour work day, his unmatched knowledge of the publishing industry, and his joy in exercising power carried him far beyond all possible rivals. By 1939 his position in the publishing field was one of unchallenged predominance. Symbolic of the concentration of this power in Rienhardt's person was the removal of the office of the RVDZV, of whose affairs he was now the sole director, to Graf-Spee-Strasse 20, where he functioned simultaneously as the powerful staff director of the administrative office of the Reich Leader for the Press.[23] Nothing significant occurred in the German publishing industry without his knowledge and approval. However, in all decisions and actions he was exercising only powers delegated by his superior. Max Amann was content to sign the articles and promulgate the orders and regulations prepared by his staff director for publication in *Zeitungs-Verlag*. He also read the addresses composed for the party congresses, although their intellectual level and literary polish strangely contrasted with the obvious meager endowments of the man who delivered them. Theirs was a relationship not at all uncommon in highly bureaucratized establishments, but even when the men are somewhat evenly matched intellectually it is a difficult relationship to maintain—one recalls Wilson and House, Bülow and Holstein, Northcliffe and Kennedy Jones, Ludendorff and Hindenburg. After the war, both Amann and Rienhardt were reticent in the matter of their

[23] *Zeitungs-Verlag*, No. 42, Oct. 21, 1939.

breach and the staff leader's abrupt and brutal dismissal. An intimate associate, whose judgment is sound and who worked closely with both men for ten years, thought that the break resulted from an accumulation of resentment and a massive inferiority complex on the part of Amann, who in mentality, education, and ability was so starkly inferior to his principal assistant. Finally subterranean forces broke through the surface and Rienhardt was brutally sacked. There is merit in this explanation.

On the factual side we know that serious friction developed in 1938, and that Rienhardt was the object of several of Amann's famous outbursts of violent wrath. Amann was also the recipient of many bitter complaints from Gauleiters who resented Rienhardt's centralized control and administration of Gau publishing enterprises. They did not always get satisfaction when they went to the Verwaltungsamt in Berlin on matters pertaining to publishing. This was embarrassing for Amann and involved him in a good bit of political fence-mending within the party leadership. On one occasion after the beginning of the war a large display of party publications was arranged for one of the Gauleiter assemblies. The display was designed to show how the press was contributing to the war effort, but it had the opposite effect. It evoked criticism because of unnecessary publishing when the country needed to conserve its resources and manpower for prosecution of the war. For this miscue Amann held Rienhardt responsible and there was an unpleasant scene between the two. Rienhardt was inclined to attribute Amann's loss of confidence in him to the dilatory handling of Hitler's order to suspend the *Frankfurter Zeitung.* But this affair, which was settled in August, could not have produced Rienhardt's dismissal notice in November, unless we assume that in the intervening period Amann was preparing the ground for Rienhardt's discharge. His staff director had served him efficiently and effectively; he had raised the imposing structure

of the party trust; he had given Germany a National Socialist press; he had established a chain of German papers
encompassing every occupied capital of Europe; and since
1938 the Eher combines had yielded large profits from
which Amann personally benefited. "The Moor had done
his work, the Moor could go."

According to Fritz Schmidt, although unconfirmed from
any other source, it was Rienhardt's application to the party
chancellery for appointment to a vacated Reichstag mandate that brought about his fall. He sought this as recognition for his service to the party. It infuriated Amann, who
reminded Hitler of Rienhardt's association with Gregor
Strasser and the party's rejection of Rienhardt as a candidate in the March 1933 election. When the requested appointment was rejected, which indicated Hitler's attitude,
Amann proceeded to sack his staff director in a characteristically brutal fashion. He first notified the military induction office that Rienhardt's deferment from military service was no longer valid. He then sent Wilhelm Baur, manager of the Berlin branch of the V-B, to Rienhardt with a
three-line letter notifying him of his dismissal with one
month's pay.

Rienhardt's departure was a minor Götterdammerung
since these events transpired on November 23, when western Berlin from the Tiergarten to Wilmersdorf was in
flames from the heaviest bombing attack Berlin had suffered to date. The offices of the RPK in Von-der-Heydt-
Strasse and the headquarters of the RVDZV and the Verwaltungsamt in Graf-Spee-Strasse were reduced to smoking ruins. Fritz Schmidt, who as a staff member was present,
describes how Baur called together Rienhardt's principal
collaborators and assistants in the conference room of the
United Press Service and presented Max Wiessner, head of
the Deutscher Verlag, as the new director of the RVDZV,
and himself as staff director of the Verwaltungsamt. "Except perhaps for Baur, none of the approximately twenty

participants in these events will ever forget the ghastliness of the scene: The fire-red, smoke-filled background, the sense of doom evoked by this dark November afternoon, and the bizarre dance of death of a system already condemned by history, but one in which the crazy dance for power and office still continued." [24]

Rienhardt was inducted into the SS Division Leibstandarte Adolf Hitler and served until the war's end. Inquiries from the party chancellery were received through military channels as to his assignments and location, but SS General Sepp Dietrich, a Munich friend of Rienhardt's, rejected all inquiries and suggestions and protected him with the cloak of military anonymity.

## Total War—The Third Press Closing Action

Wilhelm Baur, Rienhardt's successor, had served as chairman of the national book dealers association and business manager of the Berlin branch of the Eher Verlag. He was the son of the famous "Schwester Pia," the only woman holder of the Nazi Blood Order, and a frenetic female figure in the early days of the National Socialist party. As Amann's secretary, Baur grew up in the service of the Eher Verlag and became known in the publishing trade as "Amann's boy" and indubitable stool pigeon. With few ideas of his own and very modest executive ability, he attempted in his new position to carry out Amann's orders, which he received each fortnight on his reporting visits to the Eher headquarters in Munich. Max Wiessner, titular head of the RVDZV, was accustomed to taking Amann's orders as head of the Deutscher Verlag and showed about as much independence and initiative as an office boy. Thus Rienhardt's departure removed the last moderating influence, and the most radical party policies in the publishing industry now had full play.

[24] Schmidt, *Presse in Fesseln*, p. 17.

This policy, which led to further closings and consolidations in the interest of the party press, must be viewed in
connection with the last phase of the war, which began
with the Allied occupation of France and Belgium, the
collapse of the Eastern and Balkan fronts, and the advance
of the Russians to the Vistula and the Danube. The great
accumulated capital of space, which the Wehrmacht had
acquired in the early years of the war, was now dissipated
and Allied armies advanced toward the frontiers of the
Reich in the East and West. Only a handful of military
and civilian opponents of National Socialism drew the
logical conclusion from this situation and endeavored to
overthrow the regime by removing Hitler with a bomb.
The July 20 plot failed and the country was subjected to a
crash program to mobilize every man, woman, and child,
and every economic resource for a total war effort. Surpris-
ingly this had not been done before. Articles of civilian
supply had been produced in Germany long after the production of such commodities had been prohibited in Britain
and the United States.[25] Alone among the Nazi leaders
Goebbels had pressed for a policy of greater civilian sacrifice
and the proclamation of total war. Since 1942 he had
aspired to become the Führer of the home front and at
every opportunity pressed his views upon Hitler. After
July 20 his ambitions were realized as Hitler named him
"Plenipotentiary for the Total War Effort" and endowed
him with extraordinary powers over German civil life.[26]

[25] "The party leaders and Gauleiters believed that the maintenance of the civilian standard of living was essential for the morale
of the country and the health and well-being of the Nazi party in
particular. . . . As late as the fall of 1943 Hitler protested to
Speer against the latter's refusal to allocate material for the production of hair curlers." U. S. Strategic Bombing Survey, *The Effects
of Strategic Bombing on the German War Economy*, p. 70.

[26] Returning from Hitler's headquarters with his appointment
and powers in hand, Goebbels said to an associate: "If I had received these powers when I wanted them so badly, victory would be

Goebbels' program came too late to accomplish anything but further dislocation and confusion on the German home front. By the autumn of 1944 the German civilian economy was caught up in the spreading disruption caused by the concentrated Allied air attacks upon transportation, the most decisive aspect of the Allied attack upon Germany and the one that proved the keystone to final industrial collapse.[27]

During August and September were promulgated a spate of decrees designed to mobilize the maximum manpower and womanpower for the armed forces and armaments production. The draft age was lowered to 16, the work week in war industries and essential services lengthened to 60 hours, and the age limit for conscripting women raised from 45 to 50. These were obvious measures under the circumstances. What was new about the Goebbels program was the suspension or curtailment of a wide range of activities, which did not contribute directly to the war effort, and the transfer of the released personnel to some kind of essential service.

Under the slogan "a people at war" Goebbels and his associates decreed that all foreign domestic help must be transferred to industry; deferred armaments workers sent to the army as soon as replacements could be trained; all public functions—receptions, festival and theater weeks, expositions, and memorial services—not connected with the war effort, banned; theaters, cabarets, orchestras, conservatories, and all fine arts exhibitions suspended; and all

---

in our pockets today, and the war would probably be over. But it takes a bomb under his arse to make Hitler see reason." Rudolf Semmler, *Goebbels—The Man Next to Hitler*, pp. 146-47.

[27] "The attack on transportation beginning in September 1944 was the most important single cause of Germany's ultimate economic collapse. Between August and December freight car loading fell by approximately 50 per cent. . . . From December 1944 onwards, all sectors of the German economy were in rapid decline." USBS, *Effects of Strategic Bombing*, p. 13.

sports events, not local in character, canceled. The universities were emptied of all but students in the scientific, medical, and technical courses and a temporary ban was placed on vacations except for women over 50 and men over 65. Public services were drastically curtailed, mail deliveries cut to one per day, and private telephone service sharply restricted. Travel except for official business was practically prohibited. The Labor Front's "Kraft durch Freude" program was suspended and even some of the agencies and services of the Nazi party were closed or greatly reduced. Riding horseback in the parks was forbidden in Munich and Berlin.[28] Austerity was the order of the day.

These massive closings and curtailments sent swarms of unsuitable people to the labor offices and military induction centers. With the economy already collapsing and plants and factories closing, large pools of unemployment were created. The Goebbels program had its culmination in the creation of the Volkssturm (People's Army) on the anniversary of the Battle of Leipzig (October 18). Organized and trained by the Nazi party officials, it was publicized as an opportunity for every German male, age 16 to 60, who was not in military service, to share directly in the defense of the country. For workers in war industry and essential services the weekly military drill obligation became another irksome burden. "The Volkssturm seems to have epitomized not only the philosophy of the 'total war' program, but its confusion as well." [29] In short, the Goebbels program was a performance typical of a political party that from its inception had emphasized agitation and propaganda—the mill made a great noise but produced little meal. The party's order to Gauleiters and Kreisleiters to

[28] The decrees and accompanying publicity are best studied in *Deutsche Allgemeine Zeitung*, Aug. 2, 25, 26, Sept. 9, 16, 21, 29, Oct. 7; *Völkischer Beobachter*, Aug. 12, 13, Sept. 9; *Münchner, N. N.*, Aug. 3, 19, Sept. 2, 1944.

[29] USBS, *Effects of Strategic Bombing*, p. 39.

resist to the death, the organization of the Volkssturm, the proclamation of a "people's war," the incitement of German youth to become "Werewolves"—these were typical of the Nazi ethos and mentality. Words would substitute for deeds, fantasy become reality, and propaganda bring victory. But it was largely a meaningless performance, a devil's dance around the funeral pyre of the Third Reich.

When so many sectors of civil life and economy were closed or curtailed it followed as a matter of course that the newspaper and publishing industry would be severely affected. This had been forecast in one of Goebbels' pronouncements in which it was stated that the greater part of the 1,500 periodicals still appearing would be discontinued. Technical periodicals would be limited to one in each field; scientific journals would continue to publish only if they contributed directly to the war effort, and all other serial publications in the fields of literature, the arts, entertainment, fashion, and trade would disappear. It was further announced that in the book trade all literature, children's books, and entertainment fiction would be discontinued. Of the 2,000 publishing firms that existed in peacetime only 200 remained and many of these would now suspend operation.[30] A special announcement concerning the newspaper press appeared in *Das Reich* on August 20. Published under Amann's name, but prepared by Baur and his staff, it announced drastic curtailments in the area of the press. It was explained that in all cities where two or more papers still appeared, a merger of these publications would take place if it promised to effect a saving in manpower and materials. In Berlin the *Deutsche Allgemeine Zeitung* and the *Börsen-Zeitung* would combine, as would the *Lokal-Anzeiger* and the *Berliner Morgenpost*. All four papers affected were now Eher publications. In the closing action after Stalingrad the principle had been established

[30] *Deutsche Allgemeine Zeitung,* Sept. 4; *Völkischer Beobachter,* Sept. 9, 1944.

to limit cities of 100,000 population or less to one newspaper. This principle found fullest application under the
Goebbels crash program for total mobilization. Newspaper
mergers and suspensions were effected in twenty principal
cities of the Reich, including Berlin and Vienna.[31] While
many of the mergers involved two papers in the Eher combine, in all instances the title that disappeared was that of
the old established paper. The same principle was applied in
mergers between a party paper and a privately owned journal. When Amann was questioned about this after the war,
he insisted that his instructions were that the better paper
of the two should be maintained; if it were always the Nazi
paper that survived then it must have been the better publication! [32]

In this action most of the remaining privately owned papers in the provinces disappeared, notably those in Bielefeld, Brunswick, Chemnitz, Halle, Münster, Heidelberg,
Nürnberg, and Düsseldorf. Only one case, fairly typical,
may be cited. The Droste Verlag in Düsseldorf was an outstanding private publishing concern which had survived
Nazi pressures, and continued to publish the prosperous
and popular *Der Mittag* and the notable industrial journal
*Deutsche Bergwerks-Zeitung*. Heinrich Droste had maintained his papers in a leading position and had prevented
them from falling into the condition of dull uniformity
that characterized the press of the Third Reich. Anyone
who read these papers consistently during the war can testify that they were indeed white ravens in a notably "brown"
flock. It is not surprising therefore that Amann's article

[31] Notably in Augsburg, Bielefeld, Bremen, Brunswick, Chemnitz,
Cologne, Danzig, Dresden, Düsseldorf, Essen, Hamburg, Hanover,
Königsberg, Karlsruhe, Magdeburg, Münster, and Stettin. In Bo-
hemia-Moravia 35 German and 186 Czech papers were suspended.

[32] "Rienhardt (and Baur) made the decisions but my instructions were that the best paper of the two should continue. It must
have been that the National Socialist paper was the best one in the
city or locality." (Interview notes, Aug. 23, 1945.)

in *Das Reich* announced: "In Düsseldorf *Der Mittag* and the *Deutsche Bergwerks-Zeitung* will disappear." [33]

Indeed by October 1, 1944, the German newspaper scene had been transformed beyond recognition. Of German papers that had more than local or regional circulation, or were recognized and quoted abroad, only a few titles remained—the *Deutsche Allgemeine Zeitung,* the *Münchner Neueste Nachrichten,* which was Eher owned, and the *Kölnische Zeitung,* still in the hands of the Neven DuMont family but hard pressed by Nazi competition, the newsprint shortage, and the disappearance of commercial advertising. Under the Goebbels program for total war a tabulation of the papers affected shows thirty-three journals of provincial importance disappeared by merger, four were closed, and in Berlin and Vienna all suburban papers were consolidated into one newspaper of this type. Thereafter, until the end of the war, as the newsprint supply, transportation, and the condition of the printing plants worsened daily, the newspapers produced were of the war emergency type (Kriegsarbeitsgemeinschaft)—one paper publishing for those that had been merged, closed, or bombed out. In Hamburg, for example, the *Hamburger Anzeiger,* the *Fremdenblatt,* and the *Tageblatt* were issued as a single paper. Despite what the masthead proclaimed, it was simply a party paper published by the Gau Verlag director, Hermann Okrass.[34]

After October 1944 reliable statistics on the number of newspapers and their circulation are not available. Using the statistics of this date and comparing them with the data

---

[33] *Zwischen den Zeilen,* p. 55 (Droste Verlag, Düsseldorf, 1948).

[34] A complete list of the mergers and suspensions is given in *Die Tagespresse des Grossdeutschen Reiches—1944,* p. 45. This elaborate presentation folio was prepared for Amann by the staff of the Deutscher Verlag, probably in one copy. It is entirely statistical and presents the last available data on the number of papers, circulation, and location. The date of compilation was September-October 1944.

for 1937, the full measure of the revolution that had occurred becomes apparent. In 1937 in the area of the "Old
Reich," total average daily circulation of all newspapers
was 16.9 million divided among 2,075 daily papers. The
average daily newspaper circulation in October 1944, including Austria, the Warthegau, and the Sudetenland, was
26.09 million divided among 1,019 newspapers. In the
area of the Greater German Reich approximately 1,000
journals ceased publication during the war. By far the
larger number of these papers, which were suspended or
merged, were small local publications. The trend produced
by Nazi policy and wartime necessity was visibly toward
greater concentration and standardization in German newspaper publishing.[35] Between 1937 and 1944 the newspapers
with average daily circulation of 60,000 or over increased
their share of total national circulation from 35 to 60 per
cent at the expense of papers of small and medium circulation. This concentration is strikingly illustrated in the large
cities: In 1939 Berlin had twenty-two national, city, and
suburban papers; at the end of 1944 these were reduced to
nine. Vienna in 1939 had eleven national, city, and suburban dailies, which were reduced to six by the end of 1944.
Hamburg had four principal papers in 1939, but only two

[35] The following analysis by circulation groups shows the extent
of concentration in newspaper publishing between 1937 and October 1944:

| Circulation Group | Per Cent of Newspapers | | Per Cent of National Circulation | |
|---|---|---|---|---|
| | (1937) | (1944) | (1937) | (1944) |
| 1. 8,000 (or less) | 78. | 52. | 22. | 7.6 |
| 2. 8-25,000 | 15. | 26. | 21. | 14.4 |
| 3. 25-60,000 | 4.5 | 12. | 22. | 17.7 |
| 4. 60,000 (or over) | 2.5 | 10. | 35. | 60.3 |

(These statistics are from *Die Tagespresse des Grossdeutschen
Reiches—1944*, p. 51.)

by 1944.[36] All these consolidations brought the Nazi press closer to the goal of a party monopoly. By 1944 there were only eight newspapers with circulations over 50,000 remaining in private hands.

While the area of the Greater German Reich was beginning to shrink appreciably and many publishing firms were bombed out of existence, by the autumn of 1944 there remained approximately 975 newspapers appearing more or less regularly as circumstances of newsprint supply and distribution permitted. Of this number 350 were party-owned or controlled and 625 were in private hands. However, of the latter number only 25 had circulations of 25,000 or above, the remaining 600 being papers with small circulations and with only local significance. Their printing facilities served primarily as stand-by plants for larger newspapers in neighboring towns and cities. The predominance of the Eher trust papers was overwhelming. In October 1944, 350 party-owned and controlled newspapers held 80 per cent of total daily circulation, while the 625 privately owned papers had only 20 per cent of the national circulation.[37]

By February 1945 there were only 700 newspapers appearing and they barely met the definition of a daily journal—periodic publication, actuality, mechanical reproduction, and public circulation. The monthly newsprint allocation had fallen to 5,000 tons when it was available and deliverable. In January these papers were limited to two pages three times weekly and four pages three times weekly. They resembled handbills or broadsides more than newspapers, carrying little but the daily military report of the

[36] *Die Tagespresse—1944*, p. 40.

[37] This computation is based upon the statistics in *Die Tagespresse—1944*. Fritz Schmidt states that at the "end of 1944" the percentages were 82.5 party press and 17.5 privately owned papers. (*Presse in Fesseln*, pp. 177-78.) Amann estimated the circulation of privately owned papers, after the suspensions and consolidations of 1944, at "somewhere between 15 and 20 per cent."

OKW, local announcements and ordinances, unrealistic appraisals of the military and political situation, and the propaganda appeals of Goebbels, Ley, Göring, Ribbentrop, Rosenberg, Dietrich, and Weiss. Hitler's last public pronouncement issued through the German press was his order of the day to German soldiers on the Oder front appealing to the defenders to stand firm against the Russian advance on Berlin.[38] As Allied forces occupied German territory the publication of indigenous newspapers was strictly prohibited.

## Exit Hugenberg—Amann Purchases the Scherl Verlag

Alfred Hugenberg, the only publisher who, after 1936, operated in the newspaper field with capital derived from heavy industry, was finally eliminated under war-time measures in 1944. The Hugenberg trust, undoubtedly a model for the Eher combination, had its origin in 1919 with the founding of the Economic Union (Wirtschaftvereinigung). With a board of directors composed of twelve members—six from industry and six from public life—it operated as a trustee group with capital supplied by the coal, steel, and engineering magnates of the Ruhr and Rhineland. These twelve men held in trust the shares of the Ostdeutsche Privatbank which was used as the principal holding company for the majority voting stock of the various properties acquired on behalf of the interests represented by the Wirtschaftvereinigung. Hugenberg was the all-powerful executive officer of the managing board. Through purchase or development, the Hugenberg trust during the 1920's acquired a strong position in the press, motion picture, and advertising fields. This position, which was powerful but by no means exclusive, was exploited politically on behalf of the German Nationalist party.

[38] *Völkischer Beobachter*, Berlin ed. April 17, 1945.

What distinguished the Hugenberg organization, a complex capitalistic combination, was that it did not concern itself exclusively with profits but combined its economic objectives with definite political goals. It operated in five fields of public information through the following subsidiary corporations: 1) the August Scherl publishing company, one of the largest newspaper, periodical, and book publishing firms in Berlin; 2) the Vera Verlagsanstalt, which owned or managed fourteen provincial newspapers, the most important being in Munich, Stuttgart, Darmstadt, Elberfeld, Magdeburg, and Halle; 3) the Ala Advertising Agency, with branches in all important centers; 4) the Telegraph Union, an international news agency rivaling the semi-official Wolff Telegraph Bureau; and 5) the giant Universum-Film AG (Ufa), Germany's principal producer of feature films and newsreels. Vehemently attacked by the Socialists and Democrats because of its monopolistic features and propagation of the programs and policies of the Nationalist party, the Hugenberg trust was unquestionably the greatest concentration of power operating upon German public opinion. However it was not a monopoly, and in every field it met strong competition.[39]

The elements of the Hugenberg trust were not immune to the world economic crisis that began in 1929. When the Nazis came to power many of the subsidiaries were operating "in the red" and a combination of political and economic pressure led to a breakup of the combine. First, Winkler negotiated the sale of the Telegraph Union and its merger with the WTB to create a state monopoly in the distribution of foreign and domestic news. Next to go was the floundering Ala Advertising Agency, which was pur-

---

[39] Ludwig Bernhard, *Der Hugenberg Konzern, passim.* For the structure of the trust see especially pp. 94-98. In many respects this is a remarkable study in that it combines sociological and economic analysis with the hard facts of corporate finance and organization.

chased by Eher in order to improve the advertising position of the Gau papers. (Two years passed before Ala showed any profit under the new management.) In 1935 the Amann ordinances led to the sale of the Vera company and its provincial newspaper holdings to the party trust. Winkler, as has been noted, used the Vera company henceforth as a principal holding and management concern for the papers which he purchased on behalf of Amann and the Eher Verlag. In the action to nationalize the film industry, Winkler negotiated the sale of the Ufa concern, whose financial affairs he henceforth administered on behalf of his principals, the propaganda ministry and the Reich ministry of finance.

In 1935-1936 when other industrialists, who operated in the publishing field with industrial capital, were excluded —Bosch, Haniel, I. G. Farben—an exception was made for Hugenberg, who was admitted to the RPK and permitted to retain the Scherl Verlag. Whether it was a commitment by Hitler to Hugenberg, or the protecting influence of Goebbels or Göring that made it possible to retain his newspaper and publishing business, cannot be ascertained. It is not really important. The Scherl Verlag published in Berlin the mass circulation *Lokal-Anzeiger*, the popular *Berliner Nachtaugsgabe, Der Montag* and a number of illustrated magazines, trade journals, and numerous city and business directories. With large printing establishments in Berlin and Leipzig, together with other physical assets, the capital stock of the Scherl Verlag had a nominal value of 30 million RM. With the outbreak of the war, Scherl added the richly illustrated Luftwaffe periodical, *Der Adler*, and concluded a number of publishing contracts with the Wehrmacht. Hugenberg's publications survived all the suspensions and consolidations until 1943, when some of the periodicals were suspended under the general closing action put through by Rienhardt after the disaster at Stalingrad.

In the allocation of newsprint and paper, Hugenberg's

firm was in a vulnerable position compared to the Eher competitors. In 1943, those surviving publishers who had enjoyed a bonanza in the early years of the war began to feel a severe pinch as profits declined or disappeared altogether. Whether it was his age and the desire to put his house in order—he was 79—or the difficulties of continuing in a vulnerable business, the "old silver fox" approached the RPK with a request that his publisher's license and shares in the Scherl Verlag be transferred to his son-in-law. Amann countered with the usual demand that a majority of the stock be sold to the party newspaper trust. He wanted the Scherl Verlag, so he said in 1945, as a stand-by establishment for the party papers in Berlin, whose plants had already suffered damage from bombing and might be expected to suffer even more. He therefore offered to purchase the concern in its entirety, appointing as his negotiator the staff director of the Verwaltungsamt, Wilhelm Baur. The latter was no match for Hugenberg and his attorneys, and so botched the negotiations that his mandate was canceled. Amann then for the last time called on the "old pro," Max Winkler, to act for the Eher Verlag. With their attorneys, appraisers, and accountants the two old men, Hugenberg and Winkler, met again as they had on many occasions in the past to deal and haggle over publishing houses, film companies, printing plants, and newspaper titles. After a lively sparring session on inventories and balance sheets they agreed on a price—64,106,500 RM —for all newspaper and periodical titles, the book publishing house, the photo service, and all plant and equipment. They then stalled on the method of payment. Hugenberg stubbornly refused the total purchase price in cash and state securities, with which the accounts of the Eher and Herold companies were stuffed, and demanded instead that a substantial portion be paid in government held shares of the Ilseder Hütte (Ilseder Smelting Company) and the Vereinigte Stahlwerke (United Steel Company), the latter shares acquired by the Prussian state from Fritz Thyssen in 1931 when a number of the Ruhr barons had been saved from bankruptcy by state credits. Hugenberg, who was not noted for tact, said that "he did not want to be paid in paper money; he didn't think it worth much."

A year later, with the Third Reich completely smashed, Amann was still chattering indignantly about Hugenberg's lack of patriotism and confidence in the regime.[40] The obliging Walther Funk, minister of economics and president of the Reichsbank, agreed to the method of payment and the transfer of stock. The contract, signed on September 6, 1944, assigned to Hugenberg shares in the Ilseder Hütte valued at 17,118,000 RM and shares in the Vereinigte Stahlwerke valued at 21,270,000 RM, and the balance in cash. To facilitate the deal Winkler formed a company in which he held the trustee shares; this company was the legal purchaser but its shares were held in turn by the Herold and Eher companies. The transfer of the Ilseder stock was never completed and ownership of the shares was under litigation after the war.[41] Amann derived no benefit from the purchase as the Scherl Verlag was bombed out shortly after it was taken over. The principal papers disappeared when Baur merged the *Lokal-Anzeiger* with the *Eher Morgenpost* and the *Nachtausgabe* with *Der Angriff*. But Hugenberg, who must be accounted a principal gravedigger of the Weimar republic, could go back whence he came, and as he came, with a substantial block of shares of Rhenish-Westphalian industry in his briefcase.

[40] Amann, Interview notes, Aug. 23, 1945.

[41] Copies of the contract, inventories, and correspondence of the principals are in File No. 3820, "Scherl Verlag," BWB. Fritz Schmidt's account (*Presse in Fesseln*, pp. 155-58) is acceptable in broad outline but as usual much slanted, partly imaginary, and unreliable as to details. This usually appears in connection with his book when a firm documentary record is available for comparison.

## The Eher Verlag and the Economics of Publishing

After liquidation of the Vera and Phoenix holding companies the structure of the party publishing trust was considerably simplified. Two organization charts showing the corporate structure have survived. One dates from July 1, 1944, the other from about six months earlier. The earlier chart shows the percentages of Eher participation through the Herold company in former privately owned newspapers and reveals how the Nazi cancer had invaded every important segment of the press. Held directly by the parent Eher Verlag were two publishing houses in Vienna, three in Munich, and two in Berlin.[42] The Europa Verlag, a subsidiary of Eher, owned and directed 27 publishing companies which produced the German newspapers in the Protectorate of Bohemia-Moravia and the occupied territories of Eastern and Western Europe. Under the Herold Verlagsanstalt were grouped 44 publishing enterprises acquired from private owners. Of these Herold held the controlling shares in 14 companies—from 51 to 70 per cent—and by lease the newspaper rights and titles of four additional companies. The 26 remaining publishing firms, including the Ala Advertising Agency, were wholly owned by the Herold concern. The profits from stock participation and ownership of these enterprises, which had been the largest and most profitable in Germany, flowed directly to the Eher company.

In all, 72 party publishing companies were organized in the Standarte group which, in its organization and objectives, bore considerable resemblance to the Konzentration

---

[42] These were the Albrecht Dürer and Ostmärkische firms in Vienna; Knorr and Hirth, M. Müller and Son, and the Albert Langen—Georg Müller firms in Munich; and the Deutscher Verlag and Scherl Verlag in Berlin.

AG of the former Social Democratic party. Both administered a large chain of official party papers on cooperative
principles. No profits were paid to the stockholders—the
Eher Verlag and the Gau publishing companies—and all
accumulations were used to finance and further the objectives of the party. In the Konzentration AG, management
and supervision were decentralized to 24 field offices; in the
Standarte organization to 43 Gau publishing companies.
Both organizations provided similar services: financing,
centralized purchasing, uniform policies and standards, and
periodic auditing. Both systems were directed toward the
propagation of an ideology and in the party membership
both enjoyed a reserved block of subscribers. What marks
the newspaper development in the Third Reich as unique
was the displacement of the free press by the party press
of the NSDAP and the establishment of a near monopoly
in the publishing field. The single party state had as its
logical extension the single party press. By 1944 in twenty
of the Gaue, the Standarte papers accounted for 90 per cent
or more of newspaper circulation. As to the financial performance of the Standarte trust no firm conclusions can
be reached as the records of the company were destroyed
in Berlin. However, from statements of those immediately
concerned we know that the conversion, development, and
financing of the Gau press was a heavy burden down to
1936; thereafter the organization was self-supporting and
generated from its profits capital for further expansion of
the system.

The profitability of the Eher Verlag and its subsidiaries,
excluding the Gau papers of the Standarte combine, is
fully attested by the only available auditor's report prepared
by the Bavarian Trustee and Auditing company (Bayerische
Treuhand AG, Munich) for the year 1943. The profit and
loss statement in this report shows the annual profit position of the Eher company and its subsidiaries from 1936
through 1943. Since they illuminate the publishing indus-

try and correlate closely with the historical developments of these years the figures are of cardinal interest.

|  | NET PROFIT EHER VERLAG | PER CENT OF LOSS OR GAIN | PROFIT FROM EHER SUBSIDIARIES | PER CENT OF LOSS OR GAIN |
|---|---|---|---|---|
| 1936 | 3,987,000 | 8.25 (decrease) | 500,000 | 30. (increase) |
| 1937 | 8,489,000 | 112.9 | 1,670,000 | 132. |
| 1938 | 13,809,000 | 62.6 | 2,542,000 | 119. |
| 1939 | 26,225,000 | 90. | 8,776,000 | 245. |
| 1940 | 53,900,000 | 105. | 20,288,000 | 131. |
| 1941 | 63,971,000 | 18. | 32,689,000 | 66. |
| 1942 | 106,700,000 | 66.7 | 63,800,000 | 99. |
| 1943 | 99,819,000 | 6.4 (decrease) | 49,483,000 | 22. (decrease) |

Some explicit conclusions can be drawn from these statistics: 1) The decline in profits in 1936 resulted from the unsettlement and slump produced by the Amann ordinances; 2) the publishing concerns purchased in 1935-1936 did not yield profits comparable to the net profits of the parent company until the outbreak of the war; 3) beginning in 1940 the profits from the subsidiaries equaled or exceeded those from the central party publishing house; 4) 1942 was the most prosperous year, while 1943 showed a noticeable decline; 5) if a balance sheet for 1944 were available it would doubtless show a terrific slump and probably the disappearance of all profits.

There is no estimate available of the total value of capital assets of the Eher combine and its 150 corporate entities, nor were the experts who worked on its liquidation after the war able to provide one. We do know what its liquid assets were: In various current bank accounts were 5,373,440 RM, and in government bonds and securities on deposit in the Reichsbank 593,721,700 RM, making a total of 599,105,140 RM. Another item of interest revealed by the auditor's report was the credit balances of important party members whose books and articles were published by the Verlag. Hitler, who had no other significant bank account, had accumulated royalties on *Mein Kampf* in the amount of 5,525,811 RM; Göring, 67,861 RM; Goebbels, 135,164 RM; and Rosenberg, 85,673 RM.[43] The most astonishing revelation, which explains in part the high net profits, was the fact, confirmed by tax officials in 1945, that the Eher Verlag had paid no taxes—corporate, business turnover, property or excess profits—for the past five years. It was assumed by investigators, but not documented, that a special ruling by the ministry of finance was the basis of non-payment of taxes since 1940. This was altogether typical of the Nazi party and its leaders and a strange application of the party slogan—"The common good above personal advantage!"[44]

In power, prestige, and financial gain Max Amann was the principal beneficiary of the party's giant publishing monopoly. He ruled his empire like a mayor of the palace. He made no financial report to the party chancellery or the Reich treasurer of the party, but only to Hitler personally. He would confer with Hess, but no one else got a glimpse of the inner workings and conditions. Amann prepared for Hitler an annual statement of the Eher concern's affairs, but in Amann's words, "he never reacted by approving or disapproving, or giving me orders."[45] Otto Dietrich, who was constantly in Hitler's entourage, recounts that once or twice a year Amann would appear to make an accounting, to present his proposals with regard to publishing operations, and to receive Hitler's assent and suggestions. Dietrich speculates as to whether Amann's unassailable

[43] Their withdrawals during 1943 were: Hitler, 569,212 RM; Göring, 210,600 RM; Goebbels, 244,212 RM; Rosenberg, 254,908 RM.

[44] Hitler owed nearly a half million marks in back taxes when he became chancellor and had the obligation canceled through action of state secretary Reinhardt and the president of the court of tax appeals. He paid no taxes after 1934. See Oron J. Hale, "Adolf Hitler: Taxpayer," *Amer. Hist. Rev.*, July 1955, pp. 830-42.

[45] Amann, Interview notes, Aug. 23, 1945.

position with the Führer was owing to his position as Hitler's private banker or to Amann's having been his company sergeant in World War I.[46] In the matter of profits from the Eher enterprises, these were not transferred to the party but were used for further newspaper purchases or deposited in the Reichsbank. In 1938, Amann's position was consolidated by a grant of power of attorney from Hitler for all matters pertaining to the Eher Verlag and its subsidiaries. No other Reich leader enjoyed in his sphere such unrestricted and uncontested authority.[47]

Not only did Amann enjoy vast power but also vast profits. Of all the Nazi leaders he made the greatest material gains from his political and business association with the party. A principal provision of the "Denazification law" concerned the use of party membership or position to oppress or injure others, or to enrich the individual party member. In the denazification hearings of Amann's associates and staff members it could not be shown that they had personally enriched themselves, although the opportunity for corruption in the handling of large and valuable properties was certainly present. Neither in the Verwaltungsamt, the RVDZV, the RPK, in Cura, Cautio, or any of the top-level agencies, does there appear to have been corruption—only fanaticism and time-serving. Indeed, as far as material rewards were concerned, working for Max Amann was comparable to working for the King of Prussia! To all special material advantages, he made and enforced his sole claim.

Amann's denazification trial produced a complete exposure of his financial position and operations. The record shows that in 1936 he concluded a new contract as general

[46] *12 Jahre mit Hitler*, pp. 210-11.

[47] In 1945 Amann said he received this power in 1936, but he signed the 1943 auditor's report: "Auf Grund der Vollmacht des Führers vom 10. XI. 38."

manager of the Eher company, which gave him an annual salary of 120,000 RM and five per cent of the net profit of the Eher company. But before that, in December 1933, he had acquired for himself a one-third interest in the printing house of Müller and Son. There was a further reorganization of the party's printing establishment in March 1934, which allocated one third of the shares to the Eher Verlag, one third to Adolf Müller, and one third to Max Amann. It will be recalled that this firm printed the V-B in Munich, Berlin, and Vienna in over a million copies, as well as the *Illustrierte Beobachter*, and a dozen party magazines and weeklies. It also had a monopoly on the printing of all party approved books including *Mein Kampf*. The business of the Müller firm exceeded in volume that of any other printing establishment in Germany with the possible exception of the Deutscher Verlag. That Amann became a man of substantial wealth is also shown by his tax returns. In January 1940 his real property and business holdings were estimated for tax purposes at 6,220,-000 RM, and in January 1943, at 10,306,000 RM. His taxable income in 1941 was 3,479,449 RM; in 1942, 3,221,430 RM; and in 1943, 2,877,156 RM.[48] In discussions with interviewers after the war Amann posed as a business man without any ideological commitment to National Socialism, who on sound principles had developed one of Germany's largest business enterprises and the biggest newspaper chain in the world. He naïvely maintained his integrity, unable to see any conflict of interest resulting from the positions he held in the party, in the RPK, and in the business of publishing. That he had made a shambles of the German publishing industry he would never admit.

[48] All this was recorded in Amann's Spruchkammer proceedings. The records and documents are in Spruchkammer München i, Max Amann, main file; and BWB, File 3820-b, "Gutachten im Presse-sachen," excerpts from the Registergericht-München, Vol. 43.

## How the Nazi Regime Evaluated Its Press

The party monopoly developed by Amann in the publishing field was the counterpart or complement of the Editor's Law that regimented the editors and journalists and made them captives of the propaganda ministry. Basically this was what Hitler desired. The system provided him with the kind of press which he considered essential to the regime. He never had any other view of the press than that of an instrument in the hands of a party leader, or, after he came to power, in the hands of a chief of state. His views of the political role of the press, which he expounded frequently to his intimates, were those of an authoritarian dictator. Its complete control was absolutely essential—it was an instrument like the Luftwaffe. Hitler warmly praised this propaganda apparatus which had been substituted for a free press and boasted of its efficiency. "Amann has more than half of the German papers in his hands. If I call Lorenz [Dietrich's assistant] and give him my views in a few sentences, it will be in every German paper by one o'clock in the morning." Only with this organization was it possible, he said, to turn the entire press around 180 degrees on June 22, 1941. "It couldn't have been done in any other country." And with regard to internal affairs, "We have banished the idea that it is any part of political freedom for people to say what they please through the newspapers." [49]

[49] H. Picker, *Tischgespräche*, pp. 269, 282. Hitler did not hesitate to expound this view of the role of the press to representatives of the publishing and journalistic professions. At an evening reception in the Führerbau in Munich, on November 10, 1938, arranged by Otto Dietrich and attended by 200 leading editors and publishers, Hitler spoke for an hour on the propaganda strategy of the recent Sudeten crisis. He congratulated the press on the successful part it had played and told the editors and publishers exactly

With the war, the strait jacket was laced ever more
tightly. After Stalingrad, when the military situation had
to be concealed by artful propaganda, the German press
almost ceased to be a medium of important daily information. Just as Hitler extended his control of military operations, he also tightened his personal control over the press,
laying down the main lines for handling military publicity
and the waging of psychological warfare. He personally reviewed and corrected the daily OKW military report and
censored Goebbels' weekly political article in *Das Reich*.[50]
At the center of the mechanism were Otto Dietrich and his
assistant Lorenz, who prepared with Hitler's approval, and
sometimes at his instigation, the daily directive for the
German press. Before eleven o'clock each morning the
directive was telephoned by Dietrich to his deputy, Helmut
Sündermann, in Berlin, and to Erich Fischer, head of the
German press division of the propaganda ministry. At
eleven o'clock the division chiefs of the ministry met in
conference, where the directive was discussed, elaborated,
and given its final form. The guidance provided in the
directive was sometimes brief, giving only the line to be
taken toward foreign developments and the military situation. On other occasions it was detailed, specifying headlines, space apportionment, and layout. The directive was

---

how they had been used and "managed" to achieve the desired
result. At times Hitler carried on like a political cabaret performer,
evoking laughter and applause with his crude witticisms aimed at
"over-educated intellectuals," and "the hysteria of our upper ten
thousand," who felt and expressed concern at his conduct of policy
in the Sudeten crisis. Not even a summary of his remarks was
released to the news media, but a recording was made and from this
the speech has been transcribed and published by Wilhelm Treue,
"Rede Hitler vor den deutsche Presse, 10. November 1938,"
*Vierteljahreshefte für Zeitgeschichte*, 6 Jahrg. 1952, Heft 2.
   [50] Picker, *Tischgespräche*, pp. 149, 269. For this article, a conspicuous feature of German wartime journalism, Goebbels received
4,000 RM weekly. (*Memoirs of Alfred Rosenberg*, p. 172.)

communicated to the representative of the principal Berlin and provincial papers at the daily press conference in the ministry and dispatched between 2 and 3 P. M. to the Gau press offices. The smaller journals received the directive through DNB. And woe to the editor who deviated in the slightest degree from the prescribed formulations! A warning, a reprimand, a fine and, in flagrant cases, exclusion from the professional journalists' list were the penalties imposed. Hitler scanned all the important papers and frequently made complaints and suggestions to Dietrich.[51] The unpleasant task of disciplining journalists was delegated by Dietrich to Sündermann, who was known as "Dietrich's tank," and who appeared to enjoy the assignment. Increasingly during the war, the journalists' professional courts were ignored when complaints were lodged and exclusions from the professional list were effected by administrative action. According to Wilhelm Weiss, who headed the association of journalists, the number of cases handled in this manner greatly increased owing to the ever more dictatorial and stringent policies enforced by Hitler and Dietrich.[52]

What kind of profession and what kind of press did the system of total control produce? For a judgment and critique we need not go outside the circle of party leaders who were intimately concerned with the daily work of the press. Wilhelm Weiss, who supported the system enthusiastically during the early years of the regime, was completely disillusioned by the end of the war. Journalists and editors became increasingly dissatisfied and resentful of the government's policy toward the press, he said. Likewise the monopoly gained by the party through Amann's operations undermined the confidence of the public, although

[51] Eugen Maier, head of the Munich office of the Reich press chief, Interview notes, Aug. 20, 1945.

[52] Weiss, Interview notes, Aug. 31, 1945. He estimated the cases of administrative exclusion at approximately one hundred.

the full extent of his operations was not appreciated. Under the strict controls established by the Reich press chief and the propaganda ministry, editors and writers were deprived of all independence and initiative, and the newspaper became simply a megaphone. The public became uncertain and mistrustful of the press. Moreover, Weiss pointed out, a uniform press did not serve equally well all levels of education, interest, and attainment represented in the German population. One paper was just the same as another and all were directed at a mass segment of the public. People became bored or suspicious and the press as a source of information and opinion lost its standing and influence.

Weiss's experience with the military censorship also throws light on the workings of the system. At the beginning of the war, Weiss engaged Colonel Soldan, a leading military expert, as military commentator for the V-B. He wrote objectively and independently, and shortly Weiss was informed by Dietrich that Hitler did not like Soldan's articles. Soon it became impossible to get his material cleared by the military censor and his employment had to be terminated. Another attempt at professional treatment of military operations was made with the hiring of Colonel Dr. Hesse, Brauchitsch's former press officer, but with no better success. The OKW forbade him to continue publication. Henceforth the V-B depended mainly upon the OKW reports and the canned articles of the Wehrmacht Propaganda Office.[53]

Rolf Hoffman, who headed the foreign press department of the NSDAP in Munich, and who served for two years in the propaganda ministry during the war, was vehement in his criticism of the system and its effect upon the journalistic profession. All initiative was killed and no ideas were permitted outside the narrow groove of official directives. He estimated that eighty per cent of the members of

[53] Weiss, Interview notes, Aug. 31, 1945.

the profession found the system intolerable. Because of the regimentation and pressure most journalists became hypocrites without any initiative. The stronger personalities tried to get positions as foreign correspondents in Stockholm, Lisbon, Madrid, or Istanbul. Others—Fritz Hesse, Karl Megerle, Krug von Nidda, and Dr. Kries—joined the foreign office or went abroad as press attachés. This was deeply resented by Dietrich and Goebbels, who had them stricken from the professional list.[54]

And even Amann, when asked if he thought the party's monopoly of newspaper publishing produced a good daily press, admitted that although he had given it a good economic foundation, "it was impossible to edit and publish good newspapers." The editors, he said, complained to him that they received a three-inch file of directives and a one-inch file of news. Owing to exchange difficulties it was impossible to maintain an adequate foreign news service. There was no recruitment of young talent and the editors were always receiving complaints and reprimands from Dietrich. "How could an editor publish a good paper when he sat with one foot in jail and the other in the editorial room?" [55] Indeed, how could he?

[54] Rolf Hoffman, Interview notes, Aug. 20-21, 1945. Fritz Hesse, *Das Spiel um Deutschland* (Munich, 1953), pp. 220, 233.

[55] Amann, Interview notes, Aug. 23, 1945.

# CHART I. Organization of the Reich Press Chamber

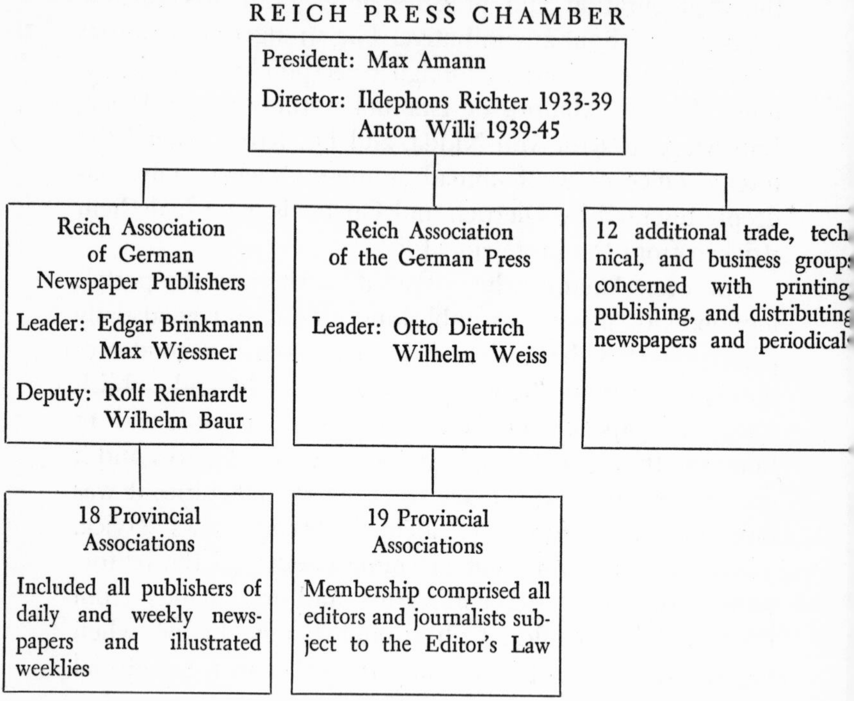

## REICH PRESS CHAMBER

| |
|---|
| President: Max Amann |
| Director: Ildephons Richter 1933-39 |
| Anton Willi 1939-45 |

| Reich Association of German Newspaper Publishers | Reich Association of the German Press | 12 additional trade, technical, and business groups concerned with printing, publishing, and distributing newspapers and periodicals |
|---|---|---|
| Leader: Edgar Brinkmann Max Wiessner | Leader: Otto Dietrich Wilhelm Weiss | |
| Deputy: Rolf Rienhardt Wilhelm Baur | | |

| 18 Provincial Associations | 19 Provincial Associations |
|---|---|
| Included all publishers of daily and weekly newspapers and illustrated weeklies | Membership comprised all editors and journalists subject to the Editor's Law |

CHART II. Organization of the Eher Verlag, 1944

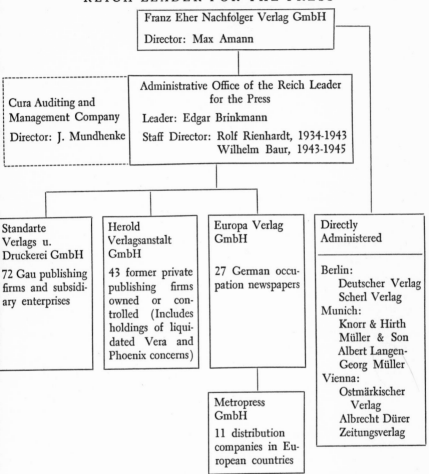

REICH LEADER FOR THE PRESS

Franz Eher Nachfolger Verlag GmbH

Director: Max Amann

---

Cura Auditing and Management Company

Director: J. Mundhenke

---

Administrative Office of the Reich Leader for the Press

Leader: Edgar Brinkmann

Staff Director: Rolf Rienhardt, 1934-1943
Wilhelm Baur, 1943-1945

---

Standarte Verlags u. Druckerei GmbH

72 Gau publishing firms and subsidiary enterprises

---

Herold Verlagsanstalt GmbH

43 former private publishing firms owned or controlled (Includes holdings of liquidated Vera and Phoenix concerns)

---

Europa Verlag GmbH

27 German occupation newspapers

---

Directly Administered

Berlin:
    Deutscher Verlag
    Scherl Verlag
Munich:
    Knorr & Hirth
    Müller & Son
    Albert Langen-
    Georg Müller
Vienna:
    Ostmärkischer
    Verlag
    Albrecht Dürer
    Zeitungsverlag

---

Metropress GmbH

11 distribution companies in European countries

# Notes on Records, Interviews, and Books · Bibliography

## The Eher Verlag

Max Amann's office and the headquarters of the Eher Verlag were located at Thierschstrasse 11, Munich. Alone among the principal buildings on the street, the Eher Verlag structure was bombed and partially destroyed by fire in the heavy air attacks of March-April 1944. Major losses of business papers and records were sustained. Following the fire, the business office, remaining records, and clerical personnel were removed to the present McGraw Kaserne on Tegernseelandstrasse. In 1945, when the main buildings in this complex were occupied by U. S. troops, they removed and destroyed the surviving business records. ("Bericht über die Tätigkeit der Abwicklungsstelle des Eher Verlages, München 1945," 15 pp. typescript, signed Stegmaier.) Doubtless this accounts for the lack of a large body of Amann correspondence and papers.

However, the business records of the Eher subsidiaries—Standarte, Vera, Herold, and Phoenix companies—and of the Administrative Office of the Reich Leader for the Press were maintained in Berlin. Altogether forty-five packages of records, including board minutes, annual balance statements, and tax documents were removed to Weissenfels a.d. Saale in April 1945. Shortly thereafter these records were taken by a member of the office staff to Hof, in northern Bavaria, and thence to Munich where they were deposited at the headquarters of U. S. Military Government in the Hubertusstrasse. It can be assumed that these are the documents now held by the Restitution Office of the

Bavarian Ministry of Finance. (Stegmaier report.) Apparently only these basic business documents of the Eher Verlag survived dispersion and destruction.

The legal and financial investigations essential to the liquidation of the Eher concern were undertaken by the Property Control Office of U. S. Military Government in Munich. A substantial quantity of documents and records were collected during this phase and these materials have been made available to the author. An important item in this collection is the auditor's report on the financial position of the parent company for the year 1943, prepared by the Bayerische Treuhand AG, Munich. Included also is a valuable analysis and commentary by Herr Willy Imhof, a former business executive in the Berlin headquarters, who worked with U. S. Property Control, and subsequently with Bavarian finance officials, in the liquidation of the Eher Verlag. An organizational chart of the Eher complex showing the percentage of its holdings in about 150 publishing firms is another item of unique importance in this collection.

## Reichspressekammer

The Reich Press Chamber was established and activated on December 1, 1933. Unlike the other chambers of the Reich Chamber of Culture, it left the major administrative tasks to the trade and professional organizations (Fachverbände), which were reorganized as control agencies. The RPK therefore operated with a small staff, as the functions were performed in the offices of the subordinate organizations. In the summer of 1943, the officials of the RPK began to move important records to the village of Hohenbruch and the estate Saaten-Neuendorf in Mark Brandenburg. Before the transfer was completed the November 1943 air attacks resulted in the destruction of unmoved records in the central office at Herkulesufer 10. In February and March 1945, as the Russians approached

Berlin, all non-essential records stored at Hohenbruch were burned on orders from higher authority. The remaining records of the RPK in Berlin, and in the storage center in the Mark, were destroyed or lost as a result of war action. The chief accountant of the RPK went twice to Hohenbruch following the end of hostilities and reported that the main house was completely burned and a nearby Gasthaus used for storing files was partly destroyed. What records survived had been removed. By whose authority this had been done the official could not learn. (Report of Dr. Rudolf Vincentz, former business manager of the RPK, Sept. 18, 1945.)

A valuable source of information would have been the individual publisher personnel files—those publishers investigated, cleared, and admitted to the RPK. For the other Chamber of Culture divisions—film, radio, literature, music, art, and theater—the personnel records survived, and were seized and administered by British authorities until they were merged in 1949 with U. S. holdings in the Berlin Document Center. They are presently consolidated into one alphabetically organized collection, comprising several hundred linear feet; but a thorough sampling of the file for the names of publishers leads to the conclusion that the membership file of the RPK was not among those seized and consolidated.

## Verwaltungsamt des Reichsleiters für die Presse

All the Nazi administrative offices dealing with publishing affairs were located between Tiergartenstrasse and Lutzowüfer, a section of Berlin that sustained heavy damage in the November 1943 air raids. The building at Graf-Spee-Strasse 20, which housed both the Administrative Office and the headquarters of the RVDZV, was totally destroyed. In 1958 the site was still uncleared, the rubble heaped eight feet high. Some records from these offices were evacuated to Hohenbruch and were destroyed there or seized by the Russians. Aside from the financial records later evacuated to Weissenfels and Munich, no large body of papers from this office seems to have survived.

## Reichsverband der Deutschen Zeitungsverleger

This was the trade association of the German newspaper publishers, formerly the Verein Deutscher Zeitungsverleger. The subordinate regional organizations (Landesverbände) were retained as executive agencies of the central office in Berlin. Of the records of this organization only two small collections, now in the Berlin Document Center, appear to have survived. One is the correspondence and general files of the executive secretary of the Landesverband Northwest Germany, A. D. Lattmann, covering the period from October 1933 to June 1934 and from January 1936 to June 1937. Although fragmentary, these files give a clear picture of the conduct of business and the relationship between the provincial offices and the central office in Berlin. The second item is a collection of the numbered circulars and directives issued by the central office from May 1, 1934, when the series began, to December 31, 1937. Included also are the protocols of the conferences of Landesverband chairmen and executive secretaries, who were summoned periodically to Berlin for staff meetings and conferences.

## Spruchkammer Records

The Spruchkammer records, or denazification files, of former Nazi leaders are not now generally available to scholars. Their classification as privileged records has not been clearly established, neither have they been classified as historical material and turned over to state archival authorities. In Bavaria they are temporarily closed under the authority of the Ministry of Justice. In the summer of 1958, the Ministry was preparing a draft law that would cover the interest of the state, the interest of the individ-

ual and his family, and meet the access requirements of
historical scholars. With special permission I was able to
use at the Ministry of Justice the case files of Max Amann
and Wilhelm Weiss, both deceased.

The Amann file consists of a "Main Case File," an "Appeals File," and the "Handakten" of the prosecutor. Altogether the complete record makes an eighteen-inch bundle.
Included are depositions, interrogations, documentary exhibits, briefs of counsel, the court's decision, and arrest,
committal, and release forms. There is much of historical
value, although the prosecutor made no effort to reconstruct in detail Amann's role in erecting the Nazi party
publishing monopoly. The Spruchkammer record of Wilhelm Weiss, editor-in-chief of the *Völkischer Beobachter*
and president of the Reich Association of the German
Press, is not as extensive as Amann's but the materials are
quite similar. It has value for the historian.

## Restitution and Indemnity Court Records

The work of restituting property and idemnifying persons who suffered losses through the action of the Nazi
state and party began with the Allied occupation and continues today through the state Restitution and Indemnity
Courts. The impact of war and revolution upon property
relationships is endlessly illustrated by the cases processed
through these courts and the Court of Restitution Appeals
at Nürnberg. Among the important and interesting cases
are those resulting from suits brought by former newspaper owners, who under pressure sold their publishing enterprises to the Eher trust. The Ullstein case in Berlin is
notorious. However, in Württemberg some of the earliest
and most important cases were adjudicated and the judgments have served as precedents in subsequent litigation.
These suits by the "old publishers," as they are frequently
designated, are well prepared with massive research and

documentation. Frequently the publisher kept his records of the sale or confiscation and these are placed in evidence. Also in the important suits surviving officials of the party agencies and the Eher concern have testified as witnesses. With permission of the president of the state courts, copies of the judgment and the Begründung can be secured. These provide a digest with extensive excerpts from the exhibits and testimony, the depositions of witnesses, and all factual material relevant to the judge's decision. The historical value of the records is substantial. Of great value for this study were the following:

Dr. Wolfgang Huck vs. State of Baden-Württemberg, Aug. 16, 1956. (48 pp. mimeo.) Druckerei GmbH, Stuttgart vs. former state of Württemberg, June 8, 1953. (10 pp. mimeo.)

Hans Rümelin, Heilbronn vs. Ministry of Finance, Baden-Württemberg, Jan. 13, 1954. (28 pp. mimeo.)

Eugen Jenz vs. Ministry of Finance, Baden-Württemberg, Feb. 4, 1954. (19 pp. mimeo.)

Heinz Becker vs. former state of Württemberg-Baden, March 15, 1954. (17 pp. mimeo.) State of Baden-Württemberg as assignee of the Druckerei GmbH, Stuttgart vs. the German Reich, Dec. 22, 1955. (13 pp. mimeo.)

Ilse Pielenz geb. Amann vs. Ministry of Finance, Baden-Württemberg, Dec. 28, 1953. (88 pp. mimeo.)

Heirs of Dr. August Madsack vs. State of Baden-Württemberg, Aug. 16, 1956. (36 pp. mimeo.)

The judgments of the Court of Restitution Appeals (subsequently Supreme Restitution Court) deal less with facts than with decisions of the lower courts and interpretation of the restitution laws. The following are important cases affecting the press:

Case No. 70: Rolf Boes vs. Bavarian Ministry of Finance, Feb. 6, 1951. (8 pp. mimeo.)

Case No. 354: Karl Richter vs. State of Bavaria, April 25, 1952. (10 pp. mimeo.)

Case No. 1771: State of Baden-Württemberg vs. Dr. Wolfgang Huck, April 25, 1958. (11 pp. mimeo.)

## Berlin Document Center (U. S. Mission Berlin)

Besides the records of the RVDZV mentioned above, the materials of the greatest value in this Center are contained in those portions of the "Hauptarchiv der NSDAP —München" that were not removed to the United States. These constitute approximately 140 linear shelf-feet; the file folders and bundles have been given record group numbers by the BDC staff. This collection has been microfilmed by the Hoover Institute and a copy of the film deposited in the National Archives. Among the items on the early history of the N-S press, from 1925 to 1933, is file No. 1766, which contains documents from the Bavarian ministry of interior on developments in the National Socialist press. An unnumbered file contains letters, circulars, and directives originating in the propaganda section of the Reichsleitung. Signed items are from Bouhler and Himmler, the latter holding the position of section chief from 1926 to 1930, with the title of Stellv. Reichspropagandaleiter.

Significant materials on the origin and development of the provincial party press are contained in the Hauptarchiv. In 1935 Reich Press Chief Dietrich instructed the director of the Hauptarchiv, Dr. Uetrecht, to prepare a history of the N-S press during the decade 1926-1935. A questionnaire was drafted and sent to the publisher of each party paper. Requested was founding date, names of founders and editors, and the number, duration, and circumstances of the paper's suspensions during the Kampfzeit. A file for each paper was established in which all relevant material was placed. The work was done by a staff member of the Hauptarchiv, Franz Hartmann. The contents of the folders, which have file numbers from 968 to 1100, constitute the documentary basis of Hartmann's completed manuscript, "Statistische und Geschichtliche Entwicklung der NS Presse, 1926-1935." (471 pp.) This study is now in the "Eher Verlag Collection" of the Manuscripts Division of the Library of Congress. Prepared with a view to publication as an official history of the party press, a bound copy was presented to Hitler as a Christmas gift in 1936. Permission to publish was withheld either by Hitler or Dietrich and the manuscript remained in the Hauptarchiv classified "Secret." (Letter from Dr. Uetrecht to the Reichspressestelle der NSDAP, Presse-Politische Amt, Berlin, March 17, 1937; Hauptarchiv folder No. 1028, BDC.) What Hartmann's manuscript reveals to an objective reader is not always flattering to the Nazi press, and even less so is much material which he screened out and left unused in the folders containing his basic documentation.

## Institut für Zeitgeschichte

The Institute archives yielded biographical and interview material not available elsewhere and the principal published books and monographs on the Nazi period are contained in the library. A special collection contains a number of limited edition volumes dealing with particular aspects of the party's publishing operations. Among these may be mentioned: *Deutscher Verlag, 1934-1941*, an elaborate folio prepared in the office of the Deutscher Verlag for presentation to Amann on his fiftieth birthday. It gives the internal and statistical history of the Ullstein publishing house after it was acquired by the Eher Verlag. *Adolf Müller—Sein Schaffen und Wirken bis zu seinem fünfzigsten Lebensjahr* (Munich, 1934), provides information on the printer of the V-B. *Die Tagespresse des Grossdeutschen Reiches—1944*, is a lavishly printed folio consisting entirely of maps, charts, and statistical tables prepared in the Deutscher Verlag by staff members. It is a mine of information, giving, for example, the number and circulation of all newspapers in each Gau, the consolidations resulting from wartime conditions, and significant correlations of population, newspaper circulation, and newspaper ownership. Dr. Sonja Noller, *Die Geschichte des "Völkischen Beobachters" von 1920-1923* (Diss. Munich 1956, 324 pp. typescript), is a highly competent study of the early history of the official party paper.

The most important book of which we have knowledge is missing from this valuable collection. According to Max Amann, the Verwaltungsamt in Berlin prepared a complete history of the Eher Verlag and its subsidiaries for presentation to him on his fiftieth birthday. It detailed all publishing enterprises acquired, the purchase price, and subsequent performance, giving in effect a complete picture of the concern and its corporate properties. At the end of hostilities this volume was in Amann's house at Tegernsee, near Munich. Since the house was occupied by General George Patton it was not possible to gain entry and search for it. Subsequently the volume disappeared and all efforts to trace the book have failed. In 1958 Willy Imhof gave this information about the volume: Confirming its preparation in the Verwaltungsamt, he stated that four copies were printed, of which one was presented to Amann, one retained in the Verwaltungsamt, and he did not know the disposition of the remaining two. The Berlin copy was destroyed in the bombing and fire at Graf-Spee-Strasse in 1943.

## Institut für Zeitungswissenschaft—Munich

The library of the Institute, with its extensive archive, is one of the best specialized collections on the history of the press to be found in Germany. The materials collected by Prof. Karl D'Ester as a basis for various Gutachten submitted in publishers' restitution cases are important items in this collection. Also of substantial value are the dissertations dealing with aspects of N-S press and publishing policy. The most useful are: Hortlof Biesenberger, *Der*

*Schwarzwälder Bote in den Jahren, 1930-1950* (Diss. Munich, 1953, 175 pp.), is a well documented study of a privately owned paper under the N-S regime, by the son of the former editor and present publisher. Claus Gottlieb, *Der Teckbote* (Diss. Munich, 1955, 217 pp.), has a chapter dealing with the period 1933-1945, which provides a case history of a small newspaper that escaped the N-S trust. H. Girardet, *Der wirtschaftliche Aufbau der Kommunistischen Tagespresse in Deutschland von 1918 bis 1933* (Diss. Leipzig, 1938, 124 pp.), is a factually based study with emphasis on the Ruhr region. The author had access to the confiscated records of the KPD publishing houses and interrogated leading KPD personnel. Ludwig Winter, *Neue wirtschaftliche Grundlagen des deutschen Zeitungswesens* (Diss. Nürnberg, 1938, 172 pp.), is based in part upon Rolf Rienhardt's statements and speeches before the RVDZV and the provincial associations. A. D. Limburg, *Der Pötz-Konzern* (Diss. Bonn, 1946, 194 pp.), is a thoroughly documented study of the largest Catholic newspaper chain and its unsuccessful struggle against the Nazi publishing trust. Heinrich Wurstbauer, *Lizenzzeitungen und Heimat Presse in Bayern* (Diss. Munich, 1952, 194 pp.), is a detailed study of the Nazi conquest of the local press in Bavaria, especially the papers allied with the Bavarian People's Party. Siegfried Walchner, *Die Neuordnung der deutschen Presse und ihre wirtschaftliche Organisation* (Diss. Giessen, 1937, 71 pp.), narrates the history of two Catholic cooperative chains in Westphalia and southern Württemberg—the Verbo and Zeno groups—and their liquidation by the Nazis.

In the archival materials in the Institute are copies of expert opinions on the N-S press policies prepared for submission in publishers' restitution cases: Ministerialrat a.D. Werner Stephan, expert opinion, March 28, 1949; Dr. Martin Löffler, brief of counsel in the case of Robert Bosch for the Restitution Chamber of the Landgericht-Stuttgart,

May 18, 1949; Dr. Karl D'Ester, expert opinion, Munich, May 14, 1949; Dr. Walther Jänecke, expert opinion, May 13, 1949.

## Interviews and Communications

In connection with assigned duties as an army historical officer in Germany, in 1945, the author interviewed a number of persons prominent in the press and publishing fields. The notes of these interviews have been used: Alfred Rosenberg, editor and publisher of the V-B; Franz Xaver Schwarz, N-S party treasurer; Max Amann, director of the Eher Verlag and president of the RPK; Wilhelm Weiss, editor-in-chief of the V-B and head of the Reich Association of the German Press; Rolf Hoffman, chief of the foreign press department of the NSDAP; Hans Schwarz Van Berk, former editor of *Der Angriff* and propaganda ministry official; Eugen Maier, head of the Munich office of the Reich press chief; and Dr. Paul Schmidt, chief of the foreign ministry press section.

In the summer of 1958 the following persons were interviewed: Herr Rolf Rienhardt, Offenburg, Baden, former staff director of the Verwaltungsamt and deputy director of the RVDZV; Dr. Martin Löffler, Stuttgart, legal counsel in numerous publishers' restitution cases; Dr. Karl Linse, special adviser in the finance ministry, Stuttgart; Dr. Walther Jänecke, publisher of the *Hannoverscher Kurier* and leading figure in the pre-Hitler VDZV; Herr E. Goldschagg, former managing editor of the *Münchner Post*, chief organ of the SPD in Bavaria; Herr Willy Imhof, former office manager in the Verwaltungsamt and member of the liquidation staff of the Eher Verlag; and Oberregierungsrat Wallner, of the Bavarian Restitution Office, Munich.

## Fritz Schmidt's *Presse in Fesseln*

Published anonymously, the book *Presse in Fesseln— Eine Schilderung des NS Pressetrusts* created a mild sensation on its appearance in 1947. It purported to show how the newspaper publishers had been persecuted and victimized by the Nazi party. Aimed at the Nazi press lords it was submitted as a major exhibit in Amann's Spruchkammer hearing. As a sensational exposé of party publishing policies and a scathing denunciation of Amann, Winkler, and Rienhardt, the work must be used with critical care. Published by the Archiv und Kartei Verlag, Berlin, the title page bore the attribution: "Cooperative Work of the Verlag Staff Based on Authentic Materials." Announcement of the work brought a prompt visit from a British official, as the Verlag had been licensed in the British sector of Berlin. From Dr. Prinz, director of the Verlag, the inquirer learned that the author was Dr. Fritz Schmidt, who had been placed on the payroll while writing the book. When the British official asked Schmidt what documentary materials he had, the author replied "that he had none except his memory." (An inquiry directed to Schmidt's widow, following his death in the summer of 1958, also evoked a reply that her husband had left no personal papers.) In the course of the interview the British official reminded Schmidt that as a Nazi party member he had violated Allied regulations by publishing his work, even anonymously, before he had been denazified. Moreover, the British official said, the book impressed him as an attempt to exonerate the German Nationalist press and give it the unmerited character of a resistance movement. Schmidt denied the charge of bias, saying that he had always been a political liberal and only wanted to show in his book "how the Nazi press trust had been built upon the bones of the private press." The official warned Schmidt that in publishing the work he had laid himself open to the charge of attempting to build up a favorable case in advance of his Spruchkammer hearing.

Schmidt's personal history is relevant to the worth and reliability of his book. To the British official Schmidt gave details of his professional employment. These statements together with information from other sources enable us to follow his checkered career. Born a Saarlander, he entered the publishing business as deputy Verlag director and general counsel of the *Saarbrücker Zeitung*, a leading liberal newspaper in the Saar. A collision with Gauleiter Bürckel led to his resignation in 1935. Sponsored by Max Winkler, with whom he had established relations prior to 1935, Schmidt was appointed chief of the newsprint allocation office of the RPK and the RVDZV in 1937. He remained in this position two years, when he was appointed Verlag director of the *Berliner Börsen-Zeitung*, acquired by the Amann trust on January 1, 1939. Not performing to his employer's satisfaction, he was shunted off into the position of business manager of the newly organized "Working Group of Privately Owned Newspapers," remaining in this position until the organization was dissolved by Amann in 1944.

In his book, Schmidt endeavors to give himself and the Working Group the character of active opponents of the Nazi party and its publishing trust. This does not accord with the record of Schmidt's political attitudes and affiliations. He joined the Nazi party in 1933 while still in the Saar, which suggests that he joined from conviction. Other persons sponsored by Winkler, who worked in the apparatus, only joined the party *pro forma*, as did Winkler himself, in 1937 and 1940. To his associates and superiors in Berlin, Schmidt never gave any impression other than that of a loyal party member. According to Rolf Rienhardt, when he commissioned Schmidt to write an appreciation of Amann as president of the Reich Press Chamber, on the occasion of Amann's fiftieth birthday, the article was so absurdly byzantine and sycophantic that he refused to authorize its publication. Schmidt's political record and party service contrast strangely with his intemperate personal assaults upon Amann, Rienhardt, and Winkler and

his denunciation of the Nazi party and its publishing policies. Equally incongruous is his affirmation of democratic
principles. In the civilian detention centers, in the summer
of 1945, interrogators encountered hundreds of Fritz
Schmidts.

As a source of information on the newspaper press in
the Third Reich, his book is not without considerable
value. Statements of fact about policies and persons in the
period 1933-1936 require careful verification, as Schmidt
had no official position at that time and was not in contact
with the central publishing agencies. Amann he knew only
slightly, with Rienhardt and Winkler he was on closer
terms but never intimate. As a specialist in the newsprint
allocation office, he had access to important information
on the structure and operations of the publishing trade.
However, on the organization of the Eher Verlag and the
ownership of specific newspapers his work has many errors
of detail. As business manager of the association of privately owned newspapers, he was of course fully informed
as to their position and the constant pressures to which
they were subjected by Amann and the party. For this
chapter in the history of the press he is almost the only
informed source.

Schmidt's book is not documented which makes evaluation difficult. It is heavily freighted with statistics—circulation, advertising rates, consolidations, and suspensions—
but this feature, which gives it apparent solidity, results
from diligent research in open sources. This information
is drawn from the files of *Zeitungs-Verlag*, the directories
of the Mosse and Ala advertising agencies, Sperling's newspaper directory, and the successive editions of the *Handbuch der deutschen Tagespresse*, issued by the Institute of
Journalism in Berlin. Dr. William R. Beyer, who has
probed deeply the corporate ramifications of the Eher Verlag and its subsidiaries, delivered this judgment on the
factual accuracy of Schmidt's book: "Highly colored and

politically slanted, the facts are often incorrect and the juristic position obscured. Also the ownership relations are oftentimes mistakenly represented." Beyond the issue of factual accuracy, the principal themes of the book must also be challenged. These are: 1) the Nationalist press bore no responsibility for National Socialism; 2) every private publisher was a Nazi victim and not a collaborator; 3) the drastic measures of consolidation effected during the war were politically motivated and not at all the consequence of wartime shortages, bombing, and transportation failures. It is not surprising that *Presse in Fesseln* has been a priority exhibit in numerous publishers' restitution and indemnity cases since the war.

# Bibliography

Altmeyer, K. A., *Katholische Presse unter N-S Diktatur. Dokumentation.* Berlin, 1962.

*Max Amann: Ein Leben für Führer und Volk.* Munich, 1941. An anniversary volume.

Aretin, Erwein von, *Krone und Ketten.* Munich, 1955.

Bernhard, Georg, *50 Jahre Ullstein.* Berlin, 1927.

Besson, Waldemar, *Württemberg und die deutsche Staatskrise, 1928-1933.* Stuttgart, 1959. A study in depth that challenges K. D. Bracher's theme of "disintegration."

Bömer, Karl, *Internationale Bibliographie des Zeitungswesens.* Leipzig, 1932.

Bracher, K. D., *Die Auflösung der Weimarer Republik.* Stuttgart, 1955. Criticized for its theoretical structure, this work is notwithstanding a masterly study of the decline of the Weimar republic.

Bracher, K. D., Sauer, W., and Schulz, G., *Die Nationalsozialistische Machtergreifung.* Cologne, 1960. Nearly the definitive work on the establishment and consolidation of the Hitler dictatorship.

Bullock, Alan, *Adolf Hitler: A Study in Tyranny.* London,

1951. Sane and solid, this is still the best biography.

Cohnstaedt, W., "German Newspapers Before Hitler," *Journalism Quarterly*, June 1935.

*Das Deutsche Führerlexikon, 1934-1935.* Berlin, 1934. Useful especially for secondary figures.

Dietrich, Otto, *12 Jahre mit Hitler*. Munich, 1955. All about Hitler but nothing on his own dubious career.

Dovifat, Emil, *Die Zeitungen.* Gotha, 1925.

Dovifat, Emil, *Zeitungslehre.* 2 vols., Berlin, 1937.

Dresler, Adolf, *Geschichte des "Völkischen Beobachters" und des Zentral-Verlags der NSDAP.* Munich, 1937. An authorized work but thin and inaccurate.

Franz-Willing, Georg, *Die Hitlerbewegung: Der Ursprung, 1919-1922.* Hamburg, 1962. Much new material presented in a questionable framework.

Groth, Otto, *Die Zeitung.* 4 vols., Berlin and Leipzig, 1928-1930. Scholarly and comprehensive, it is a starting point for all serious study of the history of the German press. Extensive bibliography.

Hadamovsky, Eugen, *Propaganda und nationale Macht.* Oldenbourg, 1933. Elaboration of a standard Nazi theme. The author became a propaganda ministry official.

Hagemann, Walter, *Publizistik im Dritten Reich. Ein Beitrag zur Methodik der Massenführung.* Hamburg, 1948. The best study of the total propaganda effort of the Nazi regime.

Hagemann, Walter, "Der Presse Niedergang im Dritten Reich," *Das Parlament*, Sept. 15, 1954.

*Handbuch der deutschen Tagespresse.* Edns. 1934, 1937, 1944. A valuable statistical and factual source published by the Institut für Zeitungswissenschaft of the University of Berlin.

Hanfstaengl, Ernst, *Unheard Witness.* Philadelphia, 1957. Recollections of Hitler by his former foreign press chief.

Heiden, Konrad, *Geschichte des Nationalsozialismus.* Berlin, 1932.

Heiden, Konrad, *Geburt des Dritten Reiches.* Zurich, 1934.

Hinkel, Hans, *Handbuch der Reichskulturkammer.* Berlin, 1937. By the general secretary of the RKK.

Hitler, Adolf, *Mein Kampf.* 2 vols., Munich, 1933.

*Hitler's Secret Conversations, 1941-1944.* New York, 1953.

Hoegner, Wilhelm, *Der schwierige Aussenseiter.* Munich, 1959. Autobiography of a leading Bavarian Social Democrat and post-war minister president.

*Jahrbuch der Tagespresse.* 1 Jahrgang, Berlin, 1928. German newspaper titles, their publishers and editors.

Kaupert, Wilhelm, *Die Deutsche Tagespresse als Politicum.* Freudenstadt, 1932. A useful classification and study of the political press in the Weimar period.

Koszyk, Kurt, *Zwischen Kaiserreich und Diktatur. Die Sozialdemokratische Presse von 1914 bis 1933.* Heidelberg, 1958. Comprehensive, scholarly, and dependable.

Koszyk, Kurt, *Das Ende des Rechtsstaates und die deutsche Presse, 1933-1934.* Reprint from *Journalismus,* Vol. ɪ, Düsseldorf, 1960.

Koszyk, Kurt, "Zeitungssammlungen in Deutschland," *Der Archivar,* April 1958, Heft 2.

Krebs, Albert, *Tendenzen und Gestalten der NSDAP. Erinnerungen an die Frühzeit der Partei.* Stuttgart, 1959. Valuable for the early history of the N-S press.

Larson, Cedric, "The German Press Chamber," *Public Opinion Quarterly,* Vol. ɪ, October 1937.

Liesenberg, Kurt, *Der N-S Verlagskonzern Saarpfalz und sein Verleger Gerhard Kuhn.* Frankenthal, 1949.

Löffler, Martin, *Presserecht—Kommentar.* Munich, 1955. The standard work.

Lochner, Louis P., *The Goebbels Diaries, 1942-1943.* New York, 1948.

Lüddecke, Theodor, *Die Tageszeitung als Mittel der Staats-*

*führung.* Hamburg, 1933. Blueprint for the Nazi party's control of the press.

Lüdecke, Kurt, *I Knew Hitler.* New York, 1937.

Manvell, R., and Fraenkel, H., *Dr. Goebbels: His Life and Death.* London, 1960. Popular and inaccurate but useful.

Matthias, E., and Morsey, R., *Das Ende der Parteien 1933.* Düsseldorf, 1960.

*Memoirs of Alfred Rosenberg.* New York, 1949. Of slight value and badly butchered by the editors.

*Nazi Conspiracy and Aggression.* 8 vols., Washington, D. C., 1948. Supp. B, Part II, chap. XVII.

*Nazionalsozialistisches Jahrbuch—1944.* Munich, 1943.

*Organisationsbuch der NSDAP.* 2d ed., Munich, 1937. Valuable for the constitutional structure of the party and its agencies.

Peters, J. F. H., *Kommentar zur Rückerstattung.* Cologne, 1949. Texts of the laws on restitution and indemnity.

Picker, Henry, *Hitlers Tischgespräche im Führerhauptquartier, 1941-1942.* German edition of Hitler's table talk.

"Die Presse der NSDAP im Überblick," *Zeitungswissenschaft,* May 1932.

*Reichsgesetzblatt.* Vols. 1933, 1934, 1935.

Rippler, Heinrich, "Das Journalistengesetz," *Deutsche Rundschau,* Oct.-Dec. 1924. Summary and analysis.

Schacht, Hjalmar, *Confessions of the "Old Wizard."* Boston, 1956. Translation of *76 Jahre meines Lebens.* Bad Wörishofen, 1953.

Schmidt-Leonhardt, H., *Das Schriftleitergesetz vom 4. Oktober 1933.* Berlin, 1934. Standard commentary by the chief of the legal division of the propaganda ministry.

Schreiber, K. F., *Das Recht der Reichskulturkammer.* Berlin, 1935. Laws, decrees, and regulations of the component chambers. Annual editions.

Schwend, Karl, *Bayern zwischen Monarchie und Diktatur, 1928-1933*. Munich, 1954.

Semmler, Rudolf, *Goebbels—The Man Next to Hitler*. London, 1947. An interesting diary kept by one of Goebbels' aides.

Seraphim, H. G., *Das politische Tagebuch Alfred Rosenbergs*. Berlin, 1956. Fragments from the years 1934-1935 and 1939-1940.

Seydewitz, Max, *Civil Life in Wartime Germany*. New York, 1945. Based on German press reports.

Sington, D., and Weidenfeld, A., *The Goebbels Experiment. A Study of the Nazi Propaganda Machine*. New Haven, 1943. Chapter VI on the press is still valuable despite inaccuracies.

*Sperlings Zeitungs-Addressbuch*. Berlin, 1937. Standard directory.

"The Story of the Völkischer Beobachter," *Wiener Library Bulletin*, Vol. 8 (1954), Nos. 36, 39.

Strasser, Otto, *Hitler and I*. Boston, 1940.

Strothmann, Dietrich, *Nationalsozialistische Literaturpolitik. Ein Beitrag zur Publizistik im Dritten Reich*. Bonn, 1960.

Sündermann, Helmut, *Die Grenzen fallen*. Munich, 1939. Informative on the take-over of the Austrian press after March 1938.

Treue, Wilhelm, "Rede Hitlers vor den deutschen Presse, 10. November 1938," *Vierteljahreshefte für Zeitgeschichte*, 6 Jahrg. 1958, Heft 2.

Ullstein, H., *The Rise and Fall of the House of Ullstein*. New York, 1943.

U. S. Bombing Survey, *The Effects of Strategic Bombing on the German War Economy*. Washington, D. C., 1945. A summary of the findings.

Walter, Heinrich, *Zeitung als Aufgabe. 60 Jahre Verein Deutscher Zeitungsverleger*. Wiesbaden, 1954. A valuable institutional history.

*Zehn Jahre Konzentration.* Bonn, 1956. Valuable for the SPD publishing enterprises.

*Zwischen den Zeilen.* Düsseldorf, 1948. Published by the Droste Verlag recounting experiences with the Nazi press trust.

# Index